PRAISE FOR
PAM JOHNSON-BENNETT

"She can, in fact, work miracles with problem cats."

—*Pet Life* magazine

"Every day is 'Caturday' for cat lovers! And to strengthen our bond with our precious feline friends, Pam's advice is simply the best. As a proud pet parent of three cats, our home is full of purrs, meows, and love, thanks to Pam's wisdom and training methods."

—Robin R. Ganzert, PhD, president and CEO,
American Humane Association

"Cats are like pieces of art that grace your home and throw up on your laptop, but oh how we love them, and *nobody* knows the ways of the mysterious feline any better than Pam Johnson-Bennett. If you are holding this book, be prepared to learn more about cats than you ever could have imagined. Seven kitties own my wife, Mary, and me right now, and we need to learn all we can! Thanks, Pam!"

—Joseph S. Bonsall, forty-two-year member
of the American music group The Oak Ridge Boys

"I have been a big fan of Pam's for a long time. Her sound advice and unique insight into cat behavior have helped thousands of cats."

—Beth Stern, spokesperson,
North Shore Animal League America

"Pam's knowledge and her books are truly lifesaving words of wisdom for countless owners of felines, and especially for the cats that would have otherwise found themselves homeless or in a shelter without her guidance." —Megan Brodbine Williams, cofounder, Nashville Cat Rescue

"Pam Johnson-Bennett's work makes an important contribution to our ability to understand, appreciate, and live in harmonious and loving partnership with the unique and amazing creature that is the cat."

—Jane Lumbatis, executive director, Georgia SPCA

"Pam Johnson-Bennett's works are staple recommendations for my cat clients. Her books are highly readable and contain information based on the true science of cat behavior. This book will benefit both cat owners and animal professionals. *CatWise* should be required reading for anyone owning or working with cats."

—Lore I. Haug, DVM, MS, diplomate,
American College of Veterinary Behaviorists,
Texas Veterinary Behavior Services

"The queen of cat behavior!"
    —Steve Dale, author of the syndicated newspaper column My Pet World

PENGUIN BOOKS

CATWISE

Pam Johnson-Bennett is one of the most popular and sought-after cat behavior experts in the world. She is the author of seven award-winning books on cat behavior, including *Think Like a Cat*, *Hiss and Tell*, *Starting from Scratch*, and *Cat vs. Cat*. Pam has a private cat-consulting practice in Nashville, is a popular guest on national TV and radio, has starred on Animal Planet UK's series *Psycho Kitty*, and has spoken on cat behavior at veterinary and animal-welfare conferences around the world. During her more than thirty-year career, she has been profiled widely, has written for many national magazines, and is the former behavior columnist for *Cats* magazine, iVillage, Yahoo!, *Cat Fancy*'s Cat Channel, *Kittens USA*, *The Daily Cat*, and *Catster*.

A certified cat behavior consultant, she was VP of the International Association of Animal Behavior Consultants and founded the IAABC Cat Division. Pam served on the American Humane Association's Advisory Board on Animal Behavior and Training. She has received many awards, including the Winn Feline Foundation Award, multiple Cat Writers' Association awards, and the IAABC Cat Division Award.

Pam lives in Nashville, Tennessee, with her husband, two children, a rescued Bengal cat, a rescued Sheltie, one well-trained goldfish, and two not-so-well-trained goldfish.

Learn more about Pam's techniques and recommendations at www .catbehaviorassociates.com.

CatWise

America's Favorite Cat Expert Answers
Your Cat Behavior Questions

Pam Johnson-Bennett

PENGUIN BOOKS

PENGUIN BOOKS

An imprint of Penguin Random House LLC
375 Hudson Street
New York, New York 10014
penguin.com

Cover photograph by Don Wright
Illustrations by Norris Hall Studio. Copyright © 2016 by Pam Johnson-Bennett

Cats featured on cover were rescued by The Cat Shoppe in Nashville, Tennessee.

LIBRARY OF CONGRESS CATALOGING-IN-PUBLICATION DATA
Names: Johnson-Bennett, Pam, 1954–author.
Title: Catwise : America's favorite cat expert answers
your cat behavior questions / Pam Johnson-Bennett.
Description: New York, New York : Penguin Books, 2016.
Identifiers: LCCN 2016000873 | ISBN 9780143129561
Subjects: LCSH: Cats—Behavior.
Classification: LCC SF446.5.J633 2016 | DDC 636.8—dc23

Printed in the United States of America
1 3 5 7 9 10 8 6 4 2

Set in Chaparrel Pro
Designed by Katy Riegel

To my husband, Scott

And to my precious children,

Gracie and Jack

You are my everything

To my mother

For a lifetime of love

Acknowledgments

"You're writing another cat book?"

"Yes, Mom."

"What else is there to say about cats?"

"Plenty."

"When are you going to get a *real* career?"

This is the typical exchange my mother and I would have whenever she learned I was working on yet another cat book. Don't get me wrong, she loved cats and had two who lived into old age, but in her mind, writing about cats wasn't going to provide professional and financial security. Up until my mid-forties, she still had hopes that I would see the light and become a music teacher or a nurse. I think it was close to my fiftieth birthday that she stopped mentioning how even people *my* age could go back to college. I guess she finally surrendered to the fact that the daughter she raised had somehow squeezed out a living writing about cats, or maybe she realized that my stubborn streak was probably inherited from her. Still, whenever we were together, she'd try to slip some money in my pocket to ensure that my family wasn't starving because of my career choice.

Before she passed away, my mother was in the beginning stages of

Alzheimer's disease. She was unaware that I had a very successful behavior business, continued to author several more books, and even had my own television series. I am so very grateful that she still knew who I was, and I cherish the fact that out of love, she continued to try to push a few dollars into my hand. Somewhere deep inside her, though, I think she knew I did OK despite the fact I never became a music teacher. I owe an unending thank-you to my mother for a lifetime of love and the stubbornness to follow my heart.

Thank you to my husband, Scott, for filling every one of my days with love. You were the answer to my prayers, and I thank God for feeling that I deserved such blessings. Thank you to Gracie and Jack for the love and joy you give me every day. I am so proud to be your mom. Thank you for being proud of me, as well. It means everything. Thank you to Don Wright of Don Wright Designs. I am so grateful to be the beneficiary of your amazing talent and friendship. We've traveled quite a long road together. Thank you to my agent, Linda Roghaar, for years of hand-holding, cheerleading, incredible wisdom, and nurturing support. Thank you to the editor of my dreams, Wendy Wolf. You always amaze me. Thank you to Bill Talmadge, my producer. Words really can't express my gratitude. Special thanks to Mike Sword and Brad Danks. Thank you to the amazingly talented Norris Hall for your illustrations. Thank you to Marilyn Krieger for many years of a cherished friendship. Thank you to the veterinarians focusing on cat health and behavior. You make a huge difference by spotlighting the needs of animals who have been viewed as second-class pet citizens for too many years. Thank you to my dear friends at Animal Care Veterinary Hospital. What an amazing group of professional and compassionate animal experts. Extra thanks to Dr. Kyle Daniel. Special mention to Dr. Mark Waldrop and the Nashville Cat Clinic for being one of the true pioneers in recognizing years ago there was a need for a cats-only clinic. You've been my cat hero for many years. Thank you to Megan Brodbine and Nashville Cat Rescue for your tireless dedication toward caring for the cats forgotten by so many. Thank you to Best Friends Animal Society for setting the standard when it comes to making sure every animal has a chance to be loved and for inspiring us to never give up until we have saved them all. Thank you to Chris Achord and the Cat Shoppe for years of love and devotion to cat welfare. Decades ago, you raised the bar for cat rescue. Thank you to the Farm at Natchez Trace for your devotion to local pet parent education through your summer lecture series. A huge thank-you to the many clients I've had since I first began in this field in 1982. It has always been my dream to make life better for cats and the people who love them. Thank you for giving me that opportunity. What an honor it has been to be a part of your lives.

Contents

Chapter 3
Social Media

Chapter 4
The Scoop on Poop and Pee

Chapter 5
Stinking Outside the Box

Chapter 6
Demolition Wars

Chapter 10
Animal House

Chapter 11
Fraidy Cat

Chapter 12
Don't Do That

(Training your cat to stop doing those things
that really annoy you)

Does my cat misbehave because he's mad at me? 211
How do I stop my cat from chewing my houseplants? 213
When my cat bites me, is it for attention? 216
Why does my cat suck on fabric? 217
Why does my cat steal things? 219
Pam's CatWise Clue:
    The must-have checklist for solving your cat's behavior problem 223
How can I keep my cat off the counter? 226
Why does my cat wake me at three A.M.? 228
How can I stop my cat from unrolling the toilet paper? 231
How can I prevent my cat from darting out the door? 232
Why does my cat chew on socks? 234
Why does my cat attack my ankles? 235
How do I keep my cat away from the Christmas tree? 236
How do I stop my cat from chewing on electrical cords? 240

Chapter 13
Bad Moods

(How to deal with feline aggression)

Why is my cat aggressive? 242
Why did my cat attack the other cat after visiting the veterinarian? 245
Why does my cat bite me when I pet him? 247
Why would my cats suddenly become enemies? 249
Pam's CatWise Clue: Ten tips for calming an out-of-control cat 252
Why does my cat attack his tail? 253
How do I find a behavior expert to help my cat? 254

Chapter 17
Old Friends
(Making the most of the golden years)

Introduction

MY OFFICE RECEIVES countless emails and calls from people with cat behavior questions. What's amazing is how often the same questions come up over and over again. I've spent over thirty years helping people understand their sometimes perplexing pets through behavior consults, my books, and now online. But an overwhelming number have asked for a kind of "best of" answer book, so we've created that and more in this book. We've combined many of the questions we receive with my best answers to help you solve your cat's behavior problem, prevent problems from beginning in the first place, or simply improve the relationship you already have with your cat.

Since I first began in this field, much has changed. We know a whole lot more than we used to, and you'd think any answer you'd need would be right there at a cat parent's fingertips through the Internet, but where did it come from? Cat behavior consulting has almost become trendy and, as a result, many unqualified and uneducated people have entered this field. Our office receives many sad calls from cat parents who have been burned by inappropriate, inaccurate, and sometimes downright dangerous advice. I know that as you browse through your favorite Internet book retail site or stand in the animal training aisle of the bookstore, you're faced with a large selection of cat training/behavior guides. I'm very honored and grateful that you've continued to trust my behavioral expertise and training methods.

I've included information in this book that at first may not seem behavior-related, such as litter box setup and maintenance, but trust me, if you get the litter box vibe wrong, it can have a *huge* impact on your cat's behavior. That goes for other topics, like feeding and health issues, as well.

Cats have come a long way in our world since humans first viewed them merely as vermin exterminators. For many, cats are as loved as our children, but just as we don't always understand our teenagers, we still make mistakes in providing what our cats need or understanding how they're hardwired. For example, even though cats long ago surpassed dogs as the most popular pet, they still aren't seen by veterinarians as often as dogs are; cat parents don't take cats' health issues as seriously, or they think, "They'll get over it," especially because the cat is rarely eager to climb into the carrier for the trip to the vet. Additionally, even though we view our cats as beloved family members, many of us don't do our part when it comes to the human/cat relationship. We declaw beloved cats for the sake of saving furniture without understanding what having claws means to a cat emotionally or how their removal affects them physically. Cats are fed free-choice food available twenty-four hours a day without thinking about whether they have enough opportunities for physical activity (and we are then puzzled when they get fat). In a free-range setting, cats would eat far enough away from each other to ensure security, but many cat parents put cats in the stressful environment of having to eat from dishes that are too close to each other. Intimate social dining has appeal for humans but not for cats.

Cats are viewed as more convenient than dogs because they can live indoors and use a litter box, but that doesn't mean you don't have to clean it out or that it's fine to make several cats share one box. It concerns me that cats are often placed in a no-win situation. We want cats in our lives but pick and choose what aspects of catness are acceptable, which usually means convenient—to us.

I love cats and I know you do too. With that love, though, can still come frustration and questions about cats. Some people just shrug their shoulders and believe cats are untrainable, while others try to change behaviors through a punitive approach without understanding the cat's true motivation behind a particular behavior. The key to successfully correcting behavior problems is to understand *why* cats do the things they do. If you think "misbehaviors" are performed out of spite, revenge, stupidity, or randomness, then you're missing the most important element in cat behavior training. Many behaviors we label as abnormal or undesirable are actually very normal in a cat's world. Cats are exceptionally smart, and they do certain things over and over or act certain ways because those strategies help them solve a problem. The payoff may not be something you like or think makes sense, but it always makes sense to the cat. The key is to figure out what problem the cat is facing, what payoff the behavior is providing, and what to offer as an alternative that meets the cat's needs and is also acceptable to you. Getting in the habit of looking at cat behavior from that angle can restore peace and harmony to the household. My wish for you is that you have the relationship with your cat that you've always wanted, and I hope that through this book, as well as through my other books, you find the road map to that joyful relationship.

Don't wait to implement training and behavior modification until your cat has developed a behavior problem. Just as we use preventive veterinary care, we should also use training and behavior modification to help prevent problems from arising in the first place. During every interaction we have with cats, they're learning something. Whether what they learn improves their behavior or worsens it is up to us.

Too many cats end up in shelters because they had behavior problems that cat parents didn't know how to correct. Many of the cats I evaluate in shelters could've easily stayed in their homes if the cat parents had had a little more information about the nature of cats and what they need. Even with the tremendous rise in the popularity of cats over the years, many people still view them as low maintenance. That's not the same as *no* maintenance! If that's how we enter into a relationship, it's no wonder it often fails. The good news is, it doesn't have to be that way. Cats are intelligent, social, trainable, affectionate, loving animals. It's time to get *CatWise*!

Pam Johnson-Bennett

CatWise

Chapter 1

Kitten: Impossible

*Getting started with that adorable
ball of nonstop energy*

Question:
How do I know which kitten to choose?

Pam's Answer:
To some people, kittens may all appear to be the same compared with the vast differences among dogs when it comes to size, shape, and appearance. The truth is, although cats tend to fall within a smaller range of weight and size, they can be very different, not only physically but in personality. If you're thinking about adding a kitten to the family, it's good that you're taking the time to figure out what type of cat might be the best match for you. Here are some of the questions you'll need to ask yourself as you start your search.

Purebred or Mixed Breed? What are the reasons for choosing one over the other? If you have specific features and traits in mind, and those might include size, coat, color, and temperament, then a purebred kitten may be what you're looking for. If not, then you'll surely be able to find the type of kitten you want by considering a mixed breed, which you're more likely to find in a shelter, vet's office, or rescue organization.

A purebred will cost you more money, unless you choose a cat from a purebred rescue organization or are able to locate one at a shelter. The need to find homes for the huge number of mixed breed cats is staggering. Choosing a kitten or cat (whether from a shelter or through rescue) has minimal, if any, cost, and you'll be saving a life. Wouldn't it be great to see empty cages at shelters around the world?

How Much Grooming Do You Want to Do? Longhair cats are gorgeous, but they also require more maintenance. Most longhair cats have coats that mat, so daily grooming, mostly brushing, is needed. With some, you may also have to do occasional bathing.

Male or Female? Once neutered or spayed, the sex of the cat won't really matter unless you have a personal preference for a male or female.

Does Age Matter? With an adult cat you can, for the most part, see the personality that has already developed, so if you're looking for a specific personality—playful, stately, cuddly, etc.—then an adult might be a better choice; you'll know what you're getting. If you choose a kitten, then you do have a good opportunity to influence the personality through socialization and handling, but you'll also have a greater time commitment. Kittens need more supervision and training, as they're just learning about their physical abilities and don't yet know the house rules. Kittens will also need more frequent veterinary visits initially to get their scheduled vaccinations and dewormings. With a kitten you'll also have the upcoming needed neuter or spay surgery if it wasn't already done. If you choose an adult cat from a shelter or rescue organization, then vaccinations will probably have been done, and you can focus on selecting one already spayed or neutered.

Are There Young Children in the Home? This is a huge factor when determining which cat would be right for your family. Some cats are better with children than others. An adult cat who has never been around young children might be fearful. If you're at the shelter looking for an adult cat, ask about ones who have a known history of having been around children. With kittens, you can expose them to children at a very young age so they get used to them, but kittens can also easily be injured if roughly handled by children.

Make your choice based on your family environment, including the ages and personalities of your children. Take the time to make a good match, so the addition of a kitten or cat becomes a safe and wonderful thing for everyone—human and feline.

Do You Already Have Pets at Home? If you already have a cat at home and want to add to the feline family, try to match complementary personalities. If your current cat is extremely assertive, then you wouldn't want to bring in a kitten who is very timid or undersocialized. Try not to go to either extreme of the personality scale. Additionally, be prepared to take the time to do a gradual and positive introduction. Unless you're dealing with a feral kitten, or one who was traumatized or undersocialized, he'll probably view everyone, whether human, canine, or feline, as a potential playmate and very likely not respect the personal territory of others. For the adult cat at home, this will be very disconcerting, so a safe, gradual introduction has to top your to-do list.

If you currently have a dog, is he already cat-friendly? Has he been allowed to chase cats in the neighborhood? Carefully think about how your dog will handle the addition of a kitten. The safety of both animals is a top priority. Be extra cautious about a little kitten and a big dog. Don't assume you know how your dog will react, because tragedy can happen in a split second, even if the dog is just being playful.

Get the Facts

Cats are incorrectly labeled as solitary animals, but in reality they're social creatures. The misconception may be due to the fact that they're solitary hunters and are territorial in nature.

Question:

I'll be adopting a kitten soon. What supplies do I need to buy? I'm a newbie when it comes to kittens.

Pam's Answer:

Here's my basic new kitten equipment checklist:

- Good quality kitten food
- An easy source for fresh water
- Uncovered litter box (low sides for easy entry)
- Scoopable, unscented litter
- Litter scoop
- Receptacle for soiled litter
- Food bowl (a size that's easy for a kitten)
- Water bowl (separate from the food bowl)
- Scratching post (sisal covered)
- Soft grooming brush
- Nail trimmers
- Safe toys for solo play
- Interactive play toys (fishing pole design)
- Cozy bed with raised sides
- Hiding places (box on its side, cat tunnel, paper bags or pyramid-style bed)
- Cat carrier
- Cat tree (for climbing)
- Identification (microchip, ID tag, breakaway collar)
- Treats for training (or you can use the kitten's food)
- Clicker (optional training tool)
- Kitten-proofing tools (outlet covers, cord protectors, etc.)
- Patience
- Love

You'll also need information. This book will get you started, but I recommend that you learn all you can about the nature of cats and the best way to train them before you arrive home with your ball of fur. Too many people view cats as easy, low-maintenance companion animals, and then they become disappointed when behavior problems crop up. You're in a position to begin a wonderful and rewarding relationship that you hope will last many years, so do a little homework first.

Question:

I just got a kitten, and I don't know the first thing about how to train or care for her. What do I need to know to start off right?

Pam's Answer:

This is a fun and exciting time as you get to know this adorable little newcomer. This is also a time when a great amount of learning takes place. Here are some general guidelines to get you going in the right direction:

Your First Stop: The Veterinary Clinic. Your kitten will need lifelong veterinary care, and the time to start is right now. Depending upon where you got your kitten and her current age, she may need to begin or continue her initial vaccinations and deworming. Even if she has had her vaccinations before you got her, an initial visit to the veterinarian for a checkup is important within the first few weeks after you bring her home.

Your veterinarian can also give you guidance on nutrition, show you how to do things such as nail trimming, and provide answers to your questions about being a first-time cat parent. It's also important to establish a client/veterinarian relationship now, while your new family member is just starting out, so the doctor will know your cat's normal behavior and be able to diagnose more easily if something is going wrong.

The Kitten Needs Safety. Even though you're probably very excited to begin your life with the new kitten, keep in mind that your home environment is unfamiliar and big, even if it seems like a small apartment to you. It's a lot for a little kitten to adjust to initially, so it's best to confine her to one room. I have always referred to this as the sanctuary room. It can be an extra bedroom or any room you can close off. This way the kitten can get her bearings without being overwhelmed.

Your kitten is also just in the learning stages of activities such as using the litter box, scratching, climbing, and exploring. It's much easier for her to have everything conveniently located right now. Depending upon how young your kitten is, have her litter box very close by, because youngsters don't have great bladder control.

Equip the sanctuary room with your kitten's litter box, a vertical scratching post, a horizontal scratch pad, a few hiding places (paper bags or boxes on their sides), and a cozy napping area, as well as food and water. Be sure to locate the feeding station as far away from the litter box as the room will allow.

Your kitten will also need toys. Leave out some safe toys for solo playtime, including soft toys she can chew and rubbery ones she can roll or bat. For interactive playtime, you will bring in toys so they can be used with your supervision. You don't want to leave any toys out that have strings or anything else that could pose a danger to your kitten.

Leave the carrier in the sanctuary room for your kitten to use as a hiding place if she wants. Line the carrier with a towel and your kitten will have a comfy spot for naps.

> ## Family Matters
>
> If possible, kittens should remain with their mother and littermates until twelve weeks of age in order to benefit from valuable social lessons.

The amount of time your new kitten will have to stay in the sanctuary room depends on her age, personality, the size of your home or apartment, and whether you currently have other pets at home. If she's the only pet and she seems comfortable and confident after twenty-four hours or so, you can begin to let her explore the house a little at a time. Always make sure she knows where her litter box is and can return to the safety of the sanctuary room. If you have other pets at home, then keep her in the sanctuary room as you do a gradual, positive introduction (see Chapter 10).

Your Kitten Will Need a Carrier. Even after your kitten is out of her sanctuary room, keep the cat carrier set up and ready all the time. This will help her become comfortable with its presence, and you'll eventually be able to do some carrier training to help desensitize her to the experience of being in a carrier and also travel itself. It's never too early to start training her to accept being in a carrier.

Your Kitten Needs Her Own Litter Box. Because your kitten is still in the early learning stages, the litter box setup needs to be conveniently located and easy to navigate. The box should be low-sided or at least have one low cutout so the kitten can easily get in and out. As your kitten grows, you'll be able to change out the box for a larger one and gradually move it into a place where it can live permanently.

Your kitten may not be able to remember where the box is located or have the bladder control to get to it in time, so don't let her have the run of the entire house until you feel she has the routine down. Also, get on a schedule of bringing her to the litter box during the times elimination might normally occur, such as after a nap, after a meal, and after playtime. For more specifics on litter box training, refer to Chapter 4.

Giving Her Food and Water. Start with getting the right food and water bowls. She needs kitten-size bowls, ones she can reach into easily without spilling, and she should eat growth-formula food.

Kittens need to be fed several meals a day. Your veterinarian can advise you as to how often and how much to feed based on her age, weight, and health.

Providing the Scratching Post. Get your kitten started off right by providing a sisal-covered scratching post. Her claws are probably out all the time right now, but as she matures, she'll become better at keeping them sheathed.

Cat Trees. Your kitten loves to climb, and climbing provides important skill building for her. She's learning about her strength, balance, and speed. Provide those opportunities for her by having a sturdy cat tree available. This way she can climb there instead of scaling your curtains or bookshelves.

Learn About Grooming and Nail Trimming. Unless you want to end up doing battle with an adult cat who won't let you near her claws or will bite you whenever she sees a brush, get started now on the training. While your kitten is still young is the time to get her acclimated. Get a soft brush and start brushing her for a minute or two several times a day. Gently handle her ears and touch her mouth as well. Get her comfortable with being touched so she'll accept it later when you start cleaning her teeth, cleaning her ears, or giving her medicine.

Claw trimming on a regular basis is a necessity. You'll just want to trim the very sharp tip off the top of the nail. If you start the process when your kitten is young and are consistent about doing it, she's more likely to accept the process without complaint (or with minimal complaining) once she's mature. You'll probably need a hands-on lesson from your veterinarian the first time so you can learn the best method to do it and also so you can be shown how to avoid cutting too much of the nail, which has a little blood vessel inside it.

> ### Not So Loud
>
> Cats have very sensitive hearing. Your kitten may become stressed or startled by loud noise or loud music. The sound systems you can buy for TVs are great, but they aren't very cat-friendly.

Let's Start Training. If you want a well-adjusted, well-behaved cat, you have to put the effort into appropriate and humane training. Start now and be consistent. Make sure all family members are on the same page as well, so your kitten doesn't get mixed messages. Training now will pay off greatly as your youngster grows into a full-grown cat.

Kittens are energetic; they go full speed ahead and can easily get underfoot. While much of their activity and playfulness is fun to watch, training is vital. Kittens need appropriate outlets for all that energy so they learn from an early age to direct their enthusiasm toward toys and designated cat furniture, not human body parts, potentially dangerous household objects, or a family member's personal things. Playfulness can easily turn to frustration if kittens aren't given outlets to burn off all that energy.

Question:
How do I kitten-proof my house?

Pam's Answer:
Your kitten will most likely view everything in the house as a potential toy. She'll also have a strong desire to go vertical, so your curtains and bookshelves are potential jungle gyms. Kittens often get themselves into trouble by squeezing into the unlikeliest places, so take the time to go room by room to kitten-proof. There are things in almost every room that you wouldn't think could be harmful but can be, so it's important to look at each room from a kitten's point of view. For example, if you have a recliner, it can be easy for the kitten to hide in there and get injured when you adjust the chair.

Washers and dryers may seem out of reach, but little leapers can easily find their way into them on their own. A kitten may also hide in a pile of dirty laundry that you might unknowingly scoop up and toss into the washer. Always put each piece of laundry into the washer separately. Check

the washer and dryer before you turn them on and then again after you
empty the laundry before you close the doors.

Here is a starter list for typical kitten-proofing:

- Secure window screens.
- Keep all medicine put away in a closed cabinet or drawer.
- Don't leave out string, ribbon, rubber bands, or other things that
  can be swallowed.
- Keep household cleansers put away in cabinets.
- Use trash cans with lids or secure them in cabinets.
- Cut handles off paper bags before offering bags as toys.
- Don't let your kitten play with plastic bags.
- Secure electrical cords so they don't dangle.
- Use museum or earthquake wax to secure breakable objects that
  can't be put away.
- Check the washer and dryer before doing laundry.
- Put laundry in the washer piece by piece, because your kitten may
  be sleeping in the laundry pile.
- Always double-check for hiding kittens when closing closets and
  drawers.
- Tie blind and shade pulls out of reach so they aren't dangling.
- Keep all indoor plants out of kitten's reach (most are poisonous
  to cats).
- Close all sewing and knitting baskets after use and double-check
  for any pins on the carpet.
- Don't leave candles burning unattended where a kitten could
  reach them.
- Make sure the fireplace has a secure screen.
- Always keep the fireplace screen in place, because a kitten may be
  tempted to play in ashes.
- Don't throw a box out without first checking if the kitten is
  hiding in it.
- Do a kitten check before leaving the house in case she's locked in a
  closet or drawer.
- Block the space behind the refrigerator so the kitten can't get
  wedged in there.
- Don't use mothballs in your drawers or closets because they're
  toxic to cats.

- Check before closing the recliner footrest, because your kitten may be hiding under it.
- Get in the habit of keeping the toilet lid closed.

> **A Sharp Little Fact**
>
> Kittens are unable to sheath their claws until a little after four weeks of age.

This list is just a small sample of the types of kitten-proofing that may need to be done. You'll have to customize it based on your specific household. Kitten-proofing may seem like lots of work, but your kitten will mature and outgrow many of the dangerous behaviors that it is meant to prevent. If you have children, you know that baby-proofing and toddler-proofing your home are needed but don't last forever. And speaking of baby-proofing, you can find many items to help you kitten-proof in the baby-safety section of department stores and baby-product stores. Electrical cord covers, outlet covers, cabinet locks, toilet paper roll covers, etc. are also very useful when trying to protect a curious little kitten.

Question:

I recently visited the shelter to adopt a kitten and saw two that seemed very bonded. Is it better to adopt two kittens instead of just one?

Pam's Answer:

There are many reasons why you should actually consider bringing home two kittens, starting off with the fact two may actually be much easier and more beneficial . . . for the kittens and for you.

I've done countless consultations over the years with people who had adopted a kitten and then a couple of years later realized they wanted a second cat. Because adult cats are territorial, the introduction process requires some finesse and lots of patience. In many cases, the pet parents had originally thought about adopting two kittens at once but were concerned about the added work. In reality, a second kitten wouldn't have added much extra work at all, and the benefits of companionship would've greatly enriched both cats' lives. Starting off now with two feline young-sters is much easier than adding a second adult cat down the road.

Fun Facts About Adopting Two Kittens:

- Twice the love.
- Twice the affection.
- It's very entertaining to watch two kittens playing together.
- Two kittens can entertain each other while you're busy or away at work.
- There's not much added cost to having a second kitten.

Being Together. Kittens are still learning; they learn from their mother, their environment, and each other. Kitten-to-kitten interaction and play-time help them develop important social skills needed later in life. They learn how to communicate and interpret each other's signals, how hard to bite during playtime, and how to share territory. In the case of a litter of kittens, the siblings have been together since birth and are already well into this process. They're already bonded by the time you come along as a potential adoptive cat parent. What a great way to start!

Kittens being adopted or rescued may have been without their moth-ers. Rescued kittens are often too young to be away from their litter-mates. If you adopt a pair, the socialization they would have had with their mother and littermates can continue as they create security and comfort for each other.

Learning from Each Other. If you've ever been around kittens, you know they're on the move and into everything. Kittenhood is such an important time for learning and developing skills. When jumping, the kitten is learning how to gauge distances. When walking along narrow objects, the kitten is learning about balance. What looks to be mere play or curiosity is actually an important part of kitten education. There are so many lessons taking place as kittens stalk, play, leap, climb, tumble, use their claws, and practice posturing. Because they learn by observa-tion too, a pair of kittens will help educate each other. This applies to everything from using the litter box to testing which objects are safe to land on and which ones aren't. A more inquisitive kitten may help a more reluctant one to blossom.

Life Enrichment. I spend a huge amount of time talking with my clients about environmental enrichment and the importance of providing a home environment encouraging play, exploration, and security. For a kitten, the ability to have a companion for playtime can also be one of the best forms of life enrichment. Let's face it, you have to work and spend time away from home, and a little kitten can get lonely and even scared. Many people are under the false impression that cats are solitary and don't want companionship, but they do have a social structure, and most truly benefit and thrive when they have a feline buddy.

The companionship two kittens can provide each other may help prevent future behavior problems, such as boredom or separation anxiety. Very often, the bond between two cats who have grown up together becomes strong and special.

What About the Extra Cost and Care? After the initial kitten vaccinations, the veterinary costs taper off in most cases. You'll likely be dealing just with routine yearly appointments until it's time to spay or neuter, and in some cases, the kittens have already been spayed or neutered. Many veterinary clinics offer multipet discounts as well, so be sure to check. You may even be able to adopt kittens who have already had most or all of their vaccinations.

With kittens, you'll have the expense of just one litter box until they grow bigger; then you'll add a second or third box. Scratching posts aren't expensive, and if you're handy, you can even make one. When it comes to food, even as kittens grow, you won't have the same food expense as you would if you adopted puppies, depending upon the dog breed. Large dogs can go through lots of food. Cats, even the largest breeds, won't eat that much, so adding the second mouth shouldn't break your budget.

When it comes to toys and cat furniture, your biggest expense will be a cat tree. I highly recommend that you get one, and you'd have that expense regardless of whether you adopted one kitten or two. And if you're at all familiar with cats, you know that some of the best cat furniture is empty cardboard boxes. My children made a cat condo by using duct tape to connect several cardboard boxes. They cut holes in the boxes and created a fun cat playground. Simple and very cheap.

It's Easier Than You Think. Whenever people ask for my advice about getting a kitten, they think I'm going to have a recommendation of breed, sex, or personality type. Instead, my best tip is to open your heart to two kittens. You'll be glad you did!

Question:

My neighbor's adult cat is so beautiful, but he hates being touched or petted. I have a new kitten, and want to make certain she grows up to be a cat who'll let me pet her. Do you have any tips?

Pam's Answer:

Start the training process now. Many cat parents are good at kitten-proofing the home and teaching the cat where the food and litter are, but people seldom plan ahead in teaching the youngster to accept being touched. Looking at your healthy, active, fun-loving kitten, it's hard to picture a time in the future when she'll need medication (either orally or topically). If you haven't gotten her comfortable with having her ears handled or having your fingers near her mouth, then there's a good chance that the first time you try to medicate her won't be a pleasant experience for anyone. If she's not amenable to being handled, a trip to the veterinarian may require armor for both of you!

It Begins with Touch. Plan ahead and prepare your cat to accept and even enjoy being touched in particular areas. Many cats are paw shy and don't like having their claws touched. Help your kitten learn to associate being touched in sensitive areas by petting near that area one or two times and then offer a treat.

If you have a kitten who dislikes having her ears handled, stroke her on the back of the head or on the chest and then offer a treat or a little portion of her regular food. Work up to being able to touch her ears. Another method is to let the kitten lick some wet food from a spoon as you gently touch her ears.

You'll quickly learn your cat's petting area preferences. Gradually ease into being able to offer one gentle stroke near an ear and then offer an additional treat. Don't forget to do the same on the other ear. Touch the ear briefly and then increase the length of time you handle the ear. Don't overdo it, though. Keep the whole experience positive. If done correctly, your kitten will learn that letting herself be touched results in something pleasurable and that the experience is quick, gentle, and safe. It's critical to your success that the petting session in those sensitive areas be over while it's still a positive experience. If you touch the ear or another body part too long, you risk having your kitten start to struggle.

Be a Gentle Teacher. Kittenhood is also the time when you want to get your furry new family member introduced to having her teeth cleaned and nails trimmed. The sooner you expose her to these experiences, the easier it'll be later on. If you don't work on nail trimming when your cat is a kitten, you'll probably have a much tougher time later on. You don't want to have to make a trip to the veterinary clinic once a month just to do nail trimming when you have the opportunity right now to begin the training process.

The Sooner the Better. Remember, start early and be gentle. Take baby steps and always end on a positive note. Consistency increases your chances of having an adult cat who comfortably tolerates teeth cleaning, ear cleaning, nail trimming, grooming, tick removal, or anything else that requires being touched.

Question:
Most of the cats we had when I was a child used to freak out over any small changes. How can I avoid having my new kitten turn out the same way?

Pam's Answer:
Gradually expose your new kitten to the various sights, sounds, and smells he'll most likely encounter as he grows up. The more your kitten is gradually exposed to unfamiliar stimuli as a kitten, the more comfortable he'll be with those sensory experiences as an adult.

Everyone wants a cat who'll be friendly and comfortable when visitors come to the house. The way to increase the odds of that happening is to gently expose him to a variety of people while he's a kitten.

Help Your Kitten Become Comfortable Through Gradual Exposure. Travel is one of the big sources of change-related stress. Your kitten may not have a problem being put into a carrier at this age, but as an adult, he may resist the idea. Keep the carrier out and line it with a towel to create a cozy hideaway. Periodically place your kitten in the carrier, carry him around the house, and also take him for rides in the car. The earlier your kitten is exposed to car travel, the less anxiety the experience will cause when he must go on trips as an adult.

And speaking of trips, take some trips to the veterinary clinic just to help your kitten become comfortable with the sights, sounds, and scents there. Periodic social visits, when a clinic staff member just holds or pets him, may help him develop a more positive association with the environment. In addition, if he gets used to hearing dogs or sniffing the scents there, the less unsettling the clinic might be as he matures.

Long-Term Benefits. While kittenhood is a wonderful and fun time, it's also a time for him to learn and to absorb experiences. The more time you spend to gradually introduce new things to your kitten, the more accepting he'll be of those experiences later in life, and that'll reduce everyone's stress level.

Question:
How can I teach my kitten to stop biting me when we play?

Pam's Answer:
The first and most important rule for teaching a kitten to play gently is to not use your fingers as toys. No matter how young your kitten is and whether it hurts when she bites or not, this isn't the message you want to send to her. Biting flesh is never to be allowed or encouraged.

From the very beginning, have appropriate toys for your kitten to bite during play. For interactive playtime, use toys based on a fishing-pole design. That will put a safe distance between your hands and her teeth. This way, when your kitten is enthusiastically involved in play, she doesn't have to worry about crossing the line.

When using smaller toys, such as fuzzy mice, be sure you toss them for the kitten to chase. Don't dangle them where she could accidentally bite your fingers or reach up and scratch you with her paws. During playtime you never want to send a mixed message, because what she learns as a kitten stays with her as she grows.

When Your Kitten Bites. If she accidentally bites you during playtime, immediately stop all action and stay still. She wants movement (her prey would be moving), so if you stay still, she won't be getting her desired result. If she bites your hand and holds on, stay still. Then, instead of pulling away, gently push toward your kitten. This will confuse her and she'll loosen her grip.

When your kitten bites, it's important to stop all movement and ignore her. You can restart play when your kitten goes back to being relaxed and in control. This will send the message that biting skin will mean an end to the game. Once she lets go of your hand, move it far enough away so she gets a clear message that you aren't engaging with her when she exhibits that behavior.

Time to Teach

Orphaned kittens who are bottle-fed may have a tendency for rough play because they didn't get the benefit of learning from Mom and littermates. It's up to you to teach your kitten proper play.

What Not to Do. If your kitten bites, don't hit her, push her away, squirt her with water, or yell at her. Although these actions may momentarily cause her to release her grip, they can have long-term negative effects. Your kitten may soon learn to become afraid of you. If you do any type of physical reprimand, then you can also send her into a defensive state, and this could actually cause her to bite harder the next time. The last thing you want is for your new kitten to become afraid and eventually start avoiding any interaction with you or for her to learn that aggression is the best form of communication.

Chapter 2

Boot Camp

*Training basics
for you and your cat*

Question:
What should we do the first night we bring our new cat home?

Pam's Answer:
It's much easier to spend the time to make sure your home is cat-safe *before* you bring in your newest family member. If you haven't lived with a cat before, you'll be surprised at the places a cat can hide and the trouble she can get into. Look at cat-proofing as you would baby-proofing, but think of this "baby" as a super toddler who can jump almost seven times her height, squeeze into spaces that seem completely impossible, and use her teeth to chew through cords, among many other talents a new cat parent probably never thought possible.

A Place of Her Own. Even though you plan on providing this wonderful and loving home for your new cat, she's not ready to see all of it yet. It'll be overwhelming for her to be placed in the middle of the living room the first day you bring her home, especially if you live in an environment larger than a small apartment. If you do that, the first thing she may do is run for cover somewhere. Instead, set up a sanctuary room (usually an extra bedroom, or any room that can be closed off) so she can take time to get her bearings.

Resources and Hiding Places. Her sanctuary room should be supplied with a litter box, scratching post, water, food bowl, and toys. In addition to the basic resources, set up some hiding places and covered navigation paths. If you just put the cat in a bedroom without any private paths, she might camp out under the bed if she's fearful. A better option is to create tunnels so she can securely go from one hiding place to the food bowl or litter box without feeling vulnerable. You can buy soft-sided cat tunnels or you can make tunnels with paper bags or boxes.

To help facilitate familiarity and comfort, you can also plug in a Feliway pheromone diffuser. The analogues of the F3 fraction of feline facial pheromones in the product are associated with familiarity and self-identification in an environment. Feliway is available at pet-product stores, online, and through many veterinary clinics.

Allow Time for the Cat to Get Her Bearings. Depending upon where she came from and her anxiety level, it's normal for her to not want to eat, use her litter box, or drink any water right away. Provide a small amount of food and give her privacy. She initially may feel more comfortable to eat when no one is around. If she doesn't show any interest in eating the first day, just keep providing small meals and fresh water. Don't put out too much food, so you can monitor whether any is actually getting eaten or not. By the second day, she should be hungry enough to start nibbling. If not, talk to your veterinarian. You don't want the cat to go more than a day without eating, but your veterinarian will provide specific instructions on how you should handle the situation based on your cat's history and circumstances.

Mood Lighting

Adjust the lighting in the sanctuary room so it's not too bright, so your new cat doesn't feel too exposed. A dimmer switch on the light would be a good idea, or just use night-lights, especially if you're dealing with a kitty who is fearful.

Let the Cat Make the First Move. Go at the cat's pace when it comes to interaction. It's tempting to try to hold, pet, or interact with your cat right away, but depending on where she came from and her current comfort level, she may not be ready to have you get too close. You can use a fishing pole–type toy to conduct a casual, low-intensity play session to ease her anxiety.

Slowly Introduce Other Family Members. Everyone in the family will be eager to get to know the new cat, but she may not be ready to have several unfamiliar people crowded into her sanctuary room. Do individual introductions slowly. If she's hiding and seems not yet ready, back off and let her continue to gain confidence in her new surroundings. There will be plenty of time later to make formal introductions.

Let Her Explore. When your new cat feels comfortable walking around her space and no longer hides when you come in, you can start to let her explore beyond her sanctuary room. If you live in a large home, don't overwhelm her by letting her wander around in every room. Let her explore slowly, a little at a time, so she always knows the route back to her sanctuary.

Introduce Other Family Pets. If there are other resident pets in the home, then the introduction of the new cat must be done with finesse and patience. Cat-to-cat introductions can be very tricky, so take the time to give the cats a reason to like each other through a gradual intro and positive associations. Keep in mind that the resident cat will feel that his territory has been invaded, and the new cat will feel that she has been dropped behind enemy lines. For information on how to do a cat-to-cat introduction, refer to Chapter 10.

If the resident pet is a dog, use care to ensure safety for all concerned. Don't leave the cat and dog alone until you've completed the introduction process and are sure the pets will be safe around each other.

Trust-Building and Training. It's never too early to start training. Your new cat is always learning, and what she learns depends on the messages you send. Be consistent and humane in your training process. Provide what she needs, use positive, force-free training that sends a consistent message, and always let her know when she's done it right. The decision to bring a cat into your life might have been a sudden and impulsive move, but providing for her health and happiness should never be. Take the time to educate yourself on what cats need for physical, emotional, and mental health.

Question:

We're about to adopt our first cat. I've seen many of my friends make mistakes with their cats. What should we watch out for?

Pam's Answer:

Seeing those errors gives you the opportunity to learn. Very often, pet adoptions are spur-of-the-moment decisions, and some pet parents aren't fully prepared to live with a companion animal. Here are some of the common mistakes I see:

Getting a Cat Who Isn't Right for You. Many pet adoptions are done without thinking it all through. As a result, far too many animals get brought back to the shelter when something goes awry. Whether you adopt or purchase a cat, make sure that she's a good fit for your family and that your environment will be safe, secure, and healthy for her.

Viewing a Cat as Low Maintenance. It breaks my heart whenever I hear people say they didn't have the time for a dog, so they adopted a cat. All too often, people adopt cats and then interact with them only at their convenience. The cat is left to his own devices, and then the cat parent is disappointed when the relationship doesn't grow. If you want to have a relationship, you have to be willing to invest in it. Don't view cats as convenience pets. They need a commitment of time that you'll devote to them, to play and share and be together, more than just to keep the bowl full of food.

Not Providing Routine Veterinary Care. Cats are the most popular pet in America, yet more dogs get seen by veterinarians. Cats aren't being taken for veterinary care as often as they should be. Don't make the mistake of thinking that because your cat never goes outdoors, she doesn't need yearly vaccinations and health exams. Your cat needs regular veterinary care.

Neglecting to Spay or Neuter. Unless you live under a rock, you know there are homeless pets everywhere and shelters are overcrowded. Animals are dying on a daily basis because there's no shelter space available. If the pet overpopulation issue doesn't have an effect on you, then I hope this will: an intact male cat *will* urine-mark, and an intact female *will* let you know that her mission is to escape outside and mate. With both male and female cats, failure to spay or neuter may also increase their chances of certain types of cancer.

Allowing Your Cat to Roam Outside. Whether to allow a cat outdoors at all is a controversial topic. My opinion is cats are safer indoors, and you can create a stimulating environment inside providing all the entertainment, enrichment, and fun a cat needs while keeping her safe. Letting your cat outdoors to roam the neighborhood puts her at risk for disease, injury, fighting, poisoning, abuse, parasites, and getting lost, stolen, or hit by a car.

No Identification. If you don't have identification on your cat you stand very little chance of ever getting her back if she gets lost. While the common form of identification is an ID tag on a collar, the safest method is to have your cat microchipped. Collars put a cat at risk of strangulation if caught on a tree branch. A breakaway collar is safest but won't provide identification if the cat slips out of it. If you do use a collar, make sure it's a breakaway one, but also have her microchipped as double protection.

Not Taking the Time to Train Your Cat. If you've lived with cats in the past and you have memories of trying to get them to the veterinarian without getting scratched or bitten, then I hope you now realize how important it is to start training from the beginning. Spend time getting your cat comfortable with being in a carrier, car travel, and being handled. In addition, take the time now to train your cat about the dos and don'ts in her environment. Is she allowed on the kitchen counter? The couch? If not, get started training her as to where she can and can't go. If you don't train her but then punish her when she does something you don't like, you're truly unfair to the cat. Be consistent and do appropriate, force-free training from the start.

Be Body Wise

Pay attention to your cat's body language to develop a stronger relationship and avoid misunderstandings.

Poor Litter Box Maintenance. You don't want to use a dirty bathroom, and your cat doesn't want to either. The most common reason people call my office with a cat behavior problem is because the cat isn't using the litter box. In many cases the reason is because the human family members aren't keeping the box clean enough. Make sure you provide your cat with a litter box that's the right size, filled with the type of litter most appealing to her, in a location convenient for the cat. And keep it clean.

Declawing. Don't put your furniture ahead of the emotional and physical health of your cat. Declawing is essentially ten amputations. Your cat's claws are a vital part of her physical and emotional health. If you take the time to understand how this instinct works and why it's beneficial for a cat, you'll realize how inhumane it is to declaw. Any cat can be trained not to claw the furniture—that's the solution, not surgery.

Not Buying the Right Scratching Post. If you bought the cute, soft, carpet-covered scratching post from your local pet-product store, you're going to be very disappointed, because your cat will prefer your furniture to that useless object. Sisal—it's scratchy!

Failure to Pay Attention to the Medical Connection in Behavior Change. A cat is a creature of habit. When she changes her behavior, she can be indicating a potential medical problem or reacting to a stress trigger. View the change as a potential red flag that something isn't right.

Failure to Prepare Your Cat for Life's Changes. Whether because of a move to a new house, a pregnancy, another pet, or a renovation, it can be very scary for your cat to suddenly find herself in an unfamiliar situation. Take the time to ease your cat through changes.

Punishment. Cats don't misbehave out of spite. If you think your cat is doing something wrong in a deliberate attempt to make you mad, you're mistaken. Punishment is inhumane and counterproductive.

No Environmental Enrichment. A cat is a hunter. She needs stimulation and the opportunity for discovery. Behavior problems can be the result of a boring environment. Your cat needs interactive playtime, solo play, places to scratch, cozy hideaways for napping, elevated areas for climbing and perching, and time with *you*.

Question:
To keep my mind sharp, I do crossword puzzles and am trying to learn a new language. Is there anything I can do to help keep my cat's mind sharp?

Pam's Answer:
Yes, absolutely! Your cat has a remarkable brain, which needs to be challenged, stimulated, and exercised to help maintain good mental fitness. Here are ten tips to get you started:

1. Play with Your Cat. Engage in daily interactive play sessions, moving the toy like prey so your cat can use her incredible hunting skills.

2. Make Mealtime Fun. Instead of heaping a pile of food into your cat's bowl, use puzzle feeders so she gets the chance to work for food. This feeding method provides entertainment for your cat while keeping her mentally stimulated.

3. Hide-and-Seek Solo Playtime. The solo toys your cat has for playtime (such as the fuzzy mice or balls) can be strategically placed around the house for her to "discover" all over again.

4. Clicker-Train. This training method is great for helping with behavior problems, but it's also just plain fun and is a great way to mentally challenge your cat. Learn about clicker training later in this chapter.

5. Do Homemade Agility Training. Start with something basic, such as having your cat go through a paper bag tunnel, and then add to the course with various obstacles. This is a great combination of mental and physical exercise.

6. Prevent Loneliness. For some cats, the addition of a companion cat is a great way to fight loneliness, especially when the human family members are away from home for long periods of time. Having a cat companion creates lots of opportunities for playtime and mental fitness. Not every cat benefits from feline companionship, though. Some cats prefer being the only cat. In terms of the human family, pay attention to your cat and maximize the bonding process. Living with a cat isn't just about providing food, a litter box, and shelter. It's about the human-animal bond. Spend time with your cat.

7. Keep Your Cat Socialized. Begin this early, and you'll have a cat who adjusts to change, accepting visitors in the home and enjoying life.

8. Minimize Stress. It's rare for a cat to just "get over it," if stressed. Address issues that could be causing unhealthy stress to your cat.

Be a Play Pal

No matter how tired you may be at the end of a workday, remember, your cat has been waiting for you. Take time to play with her.

---

9. Address Behavior Problems. If your cat is experiencing a behavior problem, address it early and appropriately so her brain can focus on the good things in her life and *you* can stop stressing.

10. Maintain Your Cat's Good Health. Help your cat stay active, feed her a diet appropriate for her age and physical condition, have routine veterinary exams, and stay on top of any potential medical issue.

It's Never Too Early or Too Late. If you have a kitten, now is the time to begin mental fitness training and maintain it as she grows. When your cat is a feline senior citizen, keep her brain active to help slow the progression of age-related deterioration and improve her quality of life.

Question:
Do you recommend using a squirt bottle to reprimand cats?

Pam's Answer:
The squirt-bottle deterrent, in many cat households, has become the popular method to keep cats off counters and tables. It's also the way

many people attempt to stop their cats from scratching the furniture. The squirt bottle is used to stop a cat who is getting too aggressive, either with another companion animal or with a human family member. The squirt bottle has become the tool many cat parents reach for immediately when the cat isn't acting the way they want him to act.

You'd think that based on the popularity of the squirt-bottle technique, it must be an extremely effective and successful method of training cats. The truth is, it's not effective at ceasing unwanted behaviors. The technique typically accomplishes three things:

- It creates frustration in the cat.
- It causes the cat to become afraid of you.
- It teaches the cat to engage in the behavior in your absence.

Punishment Doesn't Work. It's important to understand that regardless of how unwanted the behavior is in your eyes, it has a purpose for the cat. Your cat isn't scratching the sofa or jumping on the counter just to make you mad. Animals engage in behaviors that serve a function. Many of the behaviors cat parents view as unwanted, such as furniture scratching, are normal, natural behaviors. When you squirt the cat with water for scratching the furniture, you may momentarily stop the behavior, but the cat has a normal and natural need to scratch. If he gets punished every time he attempts to engage in a normal behavior, he may continue the behavior covertly. When you punish a cat for exhibiting a behavior you don't like, you stop the behavior only short-term.

Instead of trying to train a cat through force and punishment, here's a better idea:

Use CatWise Training. Figure out *why* the cat exhibits a particular behavior so you can provide a better option. If your cat scratches the furniture, then probably you either don't have a scratching post or it's the wrong kind. If your cat gets aggressive with another companion animal, then it's time to do some behavior modification work to help them develop a positive association with each other. If you squirt the cat with water when he reacts to another cat, you'll do nothing to help them form a peaceful relationship.

> ## Plan Ahead
>
> Have a clear plan for what you want your cat to do in place
> of the unwanted behavior. Rewarding desirable behavior
> is far more effective than focusing on what your cat is
> doing wrong.

When training, *trust* is essential. Your cat needs to be able to trust you
in order to form that important bond. The last thing you want is for your
cat to run from you out of fear.

Question:
How do I get my loudmouthed cat to stop meowing so much?

Pam's Answer:
I don't know any specifics of your situation, but here's some general
information. There are some breeds, such as the Siamese, that are naturally vocal. If you have a breed of cat known for running commentaries
on the day's activities, then you just have to learn to accept that. To be on
the safe side, if this is a new behavior or if your cat is up there in age,
have him checked out by the veterinarian. It's common for older cats
who have some hearing loss or are experiencing age-related cognitive
issues to vocalize more. You also want to make sure your cat isn't meowing due to pain.

Train Your Cat to Be Quiet. How do you do this? It's actually very simple, but it takes patience. Wait out the meowing and don't acknowledge
your cat until he stops. When he's quiet, immediately reward him. At
first, reward him for short intervals of quiet and then increase to longer
intervals. Don't set the bar too high, because you want him to stay
engaged in the training. He'll eventually realize that silence offers a better reward than meowing.

I've found that the easiest way to do quietness training is with a
clicker. I click when the cat isn't meowing and immediately offer a reward. Clicker training is a very effective way to let the cat know what you
want from him. See later in this chapter for the full lowdown on clickers.

Decoding the Meow

Cat parents are well trained when it comes to our ability to interpret what each particular meow means. We quickly learn the differences among the *feed me* meow, the *let me out* meow, and the *I want attention* meow.

Be Patient and Consistent. If your cat is used to getting his own way through nonstop meowing, it takes patience on your part to do the training, but because you're dealing with a very smart animal, he'll soon learn what behavior offers good rewards and what behavior offers nothing.

Consistency is extremely important in training, so don't reward him for being quiet half the time while you yell at him or do what he wants the other times. Inconsistency sends a very confusing mixed message to the cat and creates frustration for everyone involved.

Question:

As a family, we're struggling with training our cat. He sometimes listens, but other times he just does what he wants. Are we doing something wrong, or is he just a very dominant cat?

Pam's Answer:

Sometimes a cat continues to display unwanted behavior because we unknowingly reinforce it. Of course, we don't do it deliberately, but the bottom line is, the cat receives a message saying, "Keep doing what you're doing." These mistakes are very common, and even the most experienced cat parent slips up when it comes to consistent messages.

The Messages You Send. Think about whether you've offered your cat a treat, his meal, or even some attention to quiet him down due to his relentless vocalizations. You're working at the kitchen counter or sitting at the computer, and he meows and meows for attention. You pet him as he meows, or maybe you even pick him up, put him on your lap, or cuddle him. What's the message the cat just received? Relentless meowing results in a reward. Even just shouting at him to be quiet gives him some form of attention for the behavior.

You're asleep in bed, and your cat meows and walks back and forth across your chest in the wee hours of the morning. Do you pet him to quiet him down? Talk to him? Or maybe you just get up and put some food in his food bowl so he'll let you get a few more hours of sleep. Again, the message received by the cat is that the behavior displayed results in a reward.

It's important not to send mixed messages. Instead of giving attention to the cat for unwanted behavior, instead of punishing him or yelling at him, just ignore him. Reward him only for the desired behavior. This sends a clear message to your cat about what behavior will result in something good.

Help Your Cat Succeed. The other part of rewarding desirable behavior is to set your cat up to succeed. If he meows at you when you head to the kitchen to begin dinner preparations or when you sit down to work on the computer, maybe his environment is just boring, or you're not giving him enough interactive playtime. Before you start a task, engage him in a quick play session or set out a fun food-dispensing toy or other puzzle-type toy. This way, you provide him with beneficial activity and attention so the unwanted behavior never has to come into play at all.

If you've heard the myth that the proper way to correct a cat is to flick or bop him on the nose to imitate what the mother cat does, don't believe it. This is horrible and dangerous advice. Using this method will only cause your cat to view you as a threat. He may become afraid of you or even return the display of aggression. You could also hurt him. What the mother cat does for correction is unique to felines and accompanied by other forms of communication we can't mimic.

It's time to examine how you interact with your cat and whether you've been guilty of sending conflicting signals. Remember:

- Reward desirable behavior
- Don't send mixed messages
- Set your cat up to succeed

Family Members Need to Be on the Same Page. Inconsistency in the family can be a problem when it comes to cat training. One member may allow a cat to do something but another may not. The poor cat is stuck in the middle. This commonly happens with behaviors like begging at the table, counter surfing, sleeping in the cat parents' bed, drinking from the faucet, or playing with objects that aren't toys (such as pens and ponytail holders). There's always one softie in the family who just can't say no to the cat, but then the cat ends up getting reprimanded by another family member for the very same behavior. Work with your family to establish consistent rules so your cat won't get caught in the middle.

Question:

What is clicker training and can it be done with cats?

Pam's Answer:

When you think of clicker training, you probably think of dogs. Maybe you've seen it being done in the middle of your local pet-product store during puppy-training classes.

Why Clicker-Train? Clicker training helps your cat feel more in control in her environment because it offers her a choice. Choice is very powerful to help a cat feel in control as opposed to backed into a corner. When your cat feels more in control in her environment, she'll relax and be less inclined to exhibit negative behaviors. She'll also realize that offering desirable behavior gets her a reward but an undesirable behavior offers nothing. Cats are very smart, so they quickly figure out that desirable behavior is more beneficial.

Clicker training offers you an effective communication tool to use with your cat. You can click and reward for subtle behaviors you normally wouldn't be able to acknowledge. Clicker training can also be done at a distance, so it's a good option if you can't get physically close to the cat.

Your Tools. A clicker is a small device that makes a cricket-type sound. Its sound is unique in the environment, so when the cat hears it, she will know that she has done something desirable. The clicker is used to "mark" the behavior you want from your cat when it's displayed. The clicker communicates to the cat that a very specific behavior is desirable. Because most cats are very food-motivated, you'll immediately follow a click with a food reward. The cat learns that the sound of the click means a reward will follow.

Clickers are available at your local pet-product store, as well as online. For

timid cats who might be afraid of the clicker sound, you can put the clicker
in your pocket, so it's muffled, or use the click of a ballpoint pen.

Clicker Choices

I prefer button-type clickers over box clickers when training cats. The box clickers tend to be too loud.

The other important tool you'll need is the actual reward. It's important
to find the right reward that'll inspire your cat to want to do what it is
you're asking of her. The most popular reward is food that your cat finds
very appealing. Each cat is an individual, though, and your kitty may
find nonfood rewards more appealing, such as petting, verbal praise,
playtime with you, or being offered a toy for solo play. You'll have to find
what works best for your own cat. It's important to have that reward
ready to offer. Whether it's food or a toy, carry it with you so you'll always
be ready to immediately acknowledge and reward a behavior.

Getting Started. You first have to teach the cat to associate the sound of
the clicker with the food reward. This is what gives the clicker its value.
Click the clicker and then offer the food reward. Once you've clicked and
offered the food, wait for the cat to look at you before repeating the
sequence. This helps your cat associate you as the supplier of the reward.
Repeat the process about ten times or however long the cat remains
interested and engaged.

The first few sessions shouldn't be very long. If your cat isn't interested,
she may not be hungry enough or the food reward choice may not be motivating enough.

Food Rewards. When using food as a reward, measure your cat's daily
amount so you can designate a portion for training; don't make the
reward food extra, or you'll see extra pounds too. You can put a little wet
food on a rubber-tipped baby spoon or on a tongue depressor. If using
dry food, make sure you measure the daily portion so you don't overfeed
by simply reaching into the bag or container and grabbing a handful. If
you use treats, break them up into small pieces to get more training mile-
age out of them.

> ## Limit the Treats
>
> Treats should make up less than 10 percent of your cat's daily diet.

Target Training

Stage One. After you've taught your cat to make the association between the clicker and the food reward, you can now have him learn a behavior. Start by having him touch his nose to a target. This is called target training. Your target can be a chopstick, a straw, a traditional target stick, or even the eraser end of a pencil. I like using the eraser end of a pencil because it's soft and resembles another cat's nose.

Hold the target stick in one hand and the clicker and treat in the other hand. The treat needs to be within easy reach so you'll be able to reward immediately. Hold the target about eight inches off the ground (approximate nose height of a cat) and about two inches away from your cat's nose. When your cat sniffs the target or touches it with his nose, immediately click and reward. Click the instant he does what you want—not before or after. The click marks the exact behavior you want, so if your timing is off, the cat won't know what behavior you're asking of him. As soon as you've clicked and treated, put the target stick behind your back or move it away momentarily.

You'll repeat this behavior of having him touch the target stick about ten times, but be sure to get the cat's attention so he looks at you between each successful attempt. This'll help him connect this experience with you. *You* are the source of the treat, whether it's food, grooming, petting, or a favorite toy.

After about six or seven successful touches, you should be able to move the target stick a little farther away, so the cat has to take a step or two to touch it. Continue to increase the distance. This is how you work up to being able to direct the cat to specific locations.

Click and reward only when the cat touches his nose to the target. Don't reward for paw touches, body rubs, licking, or biting the target. Consistency is important. You're telling him what behavior is the magic one; he's not the one telling you.

After about ten times of successful nose touching at various distances, add the verbal cue. Cueing is important because it lets the cat know he'll now be rewarded only when you ask for the particular behavior. You can name the behavior anything you want, but keep it easy to remember so you'll be consistent in training. "Touch" is obviously a good verbal cue. When you assign a verbal cue, you'll be able to request specific behaviors with something as simple as a word or two.

Stage Two. Once your cat understands target training, you can use it to direct him to other areas. If you want to train him to go to a particular area, such as his bed, a perch, or a mat, in order to chill out and feel safe during a cat-to-cat introduction or when you are trying to keep a lid on multipet tension, target training can help.

To train a cat to go to a specific location, start by placing a cat bed, a fleece pad, or a simple mat near your cat. I often use soft cloth table place-mats when I work with my clients' cats. If the cat checks out the mat you've placed near him, click and reward. Pick up the mat and place it down again. If he touches the mat, click and reward. If the cat doesn't show any interest in the mat, you may have to lure him a bit. Hold the target stick over the mat. As soon as your cat places one paw on the mat, click and reward. Reward by tossing a treat away from the mat so you can reset the behavior.

Phase out the use of the target stick after a few repetitions so your cat starts to concentrate on the fact that the wanted behavior is to step on the mat and no longer just to aim for the target stick. If he doesn't get the idea, then reintroduce the target stick for a couple more repetitions. Your goal, though, is to eliminate the target stick as quickly as possible.

When the cat is successfully putting one paw on the mat, build up to having him put two paws on it before you click and treat. Delay the click until you see he has two paws on the mat. Then delay the click until he has three paws . . . and then four. He'll soon learn he must put his entire body on the mat in order to be rewarded. Remember to toss the treat away from the mat each time and then reset the behavior by lifting the mat and putting it back down.

When your cat successfully understands and performs the behavior, add the verbal cue of "Go to mat." By adding the verbal cue, you can use this behavior to ask him to "go to mat" whenever you need him to calm down. It can become a place he associates with safety. It's not a time-out but rather a place to feel secure. This is important to remember, because clicker training must never be used in a punitive way. If you call the cat to the mat to punish him, you'll undo all the good work you've done so far and end up creating secondary behavior problems.

Be sure the location for the mat is one your cat will enjoy and where he'll be safe. When he's on the mat, he should never be ambushed by another cat or dog or be bothered by any family member. His association with the mat must remain positive.

This behavior is helpful in multicat households because you can train each cat to go to a particular mat. "Go to mat" can be used to help calm a cat when visitors are over or when you feel he may be getting too aroused.

When doing your "go to mat" training, keep the sessions short and fun. If the cat begins to get bored, seems distracted or tired, or is in the mood to play, then end the session. Clicker training and target training should be positive and a way to strengthen the bond you share with your cat.

Multicat Clicker Training

Don't worry about how to clicker-train more than one cat. You don't need clickers with different sounds. Just turn toward the cat and focus your attention on him. The other cats will know where your attention is directed.

That's Just the Beginning. There's so much you can do with clicker training. You can teach your cat a variety of fun behaviors, but you can also use it for behavior modification by rewarding behaviors (however subtle) that you want to see again. For example, when dealing with two cats who are hostile toward each other, I will click and reward any positive or nonaggressive display, such as when one cat breaks a stare or when one enters a room where the other cat is located. Clicker training becomes a great way to refocus the cat's attention.

Question:
What's the secret to being able to trim my cat's nails without getting scratched to bits? It becomes a battle to hold her down and get the job done once a month.

Pam's Answer:
She has learned to associate the procedure with restraint, discomfort, fear, or even pain. If you've had to wrap your cat in a towel, enlist the help of

family members to hold her down, or restrain her by scruffing, or if you have punished her in any way for being a wiggle worm, then all that just compounds the problem. If she dislikes the process now, she'll absolutely hate it the next time and then go into full panic mode the time after that. Nail trimming does not have to be stressful. OK, it may never top the list of your cat's favorite things to do, but it shouldn't create a wave of panic and should definitely not result in hissing, growling, biting, or scratching. When done correctly, it should be a quick, easy, and dare I say, pleasant experience.

Develop Trust. You have to take it slow and do some trust building. For this, you won't even get out the clippers or attempt to trim one nail. Your main objective during this phase is to show your cat that having her paws touched is a good thing.

The Velvet Touch. Choose a time to begin to train when your cat is relaxed and maybe even a bit sleepy. Arm yourself with some treats. Gently touch her paw and then offer a treat. If she has never been comfortable with having her paws touched, make sure that when you do touch her, it's for no more than a couple of seconds—just one gentle stroke.

Work up to being able to pet each of her paws and then to lift and hold one paw for a few seconds. When you hold her paw don't grasp or squeeze it—just let it sit in your hand for a count of three. Reward your cat with a treat for her tolerance whenever she allows her paws to be held.

The next step is to hold a paw and gently press it to extend the nail. Be very gentle. Do this with all of the paws.

Do the above exercises a couple of times a day until you feel your cat is completely comfortable with having her paws held and gently pressed so the nails are exposed. Remember to always reward your cat with a treat for her acceptance of each move you make.

Choose the Right Nail Clipper. Get a nail clipper meant for cat nails. Don't use a dog nail clipper, because it's too big, and don't use clippers meant for human fingernails, because they'll split the nails. The cat's nails are smaller and thinner, so use clippers specifically designed for their size and shape.

Avoid Cutting the Quick. There's a blood supply running through the nail. If your cat's nails are light-colored you can see the pink part. That's called the *quick*, and it contains nerves and the blood supply. If you cut the quick, you'll cause pain and bleeding, and your cat may fear future attempts at the procedure. Cut only the very tip of the nail—don't go beyond the curve. If your cat's nails are light-colored, it's much easier to see the quick; if they're dark-colored, be even more careful. Always cut less than you think you should. If you're at all in doubt about how much to trim, have your veterinarian or one of the clinic's veterinary technicians show you.

If you do accidentally cut the quick, stop the bleeding with a little cornstarch. Keep a small container of cornstarch with your grooming supplies just to be on the safe side. I hope you'll never need it.

Trimming the Nails. If your cat has had negative experiences with nail trimming, you shouldn't attempt to do more than one or two nails during each session. It's better to have the whole procedure over and done before your cat even realizes what just happened. If you keep the experience quick and positive, she'll be more relaxed next time around.

Choose a time for nail trimming when your cat is relaxed, perhaps just after eating. Hold the nail trimmer with one hand and take your cat's paw in the other hand. Gently press to expose a nail and do a quick, but careful snip. If she reacts, don't attempt to do any more nails. If she's calm, do another. Always end on a positive note. It's better to come back and do a couple more nails later than to have her struggle.

Keep track of which paw you're working on so you'll know where you left off when it's time to do a couple more nails. The less you have to hold a paw to double-check whether you've already cut those nails, the better.

Question:
I want to brush my cat's teeth but I'm afraid to go near her mouth. What's the best way to do it?

Pam's Answer:
To make it easier on everybody (cat and human), don't attempt to brush every tooth in your cat's mouth the very first time. As with many things in a cat's life, it's much less stressful if this process is introduced gradually and under positive conditions. Coming at her with a toothpaste-covered toothbrush isn't going to be well received.

Getting Started. First get your cat used to the idea of having her mouth touched. When she's in a receptive mood and enjoying some petting from you, gently stroke her around the head and then along the sides of the mouth. Offer a small reward for this. Next, slide your finger along her lips, then advance to gently rubbing her teeth. It may take several sessions to work up to this point, so don't be discouraged.

Types of Brushes. There are multiple options when it comes time to actually start brushing your cat's teeth. At your local pet-product store you can find finger toothbrushes, pet toothbrushes, and teeth-cleaning pads. Choose the product you think your cat will accept most readily. You may have to experiment with several. You will also find oral hygiene sprays, but they are a last resort if you truly decide you're unable to brush your cat's teeth. If you have any questions about oral sprays, talk to your veterinarian.

If you don't feel comfortable with any of the choices at the pet-product store, you can try using a baby toothbrush. They're small, gentle, and easy to handle. You can even wrap a small piece of pantyhose or gauze around your finger. Just make sure you don't rub and irritate the cat's gums.

Types of Toothpaste. Choose one specifically made for pets. Don't use toothpaste designed for human use, because it can burn the cat's tongue, throat, and stomach. Pet toothpastes usually come in chicken, beef, and other cat-appealing flavors.

Keep It Quick and Fun. It may be a stretch to consider tooth brushing as a fun activity, but if you keep the process quick and casual, it'll be over before your cat has a chance to complain.

Ideally, you should brush your cat's teeth daily. I'm realistic enough to know that many people aren't going to do that, so at the very least, try to maintain a schedule of two or three times a week. Even once a week is better than nothing.

Question:
What's the best way to give my cat a pill?

Pam's Answer:
Pilling a cat who doesn't want to be pilled is often a frightening experience for a cat parent. Here are some tips to make the process easier.

Know Your Options. If you know from previous experience that it's easier to administer a *liquid* to your cat by squirting it into her mouth with a syringe, ask your veterinarian if the medication comes in liquid form. Knowing your cat's preference may reduce stress. Flavoring, such as chicken, tuna, or beef, can be added to liquid medication. Many veterinarians have the flavorings in their office, but if not, your local pharmacy may. Ask your veterinarian whether the flavoring can be added to a particular liquid prescription. A tasty liquid medication may be much easier for an unhappy cat to swallow, and you might be able to avoid the whole pilling process altogether.

Some medications can be reformulated into *transdermal* form by a compounding pharmacy. Transdermal medications are absorbed slowly through the skin. This type of medication is usually rubbed on the inside of the ear tip for absorption through the skin. Ask your veterinarian about it.

One thing to keep in mind when using transdermal applications in multicat households is that cats may groom each other, causing the cat who isn't the patient to ingest some of the medication and the intended recipient to get less than the full intended prescription. Transdermal medication may also not be a good idea for households with children, who may pet the cat where the med was applied.

Pilling 101. Don't crush a pill in food. Crushing a coated pill exposes the bitter medicine. Coated pills are meant to stay intact until they get farther along in the digestive tract, and the bitter taste will likely cause the cat to reject all or part of the food, thus not getting the full dose.

And don't try burying it intact in a bowl, either. Your cat's acute sense of smell will easily detect even the most deeply hidden pill in the tastiest food, and you'll find it left alone in an otherwise empty bowl.

Some pills shouldn't be given with food, anyhow, so if you do have a highly food-motivated cat who eats anything and everything in his bowl, find out from your veterinarian whether that particular prescription can be given with food.

If your cat likes treats, there's a product called Pill Pockets, which makes medicating much easier. The soft treat has a pocket; you place the pill in it and squish it closed. Pill Pockets are very palatable. If you decide to try them, first offer one that doesn't contain a pill and then offer the pill-filled one. The product is available at pet supply stores and online.

Some cats willingly accept pills coated with something palatable and sticky, such as hairball remedy gel, cream cheese, meat-flavored baby food, or yogurt. You can even try a bit of anchovy paste. First, give the cat a little taste of the cheese or gel without the pill. Next, coat the pill with the flavored gel and then administer it. After the cat has swallowed the pill, offer another taste of the gel or baby food immediately. If you do use baby food, make sure it's a brand that doesn't include onion powder, as onions are toxic to cats.

Another option for cat parents who don't want to put their fingers into their cats' mouths is to use a pill gun. This is a plastic syringelike device that grips the pill with little "fingers" until you push the plunger to release it.

Pilling Techniques. There are a couple ways to do this. The first way is to place the cat on a table or counter. Put the palm of your hand over the top of the cat's head. Slightly tilt his head up. Now open his mouth by applying gentle pressure with your thumb on one side and middle finger on the other against the area behind the canine teeth. With your other hand, hold the pill between your thumb and index finger. Use your middle finger of that same hand to press the cat's lower jaw open and then gently drop the pill on the back of the tongue. Don't shoot it too far back into the throat. Let go of the cat's mouth so he can swallow but keep hold of him so he doesn't escape until you're sure he swallowed the pill. Don't clamp his mouth shut or he won't be able to swallow. Gentle downward strokes along his throat will also help the pill go down.

After your cat has taken the pill, offer him some water to ensure the pill isn't lodged in the esophagus. If he doesn't want to drink water, try offering some low-sodium chicken broth.

Here's another pilling position: Kneel on the floor and then sit back on your heels with your legs open in a V position. Place the cat between your legs so that he's facing away from you. This will prevent him from being able to squirm away. You can then use the same pilling technique described above. The V position is good for cats who are very squirmy during pilling. Just be sure and wear your jeans when doing this to avoid getting scratched on the legs.

Practice Makes Perfect. Do yourself and your cat a favor by training him to become comfortable with having his mouth touched and manipulated. If you start training a kitten to accept your fingers near his mouth, opening his mouth, and touching his teeth, you'll have it easier when pilling time comes around. No matter how healthy your kitten is now, at some point in his life, he'll need some sort of medication. Train him now to accept the procedure.

If you're dealing with an adult cat who isn't comfortable having his mouth touched, do some clicker training to help him learn to tolerate physical contact.

No Trapping

Never use the fact that the cat will have to go to the litter box at some point as an opportunity to trap him there in order to pill him. That's a surefire way to create a litter box avoidance problem.

Help from Your Veterinarian. If you aren't comfortable pilling your cat, ask your veterinarian to give you a lesson in the procedure. Someone in the office with experience will be able to guide you. The more confident, quick, and casual you are when medicating your cat, the less anxious you'll both be about the process.

Question:
When it comes to spaying or neutering cats, I know the reason for doing it is to help control pet overpopulation, but are there other reasons? I'm having trouble convincing my husband that our indoor cat should be neutered for behavioral reasons.

Pam's Answer:
As you're already aware, the pet overpopulation problem is devastatingly serious, and animals are being put to death every day because shelters simply don't have the room. Healthy animals are euthanized because people don't act responsibly. But overpopulation is not the only reason to spay or neuter your cat. There are health concerns and behavioral implications as well.

What Happens If You Don't Neuter a Male Cat. If your husband is under the impression that as long as the intact male cat is kept indoors, he'll be fine, he's dooming that cat to a life of frustration, straining at the mercy of hormones. Intact male cats will be on a mission to roam, increase their territory, find a mate, and fight competitors, so they'll spray. If your cat is indoors, then that behavior will be directed at any companion cats, or just the idea of them (if he's a solo cat). The spraying will be directed at your furniture and belongings. Everybody loses.

Don't assume that just because your cat lives exclusively indoors, he won't contribute to overpopulation or endure any of the suffering associated with life outdoors as an intact cat. Cats escape from their homes every day. Your cat could easily slip out the door, especially if he's driven by hormones and determined to escape.

Once outdoors, he's at risk of injury or even death as he fights other males while in search of a female in heat. Intact males tend to roam beyond their usual territory to search for females. Your cat may enter into the territory of a rougher and tougher male, and the result of that fight could be tragic.

Even if a cat fight is not fatal, there may be other awful consequences. A cat's canine teeth are very sharp. If your cat is bitten, the wound may seal over, leaving bacteria trapped inside, and an abscess may form. This leads to infection and is very painful. Often the veterinarian must leave the wound open with a surgical drain while the infection clears. There's so much suffering involved with cat fights that could easily be avoided by neutering your cat and keeping him indoors.

In addition, the more an intact male fights and mates, the more he's at risk of contracting and spreading disease. Intact males are also at risk of developing certain cancers later in life. Neutering your young male will eliminate the risk of testicular cancer and greatly reduce the risk of prostate disease.

What Happens If You Don't Spay a Female Cat. An outdoor female will endure fights and repeated mating. Feline mating is not pretty—it's violent and extremely stressful. It also puts the female cat at risk of contracting and spreading disease. Giving birth, especially if a cat is very young, can pose a health risk to her as well.

An intact female indoor cat will vocalize, try to escape, and like an intact male, live as a victim of hormones. Life for an unspayed adult female cat is filled with stress. It's also very stressful for everyone else in the family. She won't be a pleasant companion to live with. She'll also attract every intact male in the neighborhood. Cat parents may find themselves dealing with cats who spray outside the windows or fight in the backyard because they know there's a cat in heat close by.

Repeated heat cycles are also very stressful on a cat's body. Moreover, unspayed females are at risk of mammary, ovarian, and uterine cancer.

Be Responsible. There's simply no excuse for not spaying or neutering your cat. If budget is a concern, you can find out about low-cost spay/neuter clinics in your town.

Some parents feel it's beneficial to have children experience the miracle of birth by having the female cat get pregnant, but it would be much better to demonstrate what responsible pet ownership means. Teaching them to be caring, responsible, kind, and attentive to animals will be a greater lifelong lesson than having them watch a cat deliver six kittens that'll likely end up in a shelter, outdoors, or dead.

Safe Surgery. Neutering and spaying are very low-risk surgeries. For male cats, neutering involves removing the testicles through an incision in the scrotum. No sutures are required, and post-op care involves monitoring to make sure the healing incision stays clean and dry. The cat will go home the morning after the surgery.

Spaying, the surgery for females, consists of removing the uterus, fallopian tubes, and ovaries through an abdominal incision. The few sutures across the cat's shaved abdomen are removed about ten days post-op.

Talk with Your Veterinarian. Your veterinarian can answer specific concerns you may have about the procedure itself, anesthesia risks, and post-op care, thus reassuring an anxious parent.

Chapter 3

Social Media

How cats communicate with us and each other

Question:
When a cat purrs, does that mean he's happy?

Pam's Answer:
The purr of a cat. It's the most mesmerizing sound. It's the sound that makes us smile and think all is right in our cat's world. That gentle sound relaxes and even mystifies us. Some facts about purring may surprise you, though. If you were under the impression, as many people are, that cats purr only when happy or content, you're missing out on how multi-faceted a purr truly is.

How Cats Purr. The physical basis of purring had been a mystery for many years. One theory was that purring was created by blood-flow turbulence in the chest. Most experts now believe that the sound is created by the laryngeal and diaphragmatic muscles in combination with a neural oscillator. A message from a neural oscillator in the brain gets sent to the laryngeal muscles, causing them to vibrate. Their movement controls how much air passes through the larynx.

Purring occurs during inhalation and exhalation. In some cases, the purr is so quiet and low, you may feel it more than hear it. Some cats have very loud purrs, though, and you can hear those engines clear across the room.

In the Beginning. The mother cat purrs during labor, probably to self-soothe and control pain. Endorphins, compounds that relieve pain by binding to the body's opiate receptors, are released when cats purr, which can help in pain management.

Once kittens are born, the mother's purr is crucial to their survival. Kittens are born blind and deaf, but they do feel vibrations. The mother's vibrating purr leads them to her body for nursing and critical warmth; they're unable to regulate their own body temperature yet.

Kittens can purr when they're just two days old, starting the communication among littermates and the mother cat.

When kittens reach the teats, they begin what is known as the milk tread. They press and flex their paws to stimulate milk flow. They also typically purr while kneading. This combination of purring and kneading is often carried over into adult life. You're probably very familiar with hearing or feeling your adult cat purr when kneading on soft objects (like your stomach).

This warm and wonderful feeling of being snuggled close to Mom, being safe and receiving meals on demand, certainly explains the contentment aspect of the purr.

Purrs Mean More Than Just Mom. The purr communicates several different emotional states. The one humans are most familiar with is that a purring cat is contented happiness, but cats also purr for a variety of other reasons.

The Purrfect Smile

The cat's purr has been compared to the human smile. People smile for a variety of reasons. People smile when happy, nervous and unsure, or when trying to make someone else feel comfortable. It's that way with the purr, as well.

Cats may purr when happy, but they also purr to soothe themselves. Cats may also purr in attempts to soothe potential opponents when they know there's no means of escape. They may purr when nervous, sick, in pain, or even when close to death. This makes sense because of the endorphin release that comes with the purring.

Many cats really know how to maximize the purr to their advantage. A study at the University of Sussex in the United Kingdom found that cats have developed a specialized purr referred to as a *soliciting purr*. The specialized purr includes cries at frequencies similar to those of a human baby's cry. Cats seem to be able to ramp up the high frequency in order to get their human family members to feed them. Pretty smart, wouldn't you agree?

Purring is also believed to be used by the cat for healing. Purrs vibrate at 25–150 Hz, which is also the frequency range that assists in physical healing, including bone mending. It may also be that purring during rest is a form of physical therapy to keep the cat's bones strong, for there is a connection between exposure to the frequency range of 25–150 Hz and increasing bone density. So even as a cat is napping or resting, he might be keeping his bones strong and healthy and ready for the next opportunity to pounce on prey.

How Purring Helps Humans. We benefit too when our cats purr. Just stroking a cat has been shown to lower a human's blood pressure and stress response. The sound of the cat's purr near us usually makes us feel more relaxed, because we associate purring with contentment. When you stroke a purring cat, both of you get something comforting out of the exchange.

What About Big Cats? Large cats that roar, such as lions, don't purr, but cats that don't roar, such as cheetahs and bobcats, can purr. Cats that purr have a hard hyoid bone located in the throat. Cats that don't purr have a more elastic hyoid bone. That flexibility of the bone enables roaring but not purring.

Cats don't have a monopoly on purring, though. Some other animals can purr as well, such as raccoons. Have you ever been close enough to hear the purring of a raccoon? Probably not. As for me, I think I'll stick with the cat's purr.

Question:
How do cats use scent to communicate?

Pam's Answer:
Scent is your cat's calling card. His sense of smell tells him about other cats in his environment, so scent is a valuable communication tool. Being the verbal species that we are, humans don't truly appreciate the volumes of information provided in scent, but trust me, your cat is on the case. The scent he leaves behind is an encyclopedia of feline data.

Your Cat's Scent Glands. Cats have scent glands located on various parts of the body, such as the paw pads, sides of the mouth, and base of the tail. There are also two scent glands on each side of the anus that can release a very strong-smelling liquid. Cats may release the contents of these anal glands when very frightened. It's not unusual for this to happen when a frightened cat is being handled at the veterinary clinic.

Scent glands release *pheromones*, scent chemicals that provide information. Outdoors, scent communication is vital because it reveals information about one cat to another without the risk of physical confrontation. For an outdoor cat, this is a very important survival benefit. The fewer physical altercations that occur, the greater the chances that the cat will live unscathed to hunt another day.

Then, of course, there's the scent of urine. All those who've ever lived with a cat, or had neighbors' cats visiting their gardens, are familiar with the smell of cat pee. If that urine belongs to an unneutered male, the odor is even more pungent.

How Cats Use Scent. Scent is used to identify members of the same colony, define territory, create familiarity, announce sexual readiness, learn more about unfamiliar cats in the environment, self-soothe, bond with another, or threaten.

The scent glands around the face are identified as friendly, or low-intensity. These are used when the cat marks familiar objects he considers part of his turf, or when he deposits scent as a bonding gesture, as when head bunting. You're also probably very familiar with the sight of your cat cheek-rubbing on objects in the home. This is a comforting behavior for him and reflects his sense of security and familiarity with the environment.

The scent glands in his paw pads get used when he scratches on objects for marking. In addition to leaving a visual mark from his claws, he leaves an olfactory mark from the scent glands. Now that's an animal who really makes sure his presence is known!

The pheromones associated with the back end of the cat, such as the ones released during urine marking, are high-intensity. There's nothing calm about those pheromones. Feline urine spraying is done under stressful or reactive circumstances.

Considering all the scent being deposited in a cat's environment, it's a good thing he has a highly developed sniffer to decode all the information left by other cats' pheromones.

Objects in the Environment. Besides companion cats and human family members, your cat also scent-marks objects in her environment. This is demonstrated by the familiar cheek-rubbing you see your cat do on objects such as chair legs, doors, and anything else she can reach.

The marking is usually limited to facial rubbing, but if the cat feels threatened or overwhelmed by a strange addition to her territory, she may resort to spraying the unfamiliar object.

A Nose for News

Cats have 200 million scent receptors. Humans have 5 million.

Scent Communication via Spray. The good thing about scent marking by facial rubbing, grooming, and flank rubbing is that the scent is undetectable by humans. Cats can pick up every nuance of scents left by each cat, but thankfully, our noses are none the wiser. Now, when cats scent-mark using urine, that's another story altogether. That's a scent easily detectable by us. When a cat starts urine marking, things in the environment aren't calm and peaceful. Urine marking is a high-intensity form of marking. It may indicate that the cat feels threatened or needs to self-soothe by creating a very obvious familiar scent. You may notice an indoor cat spraying near a window if she sees an unfamiliar cat outside. A cat may also spray when a new pet is brought into the home. There are many reasons why a cat may spray, and it's important to figure out the underlying cause, so you can address the situation and create security again.

Cats Have Some Special Equipment. Cats have a special organ located in the roof of the mouth. This organ, known as Jacobson's organ or vomeronasal organ, contains ducts that lead to the mouth and to the nose. This special equipment essentially functions as a chemical analyzer. It's used primarily for analyzing pheromones (scent chemicals) from other cats, especially the ones found in urine.

Question:
Do cats that live together have a group scent in common?

Pam's Answer:
Harmony in a multiple-cat environment depends partly on the feeling of comfort and safety evoked by creating a colony scent. You've probably seen this on a daily basis in your home as you watch companion cats rub against each other. You're even a part of it as your cats rub against you. In addition to being a sign of affection, this tactile form of communication is a way of creating a communal scent. The colony scent is created by allogrooming (social grooming between cats), head bunting, flank rubbing, and tail rubbing. These highly social behaviors create a common scent and strengthen the bond between friendly cats. In the case of cats who aren't so friendly to each other, the group scent helps keep things peaceful.

Group identity is important to survival in the cat social structure. The familiar colony scent is an efficient method to quickly determine if a cat is part of the colony or an intruder. It is also used to identify objects as being within the group's territory.

Top Cat
In allorubbing, the cat who is able to elicit the first rub is typically viewed as higher in status.

Threats to the Group Scent. If you've ever brought one cat to the veterinary clinic while the other cats remained home, you might've witnessed hostility on the part of those cats when the feline patient returned home.

The cat who returns from the vet clinic now smells very threatening. Rather than simply recognizing each other by sight, the cats react to the perceived threat by displaying aggression and fear toward the returning cat. It isn't until that cat has time to groom and take on the familiar scents of the home again that her feline companions begin to relax.

Don't Force the Scent Issue. Some cat parents have been given bad advice about how to use scent to create a peaceful environment during a new cat introduction or when trying to address multicat aggression. I've worked with clients who had previously been advised to put one cat's scent on another cat by either brushing all the cats with the same brush or rubbing one cat with a towel and then rubbing the other cat with the same one. This is very stressful to the cats and potentially dangerous. When you put one cat's scent on another, you deny that cat the ability to get away from it. An important and very basic rule in dealing with cats is to always provide *choice*. If a cat feels she cannot escape the scent, her aggressiveness may escalate and will probably interfere with the introduction and integration process. You have to go at the cat's pace. When you push the issue, the cat will typically retreat.

If you've ever been to a department store and shopped for perfume, you notice that there are paper strips to spritz the perfume on instead of your skin. If you spray the perfume on your wrist and you absolutely hate it, you then can't get away from it. I remember having done that and being barely able to wait to get to the restroom to wash off a terrible perfume. Even then, the scent trace still lingered.

Question:
Is there a correct way to approach a cat you're meeting for the first time?

Pam's Answer:
When it comes to properly greeting a cat, you may think all you have to do is walk right up to him, reach down, and offer a few loving strokes along his fur. If the cat is familiar with you and likes you, that may be perfectly OK, but if it's an unfamiliar cat or if he's reluctant to interact, you'll get scratched or the cat will back away.

The Cat's-Eye View. Cats are territorial and rely heavily on their sense of smell to determine whether an approaching person or animal is familiar and friendly or a potential threat. If you just abruptly approach an unfamiliar or reluctant cat and try to do an introduction on your terms, you don't give the cat time to do a scent investigation. As humans, we mostly rely on our sense of sight to determine whether a person approaching us is familiar or not. With cats, their sense of smell is in the driver's seat.

If you don't give the cat time to first do a little scent investigation, then he may feel backed into a corner. That, combined with the fact that you're advancing toward him, can set off alarm bells telling him it's better to either strike out or find immediate escape. From his perspective, it's better to be safe than sorry. The last thing you want to do when trying to greet a cat is to set off his fight-or-flight response.

A Bad Pattern. If people repeatedly use that brusque approach to greet the cat, he'll soon learn it's better to do a preemptive strike or not come out of hiding at all. A cat parent may try to "show" the cat that the approaching person is cat-friendly by forcing interaction. Even if this doesn't result in injury to anyone, it's very stressful to the cat and is counterproductive to the trust-building process.

Use Proper Cat Etiquette. A proper greeting is actually simple and requires just your index finger. When you walk into a room where the cat is located, don't approach him. Get down on his level by sitting or kneeling, and then extend your index finger. Don't put it in his face or wiggle it around like a toy as though you want the cat to bite it. Just extend your finger at the same height as his nose.

When cats approach each other, they engage in a round of nose-to-nose sniffing to determine familiarity and do an initial scent investigation. Your extended finger at the proper height becomes a substitute cat nose. When you hold your finger still and don't advance toward the cat, you give him the option to approach or not. Giving the cat that choice can immediately lower his stress level.

If the cat decides to approach, he'll sniff your finger a little. If he wishes to interact further, he may rub his cheek or head along your finger. If he advances toward you, he's probably ready for more interaction. At that point, you may pet him if his body language indicates relaxation. If, after sniffing your finger, he stays still or backs away, then he's *not* ready for further interaction . . . at least not this time.

Soft Eye Contact. In the animal world, a hard, direct stare is a challenge and indicates a willingness for conflict. When you're trying to make friends with a cat who isn't quite sure about your intentions yet, your gaze should be soft and friendly. Avoid directly staring at the cat. Instead, practice displaying a slightly sleepy, soft gaze and then look away. If you see that the cat is uncomfortable with you, avoid any eye contact initially.

Body Language. Observe the cat's body language. Is he displaying distance-decreasing, distance-increasing, or neutral behavior? An example of distance-decreasing behavior might be walking toward you with upright tail. The tail may even have a little hook at the end, and he may give it a flick or two. A standoffish or distance-increasing behavior basically means that the cat isn't comfortable with an approach by you. He might curl up, tucking his limbs underneath and wrapping his tail around his body, or he may simply walk away to a safer distance. A neutral behavior says the cat doesn't view you as a threat but doesn't necessarily want closer interaction. He may give you a slow-blink cat kiss to indicate that he's relaxed enough with the way things currently are, or he may look away.

Practice Makes Perfect. Continue to use your finger for the proper human-to-cat introduction, even if the first few times the cat doesn't want to interact further with you. Continue to give him the choice, showing that you aren't a threat and that you follow proper feline etiquette. You stand a much better chance of eventually winning him over.

Be a Good Student. Cats use multiple forms of communication (scent, body language, vocalization, touch, and sight), whereas we stay pretty much rooted in verbal exchanges. As a result, we tend to ignore or misinterpret the various ways cats are instructing us to increase or decrease our distance. We also often don't pay enough attention to what our own body language communicates to the cat.

Question:
What is my cat, Mason, trying to tell me when he meows?

Pam's Answer:
Cats communicate to humans in many ways, but the one that almost always gets our attention is the meow. That meow can have various meanings and may sometimes be difficult to interpret. Many cat parents, however, have become excellent interpreters of their cats' meows. They know

by the specific sound whether it's a request for food, play, or affection, an announcement of a successful hunt, or a signal to be left alone.

Meowing Is Directed Mostly Toward Us. In cat-to-cat communication, adult cats rarely meow to each other. Kittens do more meowing as a way of saying they're in need of something or are in trouble. Kittens seem to address most of their meows to the mother cat.

Once a cat becomes full-grown, cat-to-cat vocalization tends to occur more often in hostile situations where a growl, yowl, cry, hiss, or spit is needed because body language hasn't succeeded in keeping an opponent at bay.

The meow seems to be directed mostly at humans—probably because it works. Cats are very smart; if a meow got a desired result the first time, they figure it'll get the result every time. Moreover, because we're such a verbal species, we respond better to meows than to other forms of communication; witness the many times humans are scratched or bitten because they misread their cats' body language.

Some cats are more vocal than others, and some breeds turn meowing into an art form. The more vocal cat breeds will pretty much conduct a running narrative of everything they do throughout the day.

Captains of Communication

Cats are masters of communication. They make use of olfactory, auditory, visual, tactile, and vocal forms.

When Meows Become Annoying. We reinforce meowing behavior because we often respond quickly. If the cat meows and we know what he wants, we typically supply it right away—whether it's some petting under the chin, a play session, or refilling the empty food bowl. Even if we don't supply what he's asking for, we often still reinforce the behavior by giving attention. If your cat is meowing and it annoys you, chances are you'll tell the cat to quiet down or pet him just to stop the noise. When you respond to unwanted meowing, you reinforce his attention-seeking behavior.

Meow Warning Signs. An increase in vocalization may indicate a potential medical problem. Some older cats, especially ones experiencing age-related cognitive dysfunction, may meow or even yowl at night when the house is dark and quiet. If your older cat has begun nighttime meowing, it's time for a veterinary checkup.

If your cat meows at night because he's bored, because his environment is quiet and there's no one awake to play with him, make sure you conduct a good interactive play session right before bed, and then offer him a food reward. You can also set out some puzzle feeders and other activity toys to keep him busy while you sleep.

If your cat is vocal and way too active at night and isn't allowing anyone else to sleep, make sure you don't have too many lights on. After you've done a good interactive play session with your cat and offered a food reward, lower the lights enough so he'll get the message that it's time to settle down.

Question:
Why does my cat raise her butt up in the air when I pet her?

Pam's Answer:
Ah, yes, the all-too-familiar "elevator butt" position, in which she lowers her front end and raises her hindquarters. That very common position is meant as a friendly gesture and an invitation to continue scratching or petting her there.

You've Hit the Spot. Although elevator butt may seem rather insulting to us, it's actually the cat's very positive response to the fact that you've hit just the right spot when petting her. Typically, that spot is at the base of her tail. Not all cats enjoy being scratched or petted along the spine or at the tail base, but if yours does, that's probably when you've witnessed the elevator go up.

Intact Cat Behavior. In intact females, elevator butt has a much more specific meaning. By assuming that position, known as lordosis, the female shows the male she's ready for mating. However, intact cats in lordosis will hold the tail in a different position than in plain old elevator butt. The tail will be off to the side in preparation for entry by the male. The female may also tread with her hind paws.

If your intact cat is displaying true lordosis, she's in estrus, so it's very important to make sure you keep her indoors. When in estrus, females are noticeably more affectionate and vocal. You'll probably be presented with the lordosis position just about every time you pet her.

You may even notice one or two unfamiliar cats hanging around outside the window. These are intact males who are well aware of the fact that there's a mating opportunity nearby. Be extra careful about not letting your female cat outdoors, and then contact your veterinarian about having the cat spayed as soon as the heat cycle is over.

Question:

When I'm in bed, why do my cats come up to me and push their foreheads against my face? Are they trying to mark me as their property?

Pam's Answer:

Sometimes it's a gentle nudge, and then at other times it's almost a head-to-head bone crusher, isn't it? There are also times when a cat may just rub his chin, forehead, or cheek along your face. Although it may not be as startling as the head-on cat collision, you usually end up with a mouthful of cat hair. But he means well, and it's a friendly gesture.

Head Bunting. The behavior often described by cat parents as "head butting" is actually head *bunting*. Cats have scent glands in multiple locations on the body, and they use them to leave scent marks on objects (and in this case, *you*). Head bunting is reserved for bonding, for friendly, comforting social purposes. When your cat engages in head bunting, he's placing his scent on you as an affiliative behavior. Cat-to-cat head bunting is reserved for cats who already have a familiar and friendly relationship. Cats typically display head bunting toward other cats, dog companions, and humans. Lip rubbing is often reserved for marking objects.

Pet Me, Scratch Me, Pay Attention to Me. Bunting may also be used as an attention-seeking behavior if the cat butts his head up against you and then tucks it down or turns to the side. He may be asking for one of those wonderful neck or head scratches you often do for him. Past experience has told him that when he displays this behavior, you typically respond by petting or scratching him in his favorite places. Cats are so smart!

For the cat to place his face so close to yours and engage in this bonding behavior is quite an act of trust. For me, it's worth getting a little cat hair stuck to my lips just to experience this tender moment with my cat.

Scent Communication Is Complex. Many people inaccurately assume that whenever a cat bunts or rubs against you, he's merely marking you as his territory. Scent communication is far more complex than that. When your cat comes face-to-face with you and bunts, he's giving you the feline version of a hug.

Question:
Zooey is always a very sweet and friendly cat, so why does she like to sit with her backside facing me? Should I be insulted?

Pam's Answer:
What your cat is doing is actually very polite in terms of feline etiquette. When two cats greet each other, they depend on scent for communication. They start by engaging in nose-to-nose sniffing. Finally one cat will turn around to present her backside for some anal sniffing. Yes, in our world that's totally gross, but in the animal world, that's an area of concentrated scent that tells the sniffer a lot about the cat being sniffed. For a cat to present her anal area for sniffing is considered very polite.

What Should You Do? When your cat turns around and presents her backside to you, she's actually displaying her proper feline manners. What should you do in response? Relax, you certainly aren't expected to do you-know-what. All you have to do is pet your cat along the back or wherever she prefers most as an affectionate gesture.

Question:
Why do cats hiss?

Pam's Answer:
Even if your cat is the sweetest little cat on the planet, if she has ever felt threatened or needed to send a warning to someone, she has probably hissed. Hissing may sound comical to us, but to the cat it's no laughing matter. If a cat is hissing, she feels there's an immediate threat.

How Cats Hiss. The hiss is created when the cat forces a burst of air out through her arched tongue. If your face is close enough, you can feel the air being shot out through her mouth—but try not to be close enough to experience that. She'll pull her lips back, as well, and the ears will be flattened against the head. Typically she'll also arch her back, and her hair will literally stand on end (a response called piloerection). Her tail may look three times its normal size.

Why Cats Hiss. Simply put, hissing is a warning. Because cats don't want to engage in physical confrontations, they rely on body postures, marking, and vocalizations to deter opponents. A hissing cat is giving a verbal warning to her opponent. Hissing is a defensive vocalization, which means the cat is reacting to something in her immediate environment causing her to feel frightened and in danger. The hiss says aggression will follow if you don't back off. A cat who hisses is fearful but ready to engage in battle if necessary.

Many behavior experts believe the cat produces the sound to mimic a hissing snake in order to deter opponents. Mimicry is a common behavior in the animal world when it comes to survival. Some animals will mimic a predator vocally or visually as a deterrent. The cat is counting on the fact that the hiss provides enough of a warning. A mother cat may hiss if other cats or even humans get too close to her litter of kittens, or a cat may hiss when an unfamiliar guest comes into the house. Hissing is commonly heard when a cat is placed on the exam table at the veterinary clinic, and if you've tried to medicate a cat who is uncomfortable with the procedure, chances are you've been the recipient of a hiss.

Pay Attention to the Warning. A hissing cat is clearly giving a warning, so don't ignore it. If the cat doesn't have an avenue of escape, a scratch or bite may follow. How should you handle a hissing cat?

- Give her time to calm down.
- Unless you have to interact with her, provide an avenue of escape and let her retreat.
- If interaction is necessary, let her get used to your scent before you touch her.
- Don't punish her for hissing.
- Be aware of the triggers causing her to feel threatened.
- If handling is needed, use a towel to partially cover her so she can feel somewhat hidden.

Question:

I've heard that when cats blink slowly at you, it's their way of kissing. Is this true?

Pam's Answer:

A cat's eyes are very expressive and can tell you a lot about how she's feeling at that moment. Whether a slow blink is actually a cat's take on a kiss is perhaps open to argument, but I and many others in the behavior field believe that, in the right environment, it's a sign of calm and, yes, affection.

When evaluating the slow-blink cat kiss, take a close look at the immediate environment, and be accurate in your observation of what the cat is relaying with her eyes. For example, a long, direct stare from one cat to another may be meant for intimidation purposes. Narrowed eyes with ears at half-mast are certainly not displaying love and affection at that moment.

A slow-blink cat kiss is a totally nonaggressive display that may be meant to convey affection toward a human or animal family member. In an outdoor setting or multicat environment, it may be part of the body language used to display to others that all is calm and the cat isn't a threat. A cat may also display this behavior to convey that she doesn't view you as a threat.

If you watch how your cat uses her eyes, you'll start to notice the difference between a regular, alert eyeblink and a heavy-lidded, relaxed, slow eyeblink. Another cue to look for is whether the cat's face is relaxed. The whiskers will be hanging loosely on either side of the muzzle, and you won't see tension in the facial muscles. Pay attention to the whole body language and the cat's immediate environment to become more adept at interpretation.

Return the Kiss to Your Cat. When your cat gives you a slow-eyeblink kiss, return the favor by offering her a slow blink as well. You can even use the cat-kiss technique on unfamiliar cats, as long as you've read their body language correctly. Just don't mistake a hard stare for a cat kiss. Become more fluent in catspeak, and you'll probably find you've been getting "kissed" more often than you realize.

Question:
Why do some of my cats like to flex their claws on me? Sometimes it really hurts!

Pam's Answer:
Kneading is a behavior many cats exhibit, and cat parents find it endearing and fascinating. If the cat's nails haven't been trimmed lately, however, the behavior can also be a bit on the painful side, as you've experienced.

Where It Comes From. Kneading is a holdover from when cats were kittens. It originates when kittens are nursing on the mother. During nursing, kittens instinctively flex and relax their paws (a behavior known as the milk tread) to stimulate lactation and milk flow. Even after kittens have been weaned and have matured into adults, it's common for many cats to continue the kneading.

Kneading is often triggered when a cat is on a soft surface, such as a bed or blanket or on the lap of a familiar human. Being on that soft surface can put the cat in the same content emotional state as when he was nursing from the queen.

The Cat's Expression During Kneading. While the cat is engaged in kneading behavior he'll often have his eyes half closed and a dreamy expression on his face. Many cats also purr while kneading. In some cases, cats even start drooling.

Cats show contentment and affection in many different ways, and kneading is just one of those tender expressions. Just remember to keep your cat's nails trimmed, and the kneading behavior will be pleasant for everyone.

Question:

Why does my cat always want attention when I'm on the telephone?

Pam's Answer:

It's very common for the family cat to show up and start meowing and crawling all over the cat parent's lap whenever a call comes in. Is the cat jealous of the phone? You may think so, but the behavior is really just another example of your cat's intelligence.

When you're talking on the phone, the cat hears your voice. In some cases, there's no one else in the room except you and the cat. Perhaps the cat thinks you must be talking to her, because she doesn't see or hear another person.

Reinforcing the Behavior. Animals repeat behaviors when they have a payoff, when they serve a beneficial function. You may not even realize this, but as you talk on the phone, you might actually be reinforcing your cat's behavior. If the cat comes over to you, there's a good chance you pet her or acknowledge her somehow. Maybe she jumps up in your lap and you start stroking her without even realizing what you're doing. The cat soon learns that whenever you're on the phone, there's an excellent chance of some attention.

If your cat is exceptionally insistent when you're talking on the phone, you may have tossed a toy to distract her or even refilled the food bowl in an attempt to keep her occupied. If that's the case, your smart cat has learned just how successful that technique is for her, and she'll do it again and again. Your cat is always learning, so pay attention to the behaviors you reinforce.

Question:
Many people say dogs are affectionate, but cats aren't. Is this true?

Pam's Answer:
If you talk to people who don't like cats or who aren't familiar with them, they'll probably be quick to tell you that cats don't show affection. They may praise the way dogs show affection but refer to cats as snobby or aloof. I think a big part of the problem is that people are trying to compare dog behavior with cat behavior. It may seem ridiculously obvious to you, but there are so many people out there who still need to be told: *Cats aren't dogs.* One species isn't better than the other; they're just different. It makes sense that they would show affection differently as well.

Every cat is an individual, so there are many ways your particular cat may display affection, but here are just some of the common ways cats show their love:

Bunting. This is the name for the behavior displayed when a cat literally head-butts you—presses or even rams the top of his head into some part of your head or into your extended fist simulating a cat's head. He may come up onto your lap and bunt his head against your chin, nose, or forehead. Cats have scent glands on their faces, and it's a very common social behavior for one cat to bunt the head of another familiar feline buddy. This isn't just a scent exchange behavior, but also an affectionate greeting.

Cheek-Rubbing. Cats also have scent glands along the sides of their lips, and they may rub these against people, a cat friend, or an object. The pheromones produced along the lips and on the cat's head are associated with friendliness, affection, and familiarity. Cats facially rub on people or objects when they feel comfortable.

Kneading. This behavior originated when the cat was a kitten and used to milk-tread to stimulate the release of milk from the mother's teat during nursing. Many adult cats maintain that kneading behavior when they're on a soft surface or feeling very content.

Purring. Purring is complex, because it's something cats do when they're happy, content, and relaxed, but also when they're scared, sick, or injured. It has been theorized that cats purr to deepen an existing state of contentment or to soothe themselves and potential attackers in a tense environment.

Allogrooming. Cats who have a good relationship may engage in mutual grooming. It's an affiliative behavior and also helps create a group scent. This is important outdoors, for scent plays a huge role in recognition. Grooming is also a stress reliever and displacement behavior, so allogrooming may help cats keep each other calm. When your cat starts grooming you, it's generally his way of showing affection and mixing his scent with yours.

Slow Eyeblinks. This common display is one way a cat can convey that he's relaxed and comfortable with you. I call it a cat kiss!

Vulnerable Postures. When a cat takes a stretched-out position for resting, he shows he feels comfortable with you. When a cat is uncertain, he tends to tuck his limbs under his body and tightly wrap his tail around himself when resting. Leaving his limbs and tail totally exposed means he feels secure near you.

If the cat isn't in a confrontation, he may stretch out so much that he's on his back with his belly exposed. This is the ultimate in trust and relaxation, because he's exposing a very vulnerable body part. Don't confuse this posture with a cat exposing his tummy during a battle. In that situation, it's a defensive gesture displayed to warn an opponent that, should the battle continue, all weapons (teeth and claws) will be used. When interpreting body postures, you always have to take the immediate environment into account.

Upright Tail Flicks. A cat's tail can tell you what the cat is feeling. A tail held high with a little hook at the end usually means your cat is happy and confident. Many cats will also give the tail tip a little flick as a greeting when they see you.

Being in Physical Contact with You. Your cat may sit on your lap, sit next to you, and lie on top of you when you're in bed, or he may just lean his back against your arm as you work at the computer. Just the fact that he wants to be in close physical contact with you is quite the compliment.

Vocalization. Cats can carry on all kinds of conversations, and there's no such thing as a simple meow, but many cats issue a special mew or a little chirp as a greeting when their cat parents enter the room.

Question:
Why does our cat, Mika, like to get on my daughter's homework? She ends up pushing him away several times while she's trying to study.

Pam's Answer:
A cat has incredibly acute senses and can easily figure out where his human family member's focus is directed. Mika sees your daughter staring at a paper, directing her attention at that object, so he assumes that if he sits on it, *he* will then be in the center of her attention.

There isn't any real mystery to the behavior. It's often just a cat saying "pay attention to me." Typically, when a cat does this, we do pay attention, either petting him or shooing him away. Either way, it's attention, so he's rewarded for the behavior, and that's why it gets repeated. To try to avoid it in the future, make sure the cat is getting some interactive playtime at least a couple of times a day. Before doing homework, your daughter can also set out a puzzle feeder to keep him occupied.

Question:
Do cats communicate with their whiskers?

Pam's Answer:
Known also as vibrissae or tactile hairs, the whiskers serve several functions and are highly sensitive. Thicker than the cat's normal hair, the whiskers are really touch receptors rooted more deeply than normal hairs and rich in nerve endings.

Whisker Navigation. The whiskers are so sensitive that they aid in detecting changes in air currents, helping the cat navigate in the dark. Your cat uses her whiskers in the same way you would hold out your arms so your fingers could feel for objects. By determining changes in air currents, the cat can avoid walking into an object. This ability to detect air currents also helps the cat gauge the swift movement of prey when hunting.

A Tight Squeeze or a Perfect Fit? The muzzle whiskers also help the cat determine whether she can fit through a small opening. They are about as long, side to side, as the cat's body is wide, so if they can fit through an opening without bending, then the cat should be able to squeeze through. When a cat pokes her head into an opening, she's not only looking around in there; she's doing a whisker check to see if she can fit. Unfortunately, if the cat is overweight, that whisker function isn't always accurate.

On the muzzle, there are four rows of whiskers on each side. The top two rows can move independently from the bottom two rows.

Eye Protection. The whiskers above the eyes help when the cat is hunting in grass or bushy areas. They trigger a protective eyeblink if there's a branch or some brush that might get into the cat's eyes. The whiskers also help during contact with other animals (including us). If touched, they cause an eyeblink.

Hunting Help. The carpal whiskers, located on the underside of the cat's wrist, are very useful in hunting. When the cat has prey captured in her paws, the carpal whiskers help determine if there's any movement. Because cats can't see well up close, the carpal whiskers also help determine the position of the prey to aid in delivering an accurate killing bite.

Whisker Sensitivity. The cat's whiskers are so valuable that if cut or chewed off, lack of them can inhibit her hunting ability and even her ability to navigate around her environment. She may become fearful and disoriented. They're also sensitive. Never cut a cat's whiskers, as it's extremely cruel and will cause pain.

Don't Crowd Me

Most cats don't like having their whiskers squished when trying to eat or drink, so if a dish isn't the right size, they'll dip a paw in the food or water and then lick it or paw the food out. Make sure your cat's dish isn't too small or narrow.

Mood Indicator. Your cat's whiskers can also reflect her mood. When the whiskers are hanging loosely on either side, she's probably relaxed. When she's frightened or getting ready for battle, the whiskers are flattened against the face to prevent damage to them. When on the alert or hunting, the whiskers face forward to aid in prey detection. Keep in mind, though, that you shouldn't gauge your cat's mood by just one thing. Take other body language signals into consideration, along with the immediate environment.

The occasional whisker does fall out now and then, so don't be alarmed if you find one on the carpet. Whiskers do grow back.

Question:
Do cats communicate with their tails?

Pam's Answer:
Your cat's tail is quite the communication device. He uses it very efficiently and effectively to let you and his cat companions know just what's going on inside that brain of his. Here are a few interesting tail communication signals:

- When feeling confident, your cat usually will walk with his tail straight up. When walking through tall grass, if the cat wants others to know he's there, he'll hold his tail up as a beacon.
- An upright tail resembling a question mark usually indicates a friendly greeting or playfulness.
- When greeting you, your cat may flick his upright tail a few times. Consider that a friendly "Welcome home."
- A relaxed tail is loosely horizontal.
- When a cat lashes his tail back and forth, he's usually irritated. However, if he's watching a bird outside, he may whip his tail back and forth in excitement.
- A thumping tail can also mean irritation.
- An upright twitching tail typically is displayed when a cat is anticipating something good, such as a meal or a treat.
- When a cat sprays, his tail will twitch.
- When walking, if a cat holds his tail very low to the ground, he may be afraid or unsure. Depending upon specific circumstances, it can also mean he's feeling defensive.
- A puffed up "Halloween cat" tail is often a defensive display but can be an offensive one, depending on the circumstances. It usually occurs when the cat is startled or frightened.
- A tail wrapped tightly around or tucked under the body usually indicates that the cat is afraid and wants to be left alone.

Question:
Why does my cat chatter?

Pam's Answer:
There are a few theories behind the chattering and chirping sound that cats make. Some experts believe it expresses the frustration they feel from not being able to get to prey, such as a bird or squirrel seen through a window. Some believe that chattering is merely a reflex motion in anticipation of the killing bite to the prey's neck. Another theory is that it's the way a cat controls his over-the-top excitement at spotting a bird. There's also a theory that cats use the chattering sound to mimic the sound of prey. So I guess you can take your pick when it comes to the reason your cat engages in the behavior. There are some mysteries cats insist on keeping to themselves, and chattering is one of them.

Take Your Cue from the Cat's Chattering. If your cat sits at the window and chatters while watching the birds, you can take advantage of his excitement by engaging him in an interactive play session. That way, he'll actually get to "capture" his prey. If he's annoyed because the birds are on one side of the glass and he's on the other, a play session will change the situation from frustrating to fulfilling.

Question:
Why does my cat sometimes make such a terrible-looking face? It almost seems that he smells something rotten.

Pam's Answer:
Cats are equipped with a very special piece of equipment known as Jacobson's organ or the vomeronasal organ. Located in the roof of the mouth, it contains ducts leading to the mouth and to the nose. This is essentially a scent analyzer. It's used primarily for analyzing pheromones from other cats, especially ones found in urine.

How It Works. The scent is collected in the mouth, where the cat then uses his tongue to flick it up to the vomeronasal organ. You can tell when the cat is in the process of using his vomeronasal organ because his facial expression is similar to a grimace. His upper lip curls and his mouth will be partially open. This expression is known as the *flehmen reaction*.

The Purpose of the Vomeronasal Organ. Although all cats have this organ and can use it whenever they come across any scent they feel requires more in-depth analysis, it's often used in particular by intact males reacting to the pheromones in the urine of females in heat.

Question:
Why does Sunny always want to lick my hair? Is she grooming me?

Pam's Answer:
Let me guess: Is this the typical scenario? You're sound asleep in bed when a very strange feeling wakes you up. You reach up to your head and feel—a section of your hair is wet. Looking over, you see your cat's face. She looks at you for a moment and then goes back to what she was doing—licking your hair. Judging by the soggy strands on your head, you realize that your cat has probably been doing that for quite a while.

Social Behavior. Grooming is a common behavior between cats who have a bond. It's not unusual to see two cats engage in a session of licking each other's head and neck. I have watched as the recipient of the licking closes her eyes and seems to drift off into dreamland.

For some cats who are very bonded with particular family members, the social behavior of hair licking is very normal, and of course, because the biggest crop of hair can be found on the head, that gets most of the attention.

Appealing Taste or Scent. The taste or scent of certain shampoos, hair sprays, or gels seems to appeal to individual cats. Some may lick the hair of their cat parent just because they like that particular flavor.

How to Stop Hair Licking. The most important thing to remember is to not reinforce the very behavior you don't want from your cat. If you pet her or talk to her when she's licking your hair, then you send the message that this is a welcomed act on her part.

Move yourself away from the cat. If you're in bed, place a pillow between you. If you're sitting in a chair and she's behind you licking away, stand up and move. Show your cat that when she engages in this particular behavior, she loses your company.

If you've been able to pinpoint that certain hair products may be the culprit, switch to ones with no scent or a scent that's not so cat friendly.

Cats generally don't like the smell of citrus, so look for shampoos and gels with a citrus scent. You can also try putting a few drops of a citrus-based essential oil into your shampoo or conditioner. Another option is to mix a few drops of citrus-based essential oil in a carrier oil such as coconut oil, and rub a little behind your ears or on your neck. It's best to mix essential oil in a carrier oil to reduce chances of skin irritation. Be aware, though, that using citrus-based essential oil on your skin will make you more sun-sensitive outdoors.

If your cat has a pattern of licking your hair at the same time each day (such as when you're in bed or when you sit in your favorite chair to watch TV), provide her with something to keep her occupied, such as a puzzle feeder, right before you settle down.

Question:
Why do cats sleep so much?

Pam's Answer:
Cats have the reputation of being aloof, and although it's not an accurate assessment, some of that belief comes from the fact that cats are known for sleeping much of the day. Some people even think cats are lazy because sleeping takes up about two thirds of their lives. Lazy is about as far from the truth as you can get. To people who don't like cats or aren't familiar with them, it may seem that cats don't *do* anything but just rely on humans for an endless supply of food. If you take a moment to really look at why cats sleep the way they do, you'll end up with an entirely different perspective and a new respect for how efficiently a cat's body works.

Energy for the Hunt. Unlike animals who forage for grains and grasses, cats are predators. Food for a carnivore isn't growing in vast fields, so in order to eat, the hunter has to work. Once prey is discovered, the cat goes into stealth mode and carefully inches up to get into the perfect position to pounce. Being an ambush predator, the cat's attempt at catching prey requires short but intense bursts of energy. Cats aren't scavengers, so the prey they eat must be fresh. Requiring fresh prey means a constant need to hunt.

Hunting requires energy. Moreover, because of size, a cat is prey as well as predator, and the stress factor increases the animal's energy needs. The cat needs to make sure he's well prepared for however many hunting attempts he may make. Sleep is needed to conserve energy and recharge for the next hunt. Cats sleep anywhere from twelve to sixteen hours per day.

Sleeping with One Eye Open. OK, the cat doesn't really sleep with one eye open, but he does tend to stay in a light sleep much of the time. Because he's a "wait and see" predator, he depends on being able to spring into action if potential prey appears. Much of the sleep you notice your cat doing is a light sleep, so he can instantly engage. This level of sleep helps his body to immediately react, whether that reaction is needed to hunt or to protect himself from a larger predator. Cats do engage in deep sleep but in short cycles of about ten to fifteen minutes at a time.

When a cat is in that light catnapping phase, you may notice his ears move a bit now and then; one might even rotate in the direction of an interesting sound. His eyes won't be tightly shut and may open a bit every so often.

Sleeping positions can also be determined by the temperature. When cats are cold, they tend to sleep curled up; when the temperature is warm, they may sleep more stretched out.

The Nighttime Cat Crazies. For many cat parents, the cat's sleep cycle doesn't make sense. The cat sleeps all day and then goes into the "cat crazies" at night, bouncing off the walls, knocking things over, and pawing at your face at four A.M. while you're trying to sleep. Your cat is hardwired as a crepuscular predator, and that means he's naturally more active at dusk and dawn. Outdoors, the type of prey he would hunt would be more active during those twilight hours. His internal clock is set to rest during the day and gear up for action in the early evening.

Even though your indoor cat doesn't have to worry about hunting for his next meal, he still has that same natural sleeping pattern. But cats are very accommodating. Many cats learn to adapt to our schedules and become more active during the day.

What to Do When Your Cat Is a Hard-Core Nighttime Party Animal. If your cat keeps you up at night, provide more opportunities for exploration and hunting (of toys) during the day to keep him active. In addition to doing a couple of interactive play sessions during the day, be sure to conduct one state-of-the-art session right before bed and then offer your cat some food as a grand reward. Don't increase the amount you give him during the day; just portion it out so you can provide some after the hunt. With some food in his belly after that energetic hunt, your cat will be more likely to sleep.

Do Cats Dream? Cats experience REM sleep (rapid eye movement), as humans do, and that's the phase in which dreaming occurs. You may notice your cat's whiskers or paws twitch during this phase. What do cats dream about? The cats aren't telling, but my guess is that mice and birds play a prominent role in their dreams.

Changes in Sleep Patterns. If you notice a change in your cat's sleep pattern, be sure to talk to your veterinarian. If your cat is sleeping excessively or isn't sleeping as much as normal, there could be an underlying medical problem. Hyperthyroidism, for example, causes a release of too much thyroid hormone, which speeds up the metabolism so the cat may not sleep as much as normal. Older cats with declining senses or ones with age-related cognitive issues may sleep more soundly and for longer periods. Cats with hearing loss may startle easily while sleeping, so be mindful of how you wake them.

Chapter 4

The Scoop on Poop and Pee

Creating good vibes at the litter box

Question:
Will I have to train my kitten to use the litter box or will he instinctively know what to do?

Pam's Answer:
Unless you've rescued an orphaned kitten still in the bottle-feeding stage, chances are you won't have to teach the furry little one how to eliminate, but you will have to create a litter box setup conveniently located and easy to enter and exit. You'll also have to provide guidance and help your kitten with timing. Some kittens get the hang of litter box protocol right away, but others need more help. Don't assume that all kittens come preprogrammed to know where all the pee and poop belong. Some may need you to steer them in the right direction.

A Box Fit for a Kitten. As the kitten grows, he'll appreciate having a big box with lots of room, but for now, the litter box setup needs to be kitten-size. The box should be easy for a young kitten to navigate. A high-sided box will be too difficult for a youngster to crawl over, especially with a full bladder. Keep in mind that a kitten won't have the bladder control of an adult cat, so when he has to go, it's usually urgent.

Choose a low-sided box. Not only will it be easier to get into, but also, if the kitten can see the litter, it may serve as an added reminder. Seeing the soft substrate may remind him that this is the place to dig, eliminate, and cover his waste.

As the kitten gets older, you can then place a larger box next to the smaller one to start a gradual transition. You can even place the smaller litter box inside the larger box to get him used to the new setup.

Box Basics

Never use a covered box or an electronic box with a kitten. The box setup should be convenient, safe, simple, quiet, and hard to miss.

The Litter Choice. There are many types of litter on the market, but in general, the best choice for a kitten is one of the soft, scoopable types with a texture resembling sand. This litter will be easier on the kitten's paw pads and make it more comfortable for him to dig and cover. Standing on traditional clay litter, which has some sharper edges, or hard crystal-type litter may not be as comfortable for a kitten just learning potty etiquette.

To Clean or Not to Clean. For an adult cat, you would hear me tell you over and over again to keep the litter box conditions absolutely pristine. For a kitten though, it's a good idea to leave a little (notice, I said *a little*) of his liquid or solid waste in there. This may serve as an added reminder of where the pee and poop go. If you find a little solid waste outside the litter box, instead of tossing it into the toilet, place it in the litter box so he'll have a little scented reminder of where it should've been put.

Litter Box Location. The box needs to be very easy for a kitten to find. Don't expect your new youngster to be able to get all the way across the house or down a flight of stairs to find the box.

Confine your young kitten to a smaller portion of the house so he can easily get to his litter box. Once he starts having access to more of the house, place at least one additional litter box in another location.

Litter boxes should be in open areas, almost as if a neon arrow were flashing above them. That doesn't mean the middle of the room, though. They should also be in quiet areas, away from foot traffic, so the cat isn't distracted. The location should be safe and secure so the kitten doesn't have to worry about the family dog sticking his nose in there or a child or other family member startling him.

Gently Remind Your Kitten. Typically, cats may eliminate after a nap, after playing, or after eating. Your kitten will probably be on that schedule and then some, because he'll need to eliminate more often than an adult cat. Frequently bring him over to the litter box as he learns to perfect his potty timing.

When You Need to Be the Teacher. If your kitten isn't getting the whole dig, eliminate, and cover routine, or if he was taken from his mother too young and didn't get that lesson, you'll have to assist him. When you bring your kitten over to the litter box for a potty break, use your finger and dig a little in the litter. The sound and sight of that might entice him to do the same. If he eliminates but doesn't cover, use your finger to cover a bit so he can see what the sequence is supposed to be. *Don't* grab one of his paws and use it to cover the waste. That ploy will only cause him to pull away, and it can start you off on a case of litter box aversion. Just let him see your fingers doing the motion of covering the waste.

Never Punish for Out-of-Box Accidents. Your kitten is just learning, and he may not make it to the box in time. Don't punish him in any way for missed litter box attempts. Instead, look at what you might be able to do to make it easier for him next time. Perhaps he was playing too far away from the box, and you didn't bring him back for a potty break in time. Maybe the box is too hard to get into. Was someone in the family holding the kitten for too long while he was squirming to get away in order to get to the box? Litter box accidents aren't the kitten's fault. Any punishment will only start to create a fear of you (not what you want when you're establishing a new relationship) and potentially cause a litter box avoidance problem.

Question:

I'm confused about how to set up my cat's litter box. I see all kinds of things in the pet store, and some items are very expensive. What do I really need for my cat?

Pam's Answer:

When setting up the litter box, the more complicated you make it, the less likely the cat will want to go there. Sure, you can find litter boxes on the market that do just about everything except take the bag of dirty litter out to the trash can for you, but the price you pay for them (and I'm not talking financial price) may be too high.

I admit, scooping the litter box isn't the fun part of being a cat parent. Many humans go so far as to try to pretend there isn't even a litter box in the house at all by locating it in such a remote area, a cat would need GPS to find it. The reality is, if you live with a cat, he needs a litter box, and that box should be:

1. the right size and type
2. conveniently located *for the cat*
3. kept clean

Taking shortcuts when it comes to the setup and maintenance of a litter box puts you on a slippery slope toward having a cat with a litter box aversion problem.

The most common calls our office receives are from people who have cats with litter box problems. Many of those problems are the result of cat parents not following the three-part rule above. I've visited countless homes where litter boxes were hidden in damp basements or shoved into dark closets. I've seen boxes that obviously hadn't been scooped in days. Those poor cats had to step on mounds of soiled litter while attempting to eliminate. Would you want to use a toilet that hadn't been flushed for days?

Litter Box Size and Type. I recommend only simple, open boxes. Covered boxes reduce air circulation, so it takes longer for litter to dry. The cover offers little headroom for the cat, who has only one way in and out. If you live in a multicat household, don't use boxes with covers, or you may create an anxious situation whenever a cat has to eliminate.

The box should be large enough for your cat to eliminate several times without having to stand on soiled mounds of litter. It's not fair to ask a large cat to impersonate an accordion and squeeze into a small litter box.

Electronic and self-cleaning litter boxes are potentially too noisy (which can scare a cat) and the surface the cat stands on can be uncomfortable. Some self-cleaning boxes require the use of a special substrate, which may be a texture some cats find objectionable. I've also found high-tech boxes generally to be too small for the cat. The entire box may be large, but the actual litter surface area for the cat is too small.

Litter Box Cleanliness. Scoop the box at least twice a day. It takes only a few seconds. The entire box should be thoroughly scrubbed and replaced with fresh litter on a regular basis. If you use scoopable litter, clean the box at least once or twice monthly. If you don't use scoopable litter, then the box needs to be cleaned more often.

The Nose Knows

Stay away from scented litter. When deciding among litter brands, keep the sensitivity of a cat's nose in mind, as well as how close that little nose will be to the litter.

Location, Location, Location. Nobody wants a litter box in the middle of the living room, but make sure the location is convenient for your cat. If you live in a two-story home, there should be a box on each floor. In a multicat home, the boxes should be scattered so one cat doesn't have to pass another cat's area in order to eliminate.

The litter box shouldn't be located near the feeding station. We don't eat in the bathroom, and cats don't eat where they eliminate either. For cats this is an important survival rule that even the most pampered indoor cat will feel compelled to follow.

Be mindful of physical limitations your cat has. If he has trouble going up and down stairs, don't place the box down in the basement or in a spot that's difficult for him to access. If you have a kitten, place the box in a hard-to-miss location. Kittens don't have enough bladder control yet, so don't make them go on a litter box hunt when nature calls.

Remember, keep it simple and follow the three-part rule—the right size and type, placed for cat convenience, and kept clean. Your cat will appreciate it.

Question:
Wouldn't cats prefer the privacy of a litter box with a cover?

Pam's Answer:
You may think a covered litter box is a good choice because it offers privacy for the cat and hides what you don't want to see or smell, but there are some facts to consider before making that purchase. Let's examine whether a covered box is cat-friendly or not.

From Our Perspective. From the cat parent's perspective, a covered box seems ideal. It offers:

- privacy
- control of litter scatter
- concealment of the cat's pee and poop
- confinement of odor inside the box

From the human's point of view, a covered box appears, at least initially, to be a dream come true. It keeps everything neat and tidy, and no one but the cat has to look inside the box. Unfortunately though, many behavior problems occur because, as cat parents, we look at the environment from *our* point of view and neglect to see things from the *cat's* perspective.

The Cat's Take. If you use your CatWise skill, you'll start to look at the covered litter box in an entirely different light:

- A covered box can make a larger cat feel cramped.
- Covered boxes don't allow as much air circulation, so litter takes longer to dry.
- Odor is contained in the box, so it can be more offensive to the cat inside.
- A covered box limits a cat's ability to see if another companion animal is approaching.
- A covered box limits a cat's escape potential and can create ambush opportunities.
- A covered box may not get scooped often enough.

Privacy Versus Safety. This is, by far, my biggest issue with covered boxes. While we're busy worrying about privacy, a cat is worried about safety. Being in the litter box puts a cat in a vulnerable position.

If you have a multicat household and there's the least bit of tension between cats, imagine how stressful it could be for one cat to go into a covered box where there's only one way in and out. I've often seen situations in which one cat uses the opportunity to ambush another cat in the litter box. It's not unusual to see one cat sitting on the top of the box, ready to pounce as soon as the other cat exits. In this situation, the cat being ambushed will probably decide to choose a much safer location for elimination. That location choice is often out in the open with more visual warning time so the cat has a chance to get away when an opponent enters the room.

There doesn't even have to be tension in a multicat home for a cat to feel vulnerable in a covered box with no escape potential. It could take nothing more than a cat being surprised once or twice by another cat having to use the box at the same time. It could be the family dog sticking his nose into the box or even a toddler following the cat as he heads to the box. The bottom line is, if a cat feels the litter box isn't in a safe location, his survival instinct will tell him to seek another option for elimination.

Olfactory Assault. Another thing to think about is how a covered litter box must appear to an animal equipped with such incredible senses. Since your cat's nose is often so close to the litter substrate itself, imagine how unpleasant it is to be in a covered box that doesn't have enough air circulation to adequately dry the litter. The smell in the box could be overpowering enough to drive the cat away.

Cramped Accommodations. For many cats, the only way to use the covered box is to crouch down or stick their heads out the entrance. Many litter boxes, open or covered, are too small. I recommend to my clients who insist on a covered box that they purchase large plastic storage containers and then cut an entrance on one side for the cat to have easy access.

Out of Sight, Out of Mind. With a covered box, you might not notice that the cat has eliminated, so you may just walk by without scooping.

Inconvenient to Clean. While you may initially think a covered box will keep things neater, it actually creates more work for you. In order to scoop the box, you have to remove the cover. When it's time to thoroughly scrub the box, you now have two pieces to clean instead of one.

A Better Alternative. If you're thinking about a covered box in order to control litter scatter, or if you have a cat who sprays in the box, choose a high-sided, open box instead. A large plastic storage container with high walls will work. All you have to do is cut out a low entrance on one side. There are also some manufacturers who make high-sided litter boxes, and depending upon the size of your cat or whether he sprays in the box, one of these litter boxes may work for you. If not, a plastic storage container, such as the ones made by Sterilite, is an excellent option.

Question:

There are so many kinds of litter. Which one is best for my cat? I want to make sure I avoid a litter box aversion problem.

Pam's Answer:

There are many choices of litter substrate. Many are designed to appeal to the human family member but not necessarily the cat, who will be the one using the box. I find this to be the case with many of the alternative litters, such as crystals, wheat, pine, pelletized newspaper, and even pebbles. The strongly scented litters are also marketed for human appeal. Manufacturers spend lots of money trying to come up with the next greatest litter, but the bottom line is, the cat has to want to use it. You may want to purchase a litter that's eco-friendly or has an appealing scent, but if the cat doesn't like it, you just wasted your money.

Cats Can Have Preferences. In general, the most appealing type of litter to use is one with a soft, sandy texture. Most of the scoopable, clumping litters fit into this category because they have a very soft feel. When wet, the litter forms a solid ball that can be scooped up and removed from the litter box.

Scent. Forget all about the extra scented litter or the perfumed litter additives. All they do is attempt to cover an odor that won't exist in the first place if you scoop on a regular basis. Your cat's sensitive nose doesn't need to be bombarded by an overpowering scent of flowers when she steps into the box. What she wants is to basically smell nothing or just her own scent.

Texture. Many cats have texture preferences as to litter substrate, food, and even where they sleep. Pay attention to any preferences your cat may have when purchasing litter. Find a type your cat likes and stick with that one. Typically, cats prefer a soft, sandy texture. Stepping on sharp little pieces, as are found in traditional clay litter, can be uncomfortable and even painful, especially for cats who have been declawed.

Squeaky Clean. No matter what type of litter chosen, the golden rule is, you must keep the box clean. If the litter stinks, it's not your cat's fault. Don't cover up the odor by using sprays or additives. Scoop twice a day and completely change out the litter as often as necessary. Cats are clean animals, and they deserve to have clean litter available to them.

Don't Keep Switching Brands. Cats are creatures of habit, so don't make abrupt changes in the brand or type of litter you purchase. When the cat enters the litter box, she'll expect to feel the same texture on her paws that she felt yesterday. If you must make a change, add a little of the new litter into the current brand so the switch occurs over the course of several days.

Not Sure What Litter to Buy? If you're adopting a cat, find out what litter was being used in her previous environment and start off with that to minimize any disruptions. If it's not a litter you like, you can slowly make a change after the cat gets settled. If you're bringing home a kitten, stick with an unscented scoopable litter. A kitten is still in the learning stage, so she doesn't need to be confused by a highly scented litter or an alternative litter with a strange texture. Make it as easy as possible for the youngster.

Question:
How much litter should I put in the box?

Pam's Answer:
My recommendation is to spread a three- or four-inch layer of litter in the box. That's enough for digging and adequate covering afterward. Every cat is an individual, so pay attention to your cat's litter box habits to see whether you need to adjust that level up or down.

> ## Don't Skimp
> If you have more than one cat, don't try to get by with one litter box simply by filling it with more litter. You need to increase the number of boxes.

Maintain a Consistent Litter Level. As you do your daily scooping of the litter box, you'll have to periodically top off the box with some fresh litter to keep the level consistent.

Too Much Litter. If you use too much litter, it'll end up getting kicked out over the edge, and you'll have it tracked everywhere. Even if you have a covered litter box, if there's just too much litter in there, it'll easily find its way onto your floor or carpet. If you find you're regularly sweeping up the floor, try lowering the litter level about an inch.

Using too much litter is also very wasteful, because you still have to completely empty the litter and scrub out the box on a regular basis. Filling the box with too much litter isn't the easy way to get out of scooping or cleaning the litter.

Not Enough Litter. Not using enough litter is a litter box aversion problem just waiting to happen. An inadequate level of litter will create an odor problem, as urine will have no place to be absorbed and will sit on the bottom of the box. If the box smells dirty, it'll be far less inviting for your cat to want to go there to take care of personal business.

Question:
How often should I scoop the litter box? I typically check it every couple of days.

Pam's Answer:
The box should be scooped twice a day. A dirty litter box is a ticking time bomb.

You'd be surprised how many times I visit a client's home and discover that the cause of the cat's inappropriate elimination is inadequate scooping of the box by the cat parent. Cats are very clean, and they're not comfortable stepping over mounds of urine-soaked litter or dried-up old feces in order to find a clean square inch for elimination.

People who stock up on room fresheners, covered boxes, and litter additives or locate the box in the remotest part of the house to avoid the odor are ignoring the most important tool in odor control: the litter shovel. The best way to control odor is to get rid of soiled litter as often as you can. Some cat parents wait until the odor in the box wafts its way throughout the room, then toss the entire contents into the trash. The result is a very clean box that remains appealing to the cat for about one day.

Smooth and Sleek

When cleaning the litter box, routinely check for signs of wear. Replace deeply scratched boxes, because they hold odor. Some cats may also object to the rough texture.

Scooping = Health Monitoring. Scooping serves another extremely important but often overlooked function. It's a valuable diagnostic tool. When you scoop, you're alerted to any potential problem in its earliest stages, signaled by changes in the quantity, consistency, or color of poop or by blood in the urine.

Special-Needs Kitties. If your cat develops diabetes or is in chronic renal failure, the box may need to be scooped more often due to the increased frequency and amount of urination. An additional box may be necessary to ensure there's always enough clean litter available.

It's a Small Task That Can Make a Huge Difference. Litter box scooping may not be something you look forward to, but it's a valuable way to control odor, monitor your cat's health, and keep the cat happy. If you don't think it makes a difference, try not flushing your toilet for a day or two.

Question:
The litter I buy is too expensive, so I'm thinking of changing brands. What's the best way to do it?

Pam's Answer:
Cats don't like change. If you want to avoid creating unnecessary stress in your cat's life, keep that in mind when you plan to introduce anything

unfamiliar. For many cats, even a minor change can be upsetting. But you can switch if you plan a strategy carefully.

Gradual Changeover. This is the safest method because it gives your cat time to adjust to the difference without being overwhelmed. In most cases, if you go slowly enough, your cat won't even realize a change is taking place.

Mix a small amount of the new litter in with the current brand every day for several days. Every day use a little more of the new and a little less of the old. This changeover should typically take place over three to five days. If you have a cat who you know, from previous experience, really reacts negatively to change, then it's best to stretch out the changeover over the full five days.

If switching from a traditional nonclumping clay litter to scoopable, keep in mind that the new litter won't effectively form clumps until there's very little old litter left.

Question:
How do I know the right size litter box for my cat?

Pam's Answer:
When choosing a litter box, it's important to match the size of the box to the size of your cat. It's easy to get influenced by a desire to choose a box based on whether it will fit in a certain location. In some cases, that may still work out fine for your cat, but in other cases, it means she ends up squeezing too much cat into too little litter box. Your cat shouldn't have to become a contortionist to go to the bathroom.

Sizing. In general, the litter box should be one and a half times the length of your cat. That gives her enough room to eliminate, cover her waste and still have plenty of clean litter for a couple of return trips. A litter box that's large enough for your cat will greatly increase her comfort level. She won't have to hang some of her body over the edge. Discomfort in the litter box can be very stressful, and stress is the *last* thing you want your cat feeling there. If she becomes uncomfortable in the box, she may choose another location, and her choice will probably not be to your liking.

For a kitten, the litter box should be low-sided and easy to enter and exit. When the kitten grows, the small box can be switched out for a larger one. If you have an adult cat who has gained weight and isn't quite as svelte as she used to be, the litter box you originally bought her may no longer be adequate.

Comfort matters when it comes to time spent taking care of personal business. If you've ever had to use an airplane lavatory, you can probably relate!

Question:

I want to move Munchie's litter box out of the guest room and into the bathroom. What's the best way to do it to avoid upsetting her?

Pam's Answer:

If you need to change the location of the litter box, place a second box in the proposed new spot before moving the original box, so the cat can test-drive the new one while having the security of the old location. When your cat is comfortable with the new location and is using it consistently, gradually move the old box a few inches a day until it's right next to the new box. Once they're close together, you can dispose of one of the boxes.

If you decide not to get a temporary second box to do a gradual transition, then you'll have to move the original box a little at a time toward the new location. Key word here is *gradual*!

Time to Be a Detective

What does or doesn't happen in the litter box can be a red flag indicating a potential health issue. Stay on top of your twice-daily scooping schedule so you'll be alerted to any change in a cat's frequency of elimination or in the appearance or quantity of the waste.

Your Cat's Needs Must Come First. Make sure the new location you've chosen for the litter box is one your cat will find convenient and appealing. If you're relocating the box to a more remote area, keep in mind that it'll be less convenient for the cat and less likely to get scooped and cleaned regularly. Those two factors contribute to litter box aversion problems.

Question:

I have five cats. How many litter boxes do I realistically need? I don't want to spend my days cleaning an endless number of boxes.

Pam's Answer:

The one aspect of living in a multicat home that isn't much fun is the fact that there's more poop and pee in the litter box. This is where many cat parents drop the ball—not because they neglect to keep the box clean, but simply because there isn't enough litter box space to go around.

The rule of thumb is N+1 (number of cats plus one). It's difficult to keep one box clean enough for multiple cats. You don't want one of the cats to enter a litter box and not be able to find a spot clean enough to urinate. An overcrowded litter box can't possibly be kept clean enough, and as a result, a cat may feel he has no choice but to eliminate somewhere else. Even if you keep the litter box sparklingly clean, it distresses some cats to share a toilet.

Shortcuts Don't Work. You may think you can get around the cleaning issue by investing in a self-cleaning electronic litter box, but it won't address the fact that some cats aren't comfortable venturing into another cat's territory. In multicat environments, overlapping territories can already be stressful enough. Cats who get along in every other aspect may still feel anxiety when they have to use a litter box another cat uses.

Question:

Are litter box liners a good idea? I'm hoping they'll make it easier for me to keep my cat's box clean.

Pam's Answer:

In theory, litter box liners may seem like a convenient way to keep the box clean and make changing the litter a breeze. Unfortunately though, liners can create problems for the cats who use the litter box, as well as the humans who try to clean it.

A Less Than Perfect Fit. Liners that don't fit perfectly can end up with folds in them where urine can pool and create quite a smelly situation. If the liner isn't secured well on all sides of the box, it can fold back into the box as the cat uses her paws to cover her waste.

Claws + Plastic Liner = Holes. Cats with claws can poke holes in the liners as they scratch, and that allows urine to seep through and settle on the bottom of the litter box. Worse, if cats get their claws stuck in the plastic, they can develop an unpleasant association with the litter box itself, and they may go in search of an elimination location that won't be so uncomfortable.

How Does the Cat Feel About This? Some cats object to the feel of the liners, especially ill-fitting ones that end up with lots of folds. The box may become an unpleasant place, leading to litter box aversion.

Potential Problems During Cleanup. The litter scoop can get caught in the folds of the liner, making it difficult to gather up all the soiled litter. You can also accidentally create a hole in the liner with the sharp edge of the scoop.

To completely change out the litter, you should be able to simply lift up the litter-filled liner and toss the whole thing away without any mess, right? Well, if there are holes in the liner, litter will fall through in several tiny streams. If urine has leaked through the holes, you'll have wet or dried urine on the outside of the liner as well as on the bottom of the litter box. Suddenly the liner doesn't seem so convenient.

Don't Take Shortcuts. The best way to keep the litter box clean is to scoop it a couple of times a day and thoroughly scrub the box and change out the litter as often as needed. Don't take a shortcut by using litter box liners. Your cat will appreciate having a litter box setup that's appealing and clean and won't cause his claws to get stuck in plastic.

Question:

I saw a video on the Internet where a cat was trained to eliminate in the toilet. Should I try to train my cat to use the toilet so we don't have to have a litter box anymore?

Pam's Answer:

Toilet training your cat may sound like a convenient alternative to the litter box, but don't be in a rush to get rid of that box without knowing what you and your cat will be facing. There are serious negatives to training a cat to use the toilet. I have done many consultations for cat behavior problems as a result of cat parents attempting to train their cats to exclusively eliminate in the toilet. The cats end up in distress, and the cat parents almost always wind up very frustrated. What is supposed to be the answer to the dreaded litter box setup may end up creating a major behavior problem.

Nobody Likes the Stink. One common reason people are attracted to the idea of toilet training their cats is because they're fed up with dealing with litter box mess and smell. Many people don't want to come into even indirect contact with what comes out of the rear end of a cat even if that means only scooping the waste a couple of times a day. In reality, litter boxes don't have to be messy and smelly. A big reason why they are is they don't get scooped and cleaned enough.

Why Toilet Training Isn't the Best Idea. When the cat eliminates in the toilet, you can't accurately see whether there's a change in elimination habits. If the urine is going into the toilet, you can't tell whether there has been an increase or decrease in volume. A change in volume is a big red flag to a potential medical problem. When you scoop the litter box, you can notice changes in the urine clumps.

Toilet training goes against a cat's natural instinct to dig, eliminate, and cover. The lid must always be left open, and the first time someone forgets and closes the lid, the cat may have no choice but to eliminate on the carpet.

Cats can't flush, so that can cause lingering odor from solid waste, and cats in multicat homes may object to sharing the same toilet.

Even though you can purchase commercial toilet training kits, at some point you have to take the kit away and force your cat to straddle the toilet. For some cats, including those who are very young, old, ill, or in pain, this can be difficult and *stressful*. Toilet seats are slippery and can be difficult for a less-than-healthy cat to negotiate.

If your cat falls into the toilet, although he may be able to get out, the panic may cause him to hesitate eliminating in there in the future. If he falls into a dirty toilet, you have the added stress of having to bathe him. If he's home alone, he has to deal with the traumatic event by himself. It can take only one traumatic experience for a cat to form a complete aversion to the process.

When hospitalized or boarded, your cat will be put in a cage with a traditional litter box. Once he returns home, you may have to retrain him to the toilet again. This may cause confusion.

Going to the Bathroom Shouldn't Cause Stress. The process of eliminating waste shouldn't be a stressful event for your cat. A litter box filled with an appealing litter most closely resembles what a cat would choose outdoors. Cats dig, eliminate, and cover by instinct. Covering the waste is how they prevent predators from finding where they live. Even indoor cats have that instinct for security. In multicat homes, litter box locations are important in creating security for each cat. One cat may not feel comfortable going through another cat's area to get to a litter box. With traditional boxes, that can be addressed by locating them in various parts of the house. When you toilet train, you're limited to fixed locations.

Stick to what's most natural: an absorbent litter in the right-size box that's kept clean and placed in a location with strong cat appeal. Let your cat be a cat!

Chapter 5

Stinking Outside the Box

*When cats don't pee and poop
where you want them to*

Question:

One of my cats has started urinating on the carpet. I think he's just mad, so do I really have to spend the money on a veterinary visit?

Pam's Answer:

Elimination outside of the litter box is probably the most frustrating behavior a cat parent ever has to cope with. All of a sudden, the cat who never caused any problems has suddenly started viewing the dining room carpet or living room sofa as a makeshift litter box. Plastic coverings start making their way onto the sofa, the dining room becomes off-limits, the box is cleaned to perfection, and the cat parent starts looking at the beloved family cat as an intruder.

When a cat eliminates outside of the box, he isn't being spiteful, stupid, or willfully disobedient. For some reason, he feels he can't use the box. It may not make sense to you, but it's normal behavior for the cat. As the one with the bigger brain, you have the job of figuring out *why*.

In many cases, litter box aversion has an underlying medical cause. It could be feline lower urinary tract disease (FLUTD), the start of renal failure, diabetes, inflammatory bowel disease (IBD), constipation, diarrhea, or a number of other medical issues. Very often the cat associates the pain he feels with the box itself. He thinks if he eliminates somewhere else, it won't hurt so much. In the case of urinary issues, he may try to retain the urine as long as possible because it hurts too much to pee. When his bladder reaches maximum capacity, the cat may not be close enough to the box to get there in time. With some urinary problems, the accumulation of any amount of urine in the bladder can cause pain, so the cat will pee in small drops throughout the house. If you see traces of blood in the urine (either on the carpet or in the litter box), then you know there's definitely something going on needing immediate medical attention.

Any change in your cat's behavior, litter box habits, or eating and drinking habits should be viewed as a potential medical red flag. Always have your cat checked by the veterinarian as soon as you notice a change.

Signs of Potential Urinary Problems:

- increased or decreased urination
- elimination outside of the litter box
- frequent trips to the litter box
- crying or straining while in the litter box
- voiding only small amounts of urine
- change in urine color
- change in urine odor
- traces of blood in urine
- painful abdomen
- weight loss
- restlessness
- irritability
- change in appetite
- change in water consumption

- inability to urinate (this is an absolute *emergency*)
- frequent licking of genital area
- depression
- ammonia odor to the breath
- vomiting
- excessive vocalization

Question:
Why do some cats suddenly stop using the litter box?

Pam's Answer:
First have your cat checked by the veterinarian in order to rule out any medical cause. Once illness is ruled out, consider honestly this checklist of complaints your cat may have.

A Dirty Litter Box. If the box is too dirty, cats may seek other arrangements.

Declawing. Cats who are declawed may continue to feel pain long after the healing period. Some cats' paws remain sensitive for the rest of their lives, and the texture of the litter may be uncomfortable for them.

A Covered Litter Box. A covered box often makes the cat feel confined and makes it more inconvenient for you to scoop on a regular basis. My biggest complaint with a covered box is that it gives the cat only one escape route. In a multicat household, this can be a deal breaker, because a cat may avoid the box if he feels he'll get ambushed while in there.

Wrong Size Box. Don't choose a litter box size based on where it conveniently will fit in a location. Choose a box based on the size of your cat. The box should be about one and a half times the length of your cat.

Not Enough Boxes. In multicat homes, you should have more litter boxes than you have cats. There's no skimping on this.

Wrong Location. Location choice should be about convenience and security for the cat, not about what's convenient for the cat parent. Don't put the litter box near the food, in a damp basement, in a closet, or near household appliances that may frighten the cat. In a multicat household, scatter boxes around the home; don't line them up in one room.

Litter Box Liners. Litter box liners are created for the convenience of the cat parent, but they often tear from the cat's claws.

Not Enough Litter in the Box. Don't be stingy when it comes to filling the litter box. If you don't want to create an odor problem, put an adequate amount of litter in the box and keep the level consistent.

The Wrong Litter. In general, cats like an unscented, sandlike substrate. Texture is important. Most cats like the feel of sand on their paws, and sandlike litter makes it easy to dig and cover.

Stress and Environment. Whether the stress is due to multicat issues, household chaos, or sudden changes (such as a move, renovation, new baby, new spouse, etc.), the effect can end up being litter box aversion. Cats are creatures of habit who don't adjust well to abrupt changes or chaotic environments. A litter box avoidance problem may result if your cat is too fearful to even peek his head out from under the bed. Address multicat tension issues and/or environmental factors in order to provide your cat a sense of security and safety in his own territory.

Going High-Tech. Electronic self-cleaning boxes have so many downsides, I don't even know where to start. Many of them have motors whose noise is frightening to cats. Even in the big ones, the actual surface area for the cat is too small. Many self-cleaning boxes have covers, as well. Some of these boxes have timers that delay cleaning until ten minutes after the cat has left the box, but they don't allow for another cat entering. Some rakes in the boxes easily clog when there's a large clump.

Strong Cleansers. Strong-smelling household cleansers may leave enough of a scent on the plastic box to drive the cat away. When you clean the box, use well-diluted dish soap. You can also use heavily diluted bleach, but rinse very well after cleaning.

Litter Scatter Mats. These mats are designed to catch the litter trapped on the cat's paws as he exits the litter box. Some mats may have a texture cats find uncomfortable.

Punishment. I include this on the list because it's important to know that a cat may avoid the box if punished for eliminating in other locations.

When you punish a cat for peeing or pooping outside of the box, the messages he receives are (1) he should be afraid of you, and (2) peeing and pooping will get him in trouble. Even though you think you're teaching him that his location choice is what you objected to, the message he got was to avoid peeing and pooping when you're around. When you punish, you assume that the cat is misbehaving, but in reality he isn't. If a cat isn't using his litter box, it's because he feels he can't. Your job is to figure out why.

Keep Track

Start a log to keep track of where and when your cat eliminates outside of the litter box. This can help you establish a pattern or identify possible triggers. Once you begin behavior modification or make environmental adjustments, the record keeping can also help you recognize improvements that might otherwise go unnoticed. An easy way to do record keeping is to put a calendar on your refrigerator so all family members can record incidents.

Question:

My husband and I have four cats. Someone is peeing on the dining room carpet, but we can't figure out which one. How do we solve the problem if we can't identify the culprit?

Pam's Answer:

When addressing a litter box problem in a multicat household, the first and often most difficult step is to identify the rogue eliminator. You may think you know which cat peed on the carpet, but if you're wrong, you could create major setbacks in the behavior modification plan. So how do you find out which cat has turned your living room carpet into a giant litter box or has sprayed against your favorite antique chair?

Under Surveillance. The most accurate way to determine which cat is eliminating outside of the litter box is to set up video surveillance. Numerous companies have wireless surveillance cameras that you can monitor by an app on your mobile phone. You can also purchase a "cat cam" that attaches to your cat's collar. With the little cat cams, you won't see the cat eliminating or spraying, but you may get to see what he was looking at that triggered the spraying. Video surveillance is the most reliable detection method.

Fluorescein. If urination or urine marking is the problem, as opposed to defecation, you can also try identification through the use of fluorescein dye. This ophthalmic dye is used to detect problems on the surface of the eye, but it has also been given orally to help identify which cat is urine marking in a multicat household. The fluorescein will cause the urine to fluoresce under a Wood's lamp. You can have your veterinarian put the fluorescein in a capsule for you to administer to your cat. The problem with fluorescein is that it isn't 100 percent reliable in causing all urine to fluoresce.

Defecation Identification. Video surveillance is your best tool, and fortunately, wireless home video surveillance cameras have become much more affordable. When it comes to defecation, though, there's a simple, low-tech detection method as well. Some veterinarians suggest that clients add a small amount of brightly colored, nontoxic crayon shavings to a cat's food. Because it doesn't get digested, it often shows up in the feces after elimination. Your veterinarian will provide specific instructions on how much to use.

Confinement. A method many cat parents use is to confine one cat away from the others to see if the problem persists. Separating a cat is unreliable, because the confined cat may be causing the stress to the cat who is actually spraying, and the behavior may stop if the two cats no longer share space.

Visit the Veterinarian. Don't automatically assume that the problem is behavioral, even if your cats have been throwing hissy fits at one another. There could be a medical cause for the behavior. In addition, stress can contribute to the onset of medical issues relating to the litter box, such as idiopathic cystitis. So get out that cat carrier, because it's time to make a clinic appointment.

In a multicat household, just how do you decide which cat to take to the veterinarian? If you have just two or three cats, then it's safest to bring them all in for a checkup. In a more cat-dense household, you may want to start with the most likely suspect.

Pam's CatWise Clue

Common Mistakes People Make When Trying to Solve a Cat's Litter Box Problem. It can be extremely frustrating when a cat stops using her litter box. Anything and everything in your home can become a potential target of urine or feces. Litter box aversion is the most common problem clients call me about, and in many cases, those clients are at the end of their ropes. Cat parents seem to be able to tolerate furniture scratching or constant meowing, but peeing on the carpet day after day can be a deal breaker. Nothing sends a cat to the shelter faster than a litter box problem.

That's very sad, because many of the cats relinquished to shelters, abandoned, or euthanized due to litter box problems could've been helped. Litter box problems cause cat parents to react impulsively, emotionally, and sometimes irrationally. The sight or smell of cat pee on a cherished sofa, a bed, or an expensive carpet can easily short-circuit a person's patience. The level of frustration is understandable, but the way people handle the problem can either improve the situation or send it into a downward spiral. Here are some harmful mistakes cat parents often make:

Mistake: Waiting Too Long to Do Something About It. I can't tell you how many times people call me and request an immediate consultation because they plan on relinquishing the cat to a shelter within days. The problem has usually been going on for weeks, months, and maybe even years, and then the cat parent reaches the breaking point. The longer a problem goes on, the harder it is to correct. If you wait until the problem has caused you to reach your breaking point, you probably won't be in a good frame of mind to do the proper behavior modification. It's also not fair to the cat. When a cat feels she can't use the litter box, for whatever reason, it's stressful. If the reason is medically related, it also causes suffering. Don't wait.

Mistake: Assuming the Problem Is Behavioral. Many behavior problems have underlying medical causes. A cat may suffer pain because a cat parent assumes that the cause of the litter box aversion is a behavior problem when in fact it might be due to lower urinary tract disease, renal failure, diabetes, or any number of other medical issues. Whenever a cat displays a change in behavior, you should have her examined by a veterinarian. Once the veterinarian rules out medical causes, then you can start to tackle the problem from a behavioral standpoint.

Mistake: Punishment. This is so counterproductive, it's heartbreaking. Rubbing your cat's nose in her mess, spanking, yelling, time-outs, squirting her with water, or any other form of punishment does nothing to help retrain her and in fact can make the situation worse.

If you punish her, you add to her stress, potentially creating an added fear of you in the process, and she may start retaining her urine as long as she can, which is physically harmful. Hitting a cat is inhumane and also harmful to the behavior modification process. Your hands should never be used as weapons. How can you ever expect your cat to trust you if she doesn't know whether the hand coming near her is going to pet her or smack her? Fear, intimidation, and pain are not appropriate behavior modification tools. Don't let your frustration over a behavior problem get the better of you, because your relationship with your cat will suffer.

Mistake: Not Finding the True Cause. Animals don't repeat behaviors unless they serve a function. If the cat is eliminating outside of the litter box, there's a valid reason for it. The reason is not acceptable from the cat parent's point of view, but the cat is trying to solve a problem in the best way she knows. Let's look at a couple of examples: Perhaps she's eliminating outside of the box because it's too dirty. While you may think scooping the box once every other day is adequate, your cat may not feel that it's clean enough. She may eliminate in other areas of the house because they're cleaner. Maybe she's peeing in the dining room because every time she tries to go into the litter box, she gets ambushed by a companion cat. Perhaps the dining room offers her more escape potential because she can see her opponent approaching from a distance and has more places to run.

You may have set up a litter box that's very private, but in the cat's mind, the privacy limits her ability to feel safe. Or the box may be located in an unappealing location. Perhaps it's in a basement, so she has to go up and down the stairs, or in a closet with a narrow entrance and exit. There are numerous other reasons your cat may feel it's necessary to choose a location other than the litter box. If you just set up deterrents without getting to the source of the problem, she'll just keep looking for other locations.

Mistake: Being Inconsistent. Cats are creatures of habit, and they take comfort in knowing that things in their environment aren't going to be changing on a daily basis. Whether it's your desire to switch to a different brand of litter, the fact that you love rearranging the furniture, or the irresistible urge to buy the cat food that's on sale this week, sudden change is upsetting to cats.

Question:

I have a feeling that my cat, Midgie, doesn't like where I've put her litter box. I've had her checked by the veterinarian, and I also keep the box very clean. How do I know which place is best?

Pam's Answer:

The placement of the litter box can create anxiety for both the cat and the human. The human typically wants the box as far away as possible and out of sight. The cat, however, needs the box conveniently located. Because the cat is the one who has to use the box, look at it from her point of view. Would you want to travel down two flights of stairs and then go out to the garage when nature calls? Probably not.

Location Aversion. You may have the ideal litter box filled with the best litter money can buy and kept sparklingly clean, but if it's in a location your cat finds objectionable, then you've set the stage for a litter box aversion problem. It's important to view the litter box setup from a cat's perspective in order to figure out the best location.

Cats Don't Eat Where They Eliminate. Don't place the litter box close to the feeding station. For survival, cats are hardwired to eliminate away from their home in order to avoid attracting predators. Waste is covered for that reason. Placing the litter box near the food sends a mixed message and can cause distress. This setup can result in a litter box aversion problem because the cat can't move the food and water elsewhere, but she can take herself to another area to eliminate.

Balancing Privacy and Vulnerability. Privacy ranks high on our list when we think about what we want in our bathroom facilities. For a cat, however, the need for safety ranks higher than the need for privacy. When a cat is in the litter box, she's vulnerable to being ambushed. This is especially true in multipet households where there's any degree of hostility. Even if there isn't hostility, one cat entering the litter box area can startle another cat who's in the middle of taking care of business.

I've written many times about the need for an escape route from the litter box. When a cat is in there, she needs to have more than one option for a quick departure if she feels threatened. That's why I don't like the idea of covered boxes. Even if you have an uncovered box, however, you can create a problem if it's put in a closet, under a piece of furniture, or wedged into a corner.

Granted, both you and your cat most likely don't want the litter box in the middle of the family room or where there is a lot of foot traffic, but you need to balance privacy and vulnerability. This may mean something as simple as sliding the box out from under the desk or out of the closet.

The Noise Factor. Aside from the bathroom, the most common location for a litter box is the laundry room. This may seem the most logical spot, because it's usually not a carpeted room, so cleanup is a breeze. However, the cat may not like the sudden noise of the washing machine going through the spin cycle. I've also been in homes where washers shake and rattle during the spin cycle. When the litter box is planted right next to the washer, imagine how upsetting that must be. No cat wants to eliminate in a vibrating litter box.

Another noisy location is the garage. Some people install a pet door so the cat can simply go in and out as she needs to in order to use the litter box. There can be an extreme noise factor here (not to mention the terror factor) if the garage door suddenly opens or closes or a car pulls into the driveway.

Guarding and Territory. In a multicat household, one cat may exhibit guarding behavior by appearing to casually lounge in the hallway in front of the litter box area. To the human, it may seem that the cat is just napping, but to the other cats in the house, it can be an obvious No Trespassing sign.

In a multicat home, one cat may be afraid to cross another cat's area and so may eliminate on the carpet in a room where she feels safe. In a multicat home, it's important to have the same number of litter boxes as you have cats, plus one extra, and to scatter them throughout the house.

Question:

Our cat stopped using the litter box, and when we took him to the hospital, he was diagnosed with a urinary infection. He's on medication now but still won't use the box. How can we get him to stop peeing on the bath mat?

Pam's Answer:

Sometimes because the cat has experienced pain when attempting to eliminate, he might still associate the box with the memory of that pain. He has learned to avoid the litter box because every time he went there, he felt discomfort.

The Solution. The way to handle this is to offer an additional litter box. Sometimes you also have to offer a different type of litter. You can place the new box near, but not right next to, the original box. The fact that the cat is now on medication and presumably free of pain may help him feel more comfortable about using a litter box again.

Don't just fill the original box with a different type of litter, because cats don't like abrupt changes. The way to do it is to offer a choice to your cat and let him make the decision. In some cases, you may need to offer two additional boxes with two different types of litter, or you may need to put the additional box a little farther away from the original one. If your cat is consistently eliminating in a particular spot, place the additional litter box in that location.

There's a litter designed especially for cats with litter box aversion problems. Cat Attract litter was created by a veterinarian and contains an herbal attractant that cats associate with toilet locations. The litter is available at your local pet-product store and online. I recommend that you put Cat Attract in one of the litter boxes and see if it makes a difference.

Plan B. If your cat continues to insist on eliminating on the bath mat or other carpet even though you've offered other litter, there's another option to try. Place a litter box out in the targeted location, but don't put any litter in it. Instead, put a small piece of carpet or bath mat in it. The goal is to get the cat eliminating in the box. If he does, you can then start sprinkling in a little litter. Eventually, you can do away with the piece of carpet. If your cat still absolutely refuses to eliminate in any type of litter, you may have to continue to use carpet scraps or try lining the litter box with absorbent pads (similar to puppy pee pads). Granted, this isn't an ideal solution, but if it gets your cat eliminating inside the box, it's at least a start.

Question:

Why will my six-year-old cat pee in the litter box but won't poop in it?

Pam's Answer:

First, rule out medical issues. There are a number of ailments that could cause your cat to feel uncomfortable about pooping in the box. If she experiences constipation, for example, she may associate the box with her discomfort and attempt to go somewhere else. If you have a covered litter box, she may feel cramped in there while perching in position to poop.

There are a number of intestinal problems that commonly result in cats defecating outside of the box. The cat may experience cramping, and the discomfort may cause her to try to eliminate wherever she is at the time. She may also become so uncomfortable she can't make it to the box.

When you take your cat to the veterinarian, try to bring along a sample of her stool so the veterinarian can run some tests and also examine it for signs of blood, mucus, intestinal parasites, or hair. If you're unable to bring a fresh sample, the veterinarian will be able to get one, but it's much more comfortable for your cat if you can bring one along. Just make sure it hasn't been sitting in the litter box too long. You can also take the sample, seal it tightly in a plastic bag or container, and place it in the refrigerator—although for many people this is a psychologically unacceptable option. Keep in mind that the veterinarian doesn't need a huge sample. He or she needs just enough to do some testing and to examine the stool.

Don't overlook the important first step of visiting the veterinarian if your cat is pooping outside of the box. I have lived with a cat who had inflammatory bowel disease and know how much pain he must've felt when his intestines started cramping. I also have a number of clients who have cats with intestinal problems. Early diagnosis and appropriate medication and/or dietary adjustments will be most important.

Survival Instincts. There are some cats who don't like to defecate in the same area used for urination. For some cats, urination may have a more territorial connotation, or this may be just a quirky feline instinct. Regardless, a simple solution is to offer another box for defecation. Don't place it right next to the original box, or it'll be regarded as just one big box, and your cat will still not poop in it. You can most likely put the second box in the same room (depending on the size of the room), but if that doesn't work, you'll have to locate it elsewhere.

Safety Issues. It typically takes a cat a bit longer to defecate than urinate. In a multicat household where there is even the smallest amount of tension, it may be too stressful for a cat to hang out in the litter box long enough to poop. A box that's covered, shoved in a corner, or hidden in a closet will reduce the cat's escape potential. She may feel it's safer to poop in another location that allows her a better view of approaching opponents.

Substrate Preference. Some cats, for reasons only they seem to know, have a substrate preference when it comes to the feel of the litter for defecation versus urination. Perhaps it has something to do with the amount of time they spend in that perching position for pooping. If you think that might be the case, offer another litter box with a litter that has a different texture. In general, cats prefer a soft, sandy texture.

Last but Not Least: Cleanliness. A cat may decide that the box is too dirty if there is any waste already in there. She may urinate but then feel it's not clean enough for her to defecate. Understandably, you can't stand over the box twenty-four hours a day with a litter scoop in your hand to remove waste a nanosecond after it touches the litter. Just make sure you scoop at least twice a day and have more than one litter box, so there'll be a greater chance the cat can find a clean patch of litter for defecation.

Question:
I think my cat doesn't like the type of litter in his box. How do I tell if it's the litter he objects to?

Pam's Answer:
Two senses come into play to determine a cat's like or dislike of a particular litter substrate: smell and touch. If the litter is too dirty, it will smell bad. Even if *you* don't smell it, your cat will. If your pathetically insensitive nose were where the cat's nose is, you'd certainly know whether litter maintenance was up to snuff. If the cat's nose tells him all is not right in the litter box, he may be driven to seek other arrangements, such as your living room carpet, a sofa cushion, or the bath mat. You may even be keeping the litter box very clean, but if the litter is heavily scented or if that particular scent disgusts that particular cat, going to the litter box may still be an unpleasant experience.

The texture of the litter can also make a difference in the overall box appeal. Most cats prefer the soft, sandy texture of scoopable litter. If the litter has large granules or is pelleted, he may not like the feel against his paws. Litter that sticks to his paws or is too dusty may also lead to aversion.

Avoidance, Perching, and Hit-and-Run Eliminators. If your cat has a dislike for the litter substrate, he might not totally avoid the box but may perch on the edge. This may be his attempt to physically be in the box as much as he can while limiting his actual contact with the substrate. Some cats who dislike the litter do a hit and run—they eliminate and then dash out of there without taking the time to dig or cover. If the instinct to cover is very strong, some cats paw at the wall near the box or on the floor in front. Some cats vigorously shake their paws after exiting the box to rid themselves of the unpleasant litter. If he often sneezes near the litter, the brand you purchased might be too dusty.

Your cat may try to get as close to the box as possible for elimination, but when there's a litter aversion, he might be able to tolerate only being *near* but not actually *in* the box. Elimination results might be on the floor just inches away.

Plan of Action. Objectively evaluate your litter scooping and maintenance schedule. Make sure any litter box avoidance isn't due to your dropping the ball when it comes to keeping the box pristine. Scoop at least twice a day, and thoroughly scrub the box at least monthly (scrub weekly if using nonscoopable). Keep the level of litter consistent by topping off every few days. A good four inches is adequate for most cats.

If you're unsure whether your cat objects to a particular litter, experiment by putting out an additional litter box with a different kind of litter. If you've been using traditional clay litter, then put out a box of soft, scoopable litter. If you've been using highly scented litter, fill the second box with an unscented formula. If your cat has been sneezing when using the box, look for a low-dust or dust-free brand. If you're totally unsure what kind the cat might prefer, you can set out a third box as well—sort of a litter box buffet. Your cat will let you know his preference.

Question:

I have two cats, Cece and Chloe, who get along for the most part, but they do have periodic squabbles. I know this may sound crazy, but Chloe looks nervous when she's in the litter box. Why would she be afraid when she's in the box? Is it because of Cece?

Pam's Answer:

One important aspect of litter box appeal is not even on the radar screens of most cat parents—*safety*. I commonly find that cat parents take the privacy issue too far and try to hide the litter box in the remotest locations, or they purchase covered boxes. It's certainly not appealing (even to the cat) to have the litter box front and center in the middle of the family room, but your cat doesn't want the location to be too private or hard to get to. The reason is not only convenience, but also safety.

Even though you think you have created a comfortable and convenient environment for your cat when it comes to the litter box, she doesn't necessarily see it that way. This is especially true in a home where there are several companion animals. When a cat is taking care of personal business, she shouldn't have to worry about another cat ambushing or stalking her by waiting at the litter box entrance—even one with whom she's on good terms otherwise.

In your attempt to provide an abundance of privacy at the litter box, you may have located it in a closet or hidden it in a closed cabinet with a cat flap. There are even some litter boxes on the market these days disguised as planters or end tables. There are even top-entry boxes available. Imagine the poor cat who finds herself getting ambushed from *above*. Yikes! Don't be tempted to purchase fancy litter boxes in an effort to provide privacy for your cat. These products could end up being an expensive mistake if your cat feels too trapped in there.

Set Up for Success. Sometimes the solution is as simple as removing a litter box cover or sliding the box out from the closet. I often advise placing it on the side of the room opposite the entrance. The more warning time the cat has, the better.

It's up to the cat parent to create a safe environment around the litter box setup. Humans can lock the bathroom door to make sure no one barges in on them, but cats don't have that option.

Question:

What's the best way to clean cat urine from my carpet? I want to make sure my cat doesn't keep urinating there.

Pam's Answer:

Because cat urine has an unmistakable odor, you would think it would be easy to clean up, but if your cat has found some discreet locations, you may not be aware of the problem until he has gone back to that spot repeatedly to urinate. By that time, the urine will have soaked through carpeting and to the carpet pad and even beyond. So it's very important to first identify all the soiled areas so you can do a thorough cleanup.

Locate All Soiled Areas. You can't always tell by the smell; an odor can linger so faintly that you can't detect it but the cat can. The easiest way to locate every site is with a black light. It emits ultraviolet light, which will cause most urine stains to fluoresce (think of those old disco days when the black lights would cause white clothing to look almost electric).

Black lights are available at your local pet-product store, as well as online. They're inexpensive and an absolute must-have if your cat is eliminating outside of the litter box.

Using the Black Light. To see the fluorescence, darken the room as much as possible. If it's a very bright room during the day and there's no way to darken it, wait until evening for best detection ability.

Hold the light a few inches away from the area you're checking. If you think your cat has been spraying, be sure to check vertical surfaces as well.

The black light will cause other stains to fluoresce as well, so not everything you see will necessarily be cat urine. It can also cause stains from blood, vomit, and diarrhea to fluoresce. After using the black light for a while, you'll get familiar with the typical look of a urine stain.

Mark the Spot. Because the stain will not be visible when you turn the room lights back on, you'll need to make sure you outline exactly where you need to clean. I use painter's tape (not masking tape) to outline the stain because it's easy to peel off afterward. Don't just put a piece of tape over the stain—outline it so you'll be sure to clean the entire spot. If you don't get up all of the urine, your cat will still be able to detect the odor and may return to that area again. When using the black light and the tape, just pretend you're in a *CSI* episode.

Cleaning Urine. If you're dealing with a fresh urine stain, first soak up as much of the urine as possible with paper towels. Use a blotting technique and don't press so hard that you drive the urine deeper into the carpet or upholstery. You can also pour a little club soda on the spot so the bubbles can lift the urine to the surface; then start blotting with paper towels. Just don't rub, because you'll spread the urine around.

The product to use for cleaning urine stains is one that states it not only removes the stain but neutralizes the urine odor. Ordinary household cleaners or rug cleaning products won't do that. It has to be a product specifically made for pet urine. Don't use any products containing ammonia, because urine contains ammonia and the smell could induce a cat to return to that spot to urinate again.

There are several pet stain removers available, and the instructions for them vary a little, so make sure you follow the directions regarding how long to keep the product on the carpet or upholstery and whether it needs to be rinsed off. If using a product on upholstery, test it in an inconspicuous area first to make sure it's safe for that particular fabric.

Under carpet repeatedly soiled, urine may have reached the flooring underneath. The carpet may need to be replaced. Pet stain and odor removers can do only so much.

Once you've applied the pet stain remover and left it on for the time specified by the manufacturer (and rinsed, if also indicated by manufacturer), place a towel over the area with a flat weight on it so as to absorb as much of the moisture as possible. Keep replacing damp towels with dry ones until you've gotten up as much moisture as you can. If you've used a large amount of pet stain remover and it went down deep into the carpet or upholstery, set up a small fan to accelerate the drying process.

Calling in a Professional Cleaning Service. If you do call a pro, make sure the company states that the product used is specifically designed to remove pet stain and odor.

Question:
Why do cats spray?

Pam's Answer:
Even though you may not be able to see it, if your cat sprays in your home, you can definitely smell it. The unmistakable odor indicates that all is not peaceful in your cat's universe. When a cat sprays, everyone is in crisis mode. Sometimes the panicked human thinks her only solution is to send the cat to the shelter, give him away, or even euthanize him.

Many people don't understand why cats spray, so they don't understand how to effectively deal with it.

It's easy to misunderstand the motivation behind spray-marking behavior. All too often, cat parents simply label the behavior as territorial marking, but that isn't the only reason cats spray. Unless you can uncover the true cause of the behavior, you won't have much success in stopping it. So it's time to sharpen your detective skills and do some undercover work.

Spraying Versus Indiscriminate Urination. To start with, you need to know that there's a difference between spraying and indiscriminate urination. A cat urinating outside the litter box isn't necessarily spraying. These are two different behaviors and can have different causes. Indiscriminate urination is usually done on horizontal surfaces. Spray marking is usually done up against vertical objects, but some cats will spray regardless of whether there is a vertical surface present. In this case, the sprayed urine will form a thin line as opposed to the typical puddle during urination.

The posture for spraying is different from that of normal urination. When a cat sprays, he typically backs up to the object, twitches his tail and begins treading with his front paws. He may also close his eyes while spraying. When cats (male or female) display normal urination, they usually squat.

When a cat indiscriminately urinates, there may be an underlying medical cause, or the conditions in the litter box may be unappealing. Even if the box is kept clean, there may be something about the setup that's off-putting. There could also be something going on in the environment causing stress to the cat or making him feel that it's not safe to use the litter box.

Communication. Cat spray is a form of communication. It comes as a surprise to many cat parents, but both male and female cats can spray, although males do seem to spray more. I've seen many cases in which cat parents completely overlooked the female cat and believed (incorrectly) that the male was doing the spraying. The odor chemicals in urine spray reveal lots of information about the sprayer. It's the feline version of a résumé. It shouldn't be viewed as bad or spiteful behavior. Even though we certainly don't like the idea of cats spraying inside our homes, it's important to remember that spraying is a normal reaction to a particular situation in the feline world. The cat may be trying to find out if a cat or a person is a threat, or perhaps the cat already knows there's an immediate threat. Cats tend to spray on objects that are socially significant to them, such as on a cat parent's belongings, on a particular piece of furniture, or near doorways. They will also choose areas that will be visible to other cats.

Some Common Reasons Cats Spray:

- To define the perimeter for other cats.
- To create a familiar scent to define territory.
- Some cats spray a family member's belongings to self-soothe by mixing scents.
- A cat may spray a family member's belongings if that family member's schedule has changed or something else about the person's behavior is different and therefore concerns the cat.
- A cat might spray a family member's belongings if he's concerned the person may present a threat to the current household social structure.
- Spraying a family member's belongings or that person's side of the bed may be a cat's way of establishing a bond with that person.
- Because scent and familiarity play important roles in the feline world, some cats spray new objects brought into the environment.
- A cat may spray if he is denied access to another cat who may appear to be a threat (typically an unfamiliar cat in the yard).
- A cat might spray if anxious, even if there doesn't seem to be an obvious trigger from a human's perspective.
- Cats may spray as a challenge to another cat.
- A cat may spray as a victory display after a fight with another cat.
- A fearful cat may spray only when there are no other cats or humans around.
- Some cats spray entrance locations of rooms or even at the front door, because those areas are the most threatening.
- Intact cats spray when looking for mates.

Confident and timid cats spray. A confident cat may spray as a grand display of victory after a confrontation with another cat. A less confident cat might spray-mark as a form of covert aggression. It's a way of giving a warning without actually having to risk a physical conflict. A bold cat may spray in the presence of other cats or a human, whereas a fearful cat may spray only when no one is around.

The sprayed urine reveals information, such as age, sex, sexual availability, and status. These are important facts in cat-to-cat communication, especially outdoors, where close encounters could result in injury or death. Because urine marking is a form of communication, cats will not try to cover the urine, whereas after inappropriate elimination, they often exhibit covering behavior (although not all cats scratch to cover waste).

Not all cats spray, and if you gradually ease your cat through changes in his life, such as the introduction of a new spouse, new pet, new baby, or new house, you greatly reduce the chances he'll feel the need to spray. But of course, if you have an intact male cat, you stand a 100 percent chance of spray marking, so have him neutered.

The Blame Game

If you actually witness one cat spraying in a multicat household, don't assume that that cat is the only one responsible for all spray marks found. Others could also be spraying.

Managing a Sprayer. If you have a multicat household, the first step is to identify the sprayer. Unless you've actually witnessed the cat spray marking, the most reliable tool for CSI is video surveillance.

Address the Targeted Areas:

- Clean the soiled area with a product labeled for cleaning and neutralizing cat urine.
- Change the cat's thoughts about that area by engaging in playtime and offering meals there, so it becomes a place associated with positive feelings.
- Use clicker training to click and reward whenever the cat walks by the area without spraying or walks away from the area when called.
- Use a synthetic pheromone spray near the targeted areas to help change the cat's associations with them.
- To prevent further damage to carpets or furniture, cover the area with a shower curtain liner temporarily (cut the liner into pieces to cover multiple areas).
- In some cases, the area may need to be closed off completely while you work on behavior modification.

If your cat has targeted one or two areas repeatedly, place litter boxes there that have high sides (but not covered boxes), because the cat may be satisfied with spraying inside the litter box. You can use a plastic storage container (Sterilite makes great ones); just cut a low opening on one side.

If the spraying is due to the appearance of an outdoor cat, you'll need to block viewing access. Cover the bottom of the windows with an opaque or frosted window paper that will allow the light to come in but blur your cat's view of any feline interlopers. If cats are coming into your yard because you've set up bird feeders, you'll have to take them away or reposition them (if possible), so they aren't such an appealing target. If you know who owns the feline intruder, perhaps you can have a tactful discussion about the situation. If the appearance of outdoor cats is a real problem in your yard, you may have to consider fencing. There are companies that make cat-proof fencing. Many of my clients have also had success with motion-activated sprinklers.

Speaking of outdoors, if you allow your cat outside, that may be contributing to the spraying behavior. While some indoor/outdoor cats may restrict their marking to the outdoors, your cat may feel threatened by unfamiliar scents he encounters and might bring his spraying behavior inside as well.

Additional Guidelines for Helping a Sprayer:

- If possible, reduce causes of household stress, like chaos in the environment, erratic schedules, or improper new pet introductions.
- Increase vertical territory.
- Provide safe areas to retreat, such as hiding places, cat trees, and cat beds.
- In a multicat environment, provide numerous perching and hiding spots.
- In a multicat environment, increase the number of litter boxes and scatter them throughout the house so no one has to pass an opponent's area in order to eliminate.
- Set up more than one feeding station so no one has to compete.
- If you think your cat is about to engage in spraying, distract him with an enticing sound to change his mind-set from negative to positive. For example, roll a Ping-Pong ball away from the spray area.

- Incorporate daily individual interactive playtime to help reduce anxiety and increase feelings of confidence and security.
- Increase environmental enrichment to create positive diversions.
- In some multicat households, cats may need to be separated so a reintroduction can be done.
- If the cat is spraying a family member's belongings, have that family member offer the meals and engage the cat in interactive play.
- If the cat is spraying a family member's belongings, use a synthetic pheromone spray on some of the clothes so the cat may think he has facially rubbed those items.
- If spraying is done as a bonding behavior with a family member, increased playtime and environmental enrichment may help build confidence in that bond.
- Ease your cat through changes rather than forcing him to endure abrupt ones.

Spraying Behavior Is Complex. This answer I've provided is just a general road map for you. Your cat's situation is unique, so take time to carefully evaluate his environment and his behavior. Spraying is a normal communication tool (though not one humans like very much), but with time and a solid game plan, I hope you'll find a solution that works for both the cat and the people.

> ## Marking in the Box
>
> If you have a cat who sprays inside the litter box, don't resort to using a covered box. Instead, get a high-sided plastic storage container and cut a low entrance on one side. This way, the box stays open but the urine spray is contained.

Seeking Professional Help. If you're not having success with behavior modification, your veterinarian may recommend medication. If your cat is put on medication, keep in mind that this is to be an adjunct to behavior modification.

Your veterinarian may also refer you to a veterinary behaviorist, a certified applied animal behaviorist, or other behavior specialist. A qualified professional can help in pinpointing the cause of the behavior and set up a customized behavior modification plan.

Question:
Why does my cat pee on my bed?

Pam's Answer:
No one likes it when a cat starts eliminating outside of the litter box, but one time when steam really starts to come out of a cat parent's ears is when kitty starts peeing on the bed. It seems to be the one location humans take as a personal insult. As hard as it may be to understand why your loving cat would suddenly view your bed as a litter box, this behavior has nothing to do with spite or revenge.

Is It Anxiety Related? When the bed is the chosen area, there's a good chance the behavior is due to anxiety. That anxiety can be due to many factors in the environment, but before you start running through the list of what might be stressing your cat to the point where he feels he needs to pee on your bed, you first have to check two important things off the list:

- Time for a visit to the veterinarian to rule out medical causes.
- Make sure the litter box isn't the problem (size, type, cleanliness, location, number of boxes).

What's Appealing About the Bed? There are a number of reasons a cat may choose a cat parent's bed for elimination, such as:

- *Elevation advantage.* This is of particular appeal in a multicat household or one in which the cat may feel threatened. Perhaps the cat is bothered by the dog. The elevation of the bed provides a visual advantage so the cat can more easily see the approach of an opponent. Because most beds are placed with the headboards up against the wall, the cat needn't worry about being attacked from behind. He can eliminate on the bed and keep watch for any danger. From the cat's point of view, the bed meets the requirements of litter because it's soft and absorbent. When you add the safety element of elevation, it becomes an ideal spot.
- *Pet Parent Absence.* Because the bed holds concentrated scents of the cat parent, a cat may eliminate there if the human family member's

schedule has changed or there's a longer-than-normal absence. It's not a way of getting back at the cat parent, but rather a self-soothing behavior that relieves some of the separation anxiety. It may be comforting for the cat to mix his scent with the cat parent's scent.

■ *Conflict.* If there's a new significant other now sharing the bed or if the cat has been having trouble bonding with one of the cat parents, he may eliminate on that person's side of the bed. This mixing of scents may be soothing to the cat and may also be a way of trying to communicate information about himself.

■ *Appealing Substrate.* Sometimes it just comes down to the fact that the particular comforter or blanket material texture is very appealing, especially if the current litter box conditions aren't. The bedding may be the perfect softness or texture for elimination.

■ *Unexpected Change.* After a move to a new home, the cat may be having trouble with the new litter box location. The cat parent's bed is a source of familiar and comforting scents. Even renovation or other household upheaval could result in the cat choosing to eliminate on the bed. If the cat doesn't feel safe (maybe due to the addition of another cat), he might camp out in the cat parent's bedroom. When it comes time to eliminate, the soft bed meets all litter-related requirements and has that elevation benefit for added safety.

Reclaiming Your Bed. After you've taken the cat to the veterinarian and have carefully reexamined the litter box setup, it's time to ask what environmental factors could contribute to the problem. If it's a texture issue, switch to a different type of comforter. Look for one that has a feel completely different from the current one. You may even have to keep your bedroom door closed during the day to prevent the temptation of being on the bed. To limit the risk of more damage to the bed if the door is open, keep a shower curtain liner on top of it.

Normally I advise cat parents not to conduct play sessions on the bed, because doing so may send a mixed message to the cat about pouncing and soliciting play during the night. In the case of a cat eliminating on the bed, though, it may help to do a little playtime there so he starts to view the location as somewhere fun and positive. You can also offer treats in that location.

Examine multicat issues. The cat may not feel safe enough venturing out of the bedroom to get to the litter box. Make sure you have an adequate number of boxes scattered around, and work to improve the relationship between the cats. Provide more resources, and increase the hiding and perching options; in some cases, you may need to reintroduce the cats.

Address conflicts the cat may have with other family members. If the cat is having trouble bonding with a new significant other, then it's time to set up a program in which that person does the feeding, treat giving, and much of the playtime. This will help change the cat's feelings associated with the new person.

If the problem is due to long absences by you, it's time to up the fun factor in the house so the cat has opportunities for playtime and exploration when alone. This is where environmental enrichment is important. Set up a cat tree near a window, and make use of puzzle feeders and toys, calming pheromone therapy, cat entertainment videos, and music. Be creative to provide a more interesting environment. In addition, improve the quality of the time you do spend with the cat when you're home. Make sure you get in a couple of great interactive play sessions every day.

If the cat is lonely, it may be time to think about adopting another cat so he'll have a companion. If you do this, make sure you take enough time to do a proper introduction.

Extra Help. If you can't figure out the cause or are unsuccessful in correcting the behavior, talk to your veterinarian. A referral to a qualified behavior expert may be needed. Your veterinarian or veterinary behaviorist may also make the decision to prescribe antianxiety medication or an alternative medication (such as L-theanine).

Question:

Why is my cat urinating in my potted plant? He has a perfectly good litter box but goes in the plant soil instead.

Pam's Answer:

Cats can choose locations other than the litter box for a variety of reasons. There may be an underlying medical problem. The litter box may be too dirty, in an off-putting location, or filled with unappealing litter. The box may be uncomfortable, it may be in a place that makes it hard for the cat to get to it in time, or there may not be enough boxes to go around in a multicat household.

Large planters can be an appealing choice, because they are often located in more open, safer areas. If your cat's litter box is currently a covered one, the cat may have opted to use the planter because it's more comfortable.

If it's a substrate preference issue, he may prefer the soft texture of the soil in the planter over the litter in his box. If you currently have traditional clay litter or one of the alternative litters, such as pelletized newspaper, crystals, or pebbles, then the issue may be the texture.

In a multicat environment, it's important to make sure you have an adequate number of boxes and that they're scattered throughout the house to provide security and convenience. Look at the location of your cat's favorite planter for clues to its appeal. For example, it may provide safety due to its location. Is it in an open area where your cat feels he has the best visual warning time to see if another cat is approaching? Or maybe it's located in a private spot where your cat can be invisible or have his own claimed space. If you don't currently have a litter box in that room, place one near the potted plant. Your cat may be telling you that this is the location he prefers and the planter was the closest thing that resembled a litter box.

Elevation may play a factor in the appeal of a potted plant if it's in a large container. The cat may feel the slight elevation is enough to provide security in his ability to see more of the room around him.

If the soil used in the potted plant came from your yard or if it's a plant you brought inside for the winter, it may contain the scent of another animal or even the scent of animal urine.

Then there is also the possibility that your cat has chosen the potted plant merely because it's similar enough to a litter box. It's a container filled with a soft, sandy substrate, so from his point of view, it meets all requirements of a feline latrine.

If the potted plant is located near a window, use your black light to check the sides of the pot and the surrounding wall to make sure your cat isn't also spraying due to the appearance of an unfamiliar cat in the yard or some other animal out there that causes him concern.

Decrease the Appeal of the Potted Plant. Because the cat has already eliminated in there a number of times, the soil contains urine, and you certainly don't want to freshen that scent with every watering. The scent will attract him to return there. Replace all the soil with fresh soil.

To keep your cat from returning to that spot, place large smooth stones across the surface of the planter. Do this for all large planters in your home. The stones should be large enough to make it difficult for your cat to scratch them away in order to get to the soil. The stones also have to be large enough to prevent any pets in your home from swallowing them. Covering the surface with stones enables you to easily water the plant, and the stones can look decorative, so no one has to know that they're there as a defensive strategy.

Another option is to place strips of Sticky Paws for Plants across the planter. This is an inexpensive and effective way to deter your cat from gaining access to the soil. You can also cover the planter with plain garden netting. You can purchase this in a roll from your local garden and home improvement center.

Increase Litter Box Appeal. Now that you've created the deterrent, it's important to revisit the cat's litter box setup. Remove lids from any covered boxes, increase your scooping schedule to a minimum of twice a day, increase the number of litter box locations if necessary, and make sure the boxes are large enough.

If you think it might be the litter itself the cat objects to, set up an additional box next to the current one and fill it with a soft, sandy, unscented scoopable litter. Cat Attract is a good litter to offer in the additional box. It's a soft litter developed by a veterinarian and contains an herbal attractant that cats associate with toilet areas.

Evaluate Household Dynamics. If your cat eliminates in the potted plant because he feels safer there, then it's time to examine what's happening in the household. Address multicat tension issues. Doing so may even include a complete reintroduction if the hostility is severe enough. Take a good look at possible stress triggers that might be affecting your cat. Keep in mind that the possible cause of stress may appear to be very minor from your viewpoint. To learn more about stress in cats, refer to Chapter 11.

Chapter 6

Demolition Wars

*Cat versus furniture—how to help
your furniture win the war*

Question:

*I'm getting a kitten from the shelter soon and am considering having her declawed
when I have her spayed. Is this a good idea? I don't want my furniture ruined.*

Pam's Answer:

Many new cat parents decide to declaw the cat without really understanding what this permanent procedure actually involves. Too many
people look at the cat's claws as weapons of destruction and injury,
not understanding how important claws are to the cat physically and
emotionally. In too many cases, cat parents aren't given accurate information about this surgery, and they certainly aren't given enough information about how to properly train their cats so declawing wouldn't
even be needed.

Any procedure that can never be reversed requires adequate understanding of what's involved. Please try proper training before making that surgery appointment. We owe it to our cats to not make quick decisions about something that will affect their lives forever.

Legal Protection for Cats

Declawing is illegal in Britain and many European countries.

Kittens Are Getting to Know Their New Equipment. A new kitten's sharp little claws always seem to be doing something unwanted, but that's actually normal, because the youngster is just learning about her innate skills and the role her claws play in helping her navigate her environment. The act of scratching is a normal and vital part of being a cat. If you give proper positive training and purchase (or make) a scratching post that meets a cat's needs, your kitten will learn where it's acceptable to scratch and where it isn't. In addition, as your kitten grows, you'll find that her claws are kept in the sheathed position more often than not. Without humane, proper training and an effective and conveniently located scratching surface, your cat will probably end up scratching furniture because you have given him no other option.

Sharpen Your Cat Claw Knowledge

We often refer to cats "retracting" their claws as if it were a more natural position for them to be unsheathed. Actually, being sheathed is the relaxed, natural position. To expose the claws takes a conscious effort involving voluntary movement of muscles and ligaments.

As with any aspect of having a kitten, you have to allow time for that animal to learn about her emerging skills and to become trained. It's also up to us to do the proper training.

What's Involved in the Declaw Surgery? It's important to understand what declawing is. It's not just removal of the claw; it's removal of the entire first joint of each digit. It's an amputation, or rather, ten amputations. After surgery, the cat's paws are tightly bandaged, and she's kept overnight at the veterinary clinic. In some cases, cats aren't even given pain medication after this surgery. Pain medication costs extra, and some veterinary hospitals require you to sign off on the additional cost. If you choose not to pay for the meds, your cat will suffer extreme pain.

Once the bandages are removed the morning after surgery, the cat is able to go home. Imagine how painful it must be for the cat to go home and have to start walking on those very tender paws. In extremely inhumane cases, when cat parents elect to have *all* of the cat's claws removed (from front and back feet), I can't even imagine how painful movement must be.

Many cats recover without complications, but some experience tenderness or sensitivity in their paws long after the initial healing period. Some cats remain reluctant to have their paws touched for the rest of their lives. Improperly done surgery (it does happen) can cause paw deformities.

Life After Declawing. Once declawed, the cat must never be allowed outdoors again. A cat without claws can't defend herself and can't climb to escape predators. I'm amazed by how many declawed cats I do see outdoors because their cat parents are sure that they stay close to home or just sun themselves on the back deck. That doesn't prevent another cat, a dog, or some other predator from entering the yard and going after your cat. That also doesn't stop your cat from running off if she becomes afraid of something or spots prey worth chasing. Once the cat is outdoors, she's vulnerable. You must never put a declawed cat in a position where she could be at risk. If you have chosen to have your cat declawed, you must never let her outdoors, period.

Scratching Is an Important Part of Feline Life. Declawing denies the cat some very important aspects of being feline. Scratching isn't only a way for a cat to maintain the health of her claws; it's also a marking behavior. It leaves a visual and olfactory mark and is a vital form of communication.

Scratching is also a great way for your cat to get a full stretch of her back and shoulder muscles. She can dig her claws into the post, lean her weight against it and fully unkink all those muscles. Scratching is a displacement behavior, as well, and your cat may often go over to her scratching post when she's excited or anticipating something pleasant (such as dinner) or when she's anxious or frustrated. It's important to have that option available for your cat.

Be Informed Before Making That Permanent Decision. To declaw or not is obviously your decision. Before agreeing to this permanent surgery, however, make sure you have all the information about the procedure and have a good understanding of why cats scratch and how they can be trained to use a scratching post. In other words, please spare your kitten this painful, inhumane, and completely unnecessary surgery.

Question:
Why do cats love to destroy the furniture? I can't seem to train my cat to stop scratching the chairs.

Pam's Answer:
You're going at this the wrong way. You're trying to train your cat to *not* do something that's actually a normal and essential part of being feline. Scratching is important and more complex than you may realize. You may think that scratching is merely a cat's attempt to hone his claws to razor-sharp perfection or that it's a willful attempt to get back at you or destroy his surroundings. In truth, scratching serves many purposes.

Territorial Marking. Scratching is a marking behavior among cats. The marks left when the cat rakes his claws vertically create a visual sign for others who pass by. Outdoors, these visual markers are important because they let any approaching cats see that they're entering an area where another cat has been or is currently residing. This advance warning system reduces the number of physical confrontations cats would otherwise have.

When the cat scratches an object, he also leaves an olfactory mark from scent glands in the paw pads. If another cat approaches the scratch mark, he can gather information from the pheromones.

Scratching Relieves Tension. Scratching is also used as an emotional release or displacement behavior. When your cat is anxious, happy, excited, or frustrated, he can release some of that built-up emotion by scratching. Think of the times you've seen your cat scratching on an object after a nap or when you've come home from work. You may even have noticed him scratching after an encounter with a companion cat. This emotional release through scratching is healthy for the cat.

Because scratching is so complex and such a vital part of feline life, you'll need an effective training method to redirect the cat. You can't just shoo him away from the sofa. Behavior modification begins by making sure you have a scratching post that meets his needs.

In general, the most appealing texture for cats is sisal. The rough texture makes it easy for cats to dig their claws in and get an effective scratch. Carpet-covered posts are too soft, and many cats end up getting their claws caught in the carpet loops.

Not Just Any Scratching Post. The height of the scratching post should enable the cat to get a full stretch. If the post is too small, the cat has to hunch over to use it, and that doesn't allow for a good back and neck stretch. If that's the case, the cat seeks out a taller option, and I'll bet you can figure out what that option will be—your sofa!

The Ideal Location. Even a great scratching post will just gather dust if you stick it in some far-off location. When a cat needs to scratch, he'll look for the closest object that meets his needs. Keep the post where the cat likes to spend time.

If you have more than one cat, you'll need more than one scratching post. Although you can't assign a post to a specific cat, if you place them in areas where various cats tend to spend the most time, you may find they'll choose their favorites.

For cats who like to scratch horizontally, there are inexpensive corrugated cardboard scratching pads available at your local pet-product store.

A Soft Touch

A cat's paws may feel rough and tough but they're actually extremely sensitive. Cats feel movement, texture, and temperature via nerve endings in the paw pads.

Turn No into Yes. If your cat has been scratching a piece of furniture, place the scratching post right next to it. You can cover the piece of furniture with a sheet, being sure to tuck it in tightly so the cat can't slip in underneath. If the area being scratched is isolated to just a few spots, place a few strips of Sticky Paws on it. This is a double-faced tape made specifically for this purpose. The product is available at your local pet-product store and online. This way, when the cat comes over to scratch the furniture, he'll see that the area isn't as appealing as it used to be, and at the same time, he'll notice a much better option, a dream-come-true scratching post.

Question:

Scratching posts look alike to me. How do I know which one to buy?

Pam's Answer:

The post has to be as appealing to the cat as your sofa was to you when you bought it, but when I say appealing, I don't mean whether your cat likes the way it looks but whether it gets the job done. The only reason your cat may decide to scratch on the furniture instead of the post is because the furniture meets her needs. If the post you provide looks pretty but isn't effective from a cat's point of view, then it'll just sit in the corner and gather dust. Watch your cat and see whether she goes for the sofa or the carpet. That will tell you whether she's a vertical or horizontal scratcher, and you can plan accordingly.

There are three must-haves for scratching posts:

The Scratching Post Must Have an Appealing Texture. Many of the cheap posts you find in your local pet supply store are covered in carpet—pretty to look at, soft to touch, but totally ineffective for scratching. The post needs to have a rough texture in a material that lets the cat rake her nails across the surface. When a cat scratches, she digs her nails into the surface in order to remove the dead outer nail sheath. If the post is covered in carpet, what likely happens is the cat's nails get stuck. That's a sure way to drive her back to your sofa again.

For texture, think rough, not soft, loopy carpet covering. Overall, sisal is typically the best choice because it's rough and durable and gives the cat an effective, satisfying scratch.

Even though most cats prefer sisal, some have other preferences. If your cat doesn't like sisal you can try other rough materials. Some cats even prefer to scratch on bare wood. I know of several cats who go crazy for tree bark, so if you don't mind the mess, bring in a log for your cat to scratch on.

Corrugated cardboard is another popular scratching material. If you happen to have a cat who likes to scratch horizontally, consider getting a few corrugated-cardboard scratching pads. They're inexpensive and can be moved around as needed.

In general though, sisal is a pretty sure bet when it comes to texture preference.

The Scratching Post Must Be Sturdy and Tall. You can get a scratching post covered in the best material, but if it's wobbly or unstable, your cat will head right back to that trusty old sofa for her scratching needs. She has to be able to lean her full weight against the post without having it topple over.

The height of the post is also important. A kitten can use a shorter post, but as your cat grows, she'll need a post that will allow her to fully stretch when she reaches up to scratch. Make sure one you buy or build is tall enough for your cat. Remember: The taller the post, the wider the base needed. When you get a tall post, the base should be wide enough to maintain stability.

The Scratching Post Location. Like the litter box, the scratching post isn't one of the most beautiful pieces of furniture. Although I have seen some very attractive and creative posts in my time, I recognize the natural tendency to want to hide it in the corner. Wrong! The post should be placed where the cat likes to scratch.

If you're retraining a cat who is currently scratching a piece of furniture, then the post should be placed right next to that object. Make it as easy as possible for your cat to recognize the better option you've provided for her.

Pay attention to your cat's scratching habits so you'll know where to locate the post. Some cats like to scratch after a nap or after a meal. Others scratch when tense, as a way to displace anxiety. Locate the post where you think your cat would appreciate it most. You don't have to limit yourself to one, either.

Question:
I know I need three litter boxes for my three cats but is one scratching post enough?

Pam's Answer:
You may be fortunate enough to have cats who are completely happy sharing one scratching post. In most cases, though, one or more of the cats may not feel comfortable using the community post. Just as with litter box placement, it may cause anxiety for one cat to have to cross through another cat's area to get to the post. In that case, the cat may look for any convenient surface, perhaps on a piece of furniture—not a very good solution at all.

Offering Choice May Ease Tension. Even though you can't direct each individual cat to exclusively use a designated post, it's beneficial to provide multiple scratching options. One of the best and easiest ways to relieve cat tension is by providing choice.

Allow for Different Preferences Among Cats. Some cats have very particular preferences in scratching material and orientation. When you provide multiple options in texture, type, and location, some horizontal and some vertical, you stand a better chance of easing tension and satisfying individual preferences.

Provide more than one scratching post and more than one type for multicat homes. Place posts and horizontal scratch pads around different rooms so a cat doesn't have far to go if she has the urge to scratch.

Observe your cats and you'll soon learn which one likes to scratch after a nap and which one scratches after playing, after using the litter box, or when anticipating dinner. When you learn a cat's preference, you can place posts in the best locations for scratch time.

Even Small Environments Need Multiple Options. Even if you live in a small apartment, you can provide multiple scratching options. Scratch pads can be attached to walls. If you have a cat tree, wrap the support posts with sisal so it can do double-duty. If you have a cat who prefers scratching on bare wood, leave one of the support posts unwrapped. Corrugated cardboard scratching pads are great for small environments because they don't take up much room.

Marking Behavior. Because scratching is both visual and olfactory marking, it can add to overall tension if one cat goes over to scratch and is faced with evidence that an opponent cat has recently just scratched there. Supply more than one post so the cats have the option to claim their own little scratching turf. Because scratching is also a displacement behavior, the ability to scratch instead of engaging in conflict may help maintain harmony.

Post Placement. In addition to placing posts where particular cats spend time, it can also be helpful to place posts or scratching pads along common pathways or high-traffic areas. For example, if the living room is an area where all cats tend to hang out in order to be close to you, it may be helpful for a cat experiencing conflicting emotions or anxiety to be able to displace some of that through scratching. Being in the room with his companion cats might create a higher level of excitement, but he'll be able to scratch.

You can even use the convenient location of posts to your benefit when cats are together. If you notice an increase in tension, go over to the post yourself and rake your own nails up and down the surface. Very often, the enticing sound triggers a cat to run over and start scratching as well.

Question:

I have a great scratching post for Bluejay, my two-year-old Bengal, but she only wants to scratch the carpet. How do I get her to stop?

Pam's Answer:

You might have a horizontal scratcher on your hands. The easiest way to provide a horizontal scratching surface for your cat is to purchase a corrugated cardboard scratch pad. These pads are readily available at your local pet-product store and online. They come in various widths, so you can easily find one to fit any location in your home. The cardboard scratching pads are usually treated with catnip for added enticement. There are even scratching pads designed on an incline for the cats who like the angle midway between horizontal and vertical.

Question:

I'm so lucky that my cat has never scratched the furniture and will only sharpen her claws on her scratching post. After six years, though, the post is looking very tattered. Should I buy her a new one, or will she miss the old one?

Pam's Answer:

There's a right way and a wrong way to go about it. Imagine it from your cat's point of view. She spends all this time marking the scratching post and then suddenly it's gone and replaced with one that doesn't have any of her familiar scents or marks. Her old scratching post was a comfort to her. The more a surface is scratched, the more valuable it is to the cat.

The Better Way to Replace an Old Scratching Post. Purchase the new post and place it next to the cat's current one. Let her take it for a test drive. She might start scratching on it exclusively, or she may go for it only periodically. Have both posts there so she'll have the choice. You can increase the new post's appeal by rubbing a little catnip on it. To add some of your cat's own scent to it, take a clean sock and rub the old post down and then rub the new post. Don't rub your cat with the sock because you don't want to get her facial pheromones on it. Cats don't typically scratch where they facially rub. Rubbing the old post will capture some of the scent from the scent glands on the paw pads.

When to Toss the Old One. When you see your cat routinely using the new post, you can then remove the old one. Make sure it really is no longer functional for your cat. The shredded surface may not be appealing to a human but may still make it the ideal post for your cat.

Chapter 7

Party Animal

The benefits of play therapy and how to play with cats—yes, there is a wrong way

Question:
I heard you talk about interactive play therapy when I attended one of your lectures. Could you explain just how it works?

Pam's Answer:
Interactive play is a very powerful tool you can use to help your cat in a variety of situations. It's great for trust building, helping two cats become friends, exercise, stress relief, and the list goes on. Even though your cat may be one who is so revved up, she can make a game out of playing with the dust bunnies under your furniture all by herself, don't overlook how valuable it is to incorporate interactive playtime into your daily schedule.

You Are the Key Ingredient. Interactive play involves *you*. The concept is simple. You use a fishing pole–type toy to create preylike action. If you want to be truly CatWise about cat behavior, you have to conduct a game that lets your cat act like the hunter she was born to be. You move the interactive toy so the target at the end of the string wiggles, slides, darts, and creeps around the room. If you have room, you can trail it behind you while you walk or trot down a hallway. When you move the toy like prey, it'll stimulate the hunter in your cat.

While you may have lots of toys around the house for your cat, the problem is that they're essentially "dead" prey. They don't move. Your cat has to bat at them to create action. With the interactive toy, however, she doesn't have to be both predator and prey; she can focus on the hunt.

Match the Toy to Your Cat's Personality. There are many interactive toys available. The basic concept: pole, string, toy dangling on the end. When shopping, try to match the toy to your cat's personality. If you have a somewhat timid cat, go for a basic toy that's easy and comfortable for her to conquer. If you have a very confident, athletic cat, you can still get the basic toy, or you can choose something more challenging, such as a toy with more dangling pieces or one with Mylar wings that are harder to detect. Don't get one with too big a target, because you don't want it to become an opponent. Cats go after small prey and don't want to risk injury by attempting to take down something their own size.

Scheduling Play. Maintain a regular schedule of interactive play with your cat. It won't do any good to do a great playtime today and then not do another one for a week. Your cat needs consistency. Schedule playtime once or twice a day, about fifteen minutes each session. You'd be surprised what a half hour a day of playtime and fun can do for a cat's emotional and physical health (and yours).

For some cats, fifteen minutes may be too long. As you engage in play sessions with your cat, you'll become familiar with the length of time that works best for her. Sometimes as a cat plays and conquers a toy, she may get bored with it and lose interest. If so, bring out a different toy in a few minutes to spark her interest again.

All the Right Moves. How you move the interactive toy is important. Don't wave it around frantically just to give your cat an aerobic workout. That's not how cats naturally hunt. Stick to what's natural for your cat. In the wild, a cat would stalk her prey while staying as quiet and invisible as possible. She would inch closer and closer, and then, when she gets within striking distance, she would pounce. Cats don't have the lung capacity to chase prey to exhaustion, so don't conduct marathons throughout the house. Move the toy like prey, alternating between fast and slow motions so as to give your cat time to plan her next move. Here's a tip: Movements that go away from or across your cat's visual field will trigger her prey drive. Don't dangle the toy in her face or move it toward her.

Keep It Fun

When choosing toys for your cat, keep size in mind. Cats are small predators. The size of the "prey" should be that of a mouse or bird. If the toy is too big, it may be viewed as threatening.

Hunting is just as much mental as it is physical. For interactive playtime to be beneficial for your cat in terms of confidence, trust building, and stress relief, she has to be able to plan her moves and have successful captures so as not to become frustrated. Keep that in mind as you move the toy around. Also, to build confidence, let her have plenty of captures throughout the game. If you were a cat, it would be pretty frustrating if you never got your paws on the toy. Remember the game needs to be fun for your cat.

Ending the Game. When it's time to end the game, don't just suddenly stop and put the toy away. Your cat may still be very revved up. Instead, wind the action down, in the same way you would do a cooldown after exercise. Let the "prey" get tired or injured, so the cat's movements will naturally slow down as well. Then leave your cat with one final grand capture.

Put Interactive Toys Away. When the game is over, store all interactive toys out of your cat's reach. The most important reason is that you don't want her to chew on the strings. The second reason is, you want to keep the toys special. Mice don't lounge around in the open all day, waiting to be offered up on the feline dinner menu.

Question:

I'd like to buy my cat some new toys, but she never seems to respond to any of them. Which toys do cats like best?

Pam's Answer:

Every cat is an individual, so you may have to experiment some more. The type of toys your cat enjoyed in her youth, for example, may not be as appealing if she's now less mobile and has stiff joints. Some cats, no matter their age, have strong toy preferences, and others don't care at all as long as the toy is in motion and they have the chance to hunt.

Respect Toy Preferences. There are many cat toys to choose from, both solo and interactive toys. When shopping, keep your cat's size, athletic ability, personality, and texture preferences in mind. A small, timid cat, for example, may not want to play with a large cat kick-bag toy because it resembles an opponent more than prey. Your cat may have a texture preference and prefer a soft toy she can sink her teeth into rather than a hard plastic one.

Pay Attention to Your Cat's Senses. Sound also helps determine whether your cat enjoys or ignores the toy. A toy that makes a rustling sound may be very appealing, as it resembles the sound of a chipmunk or mouse darting through the leaves. Some cats like toys with feathers; others prefer fur-covered ones. Take the sense of touch into account as well as sight and hearing.

Cats Don't Knit

Pictures of cats playing with yarn are very popular, but it's actually a dangerous practice. If swallowed, yarn is a serious choking hazard. Cats have backward-facing barbs on their tongues. As efficient as the barbs are when it comes to rasping meat from the bones of prey or removing dead hair, dirt, and external parasites from the cat's coat, their positioning make it impossible to spit anything out that gets caught on the tongue.

Toy Safety. Do your own quality-control inspection of any toy you buy. Make sure it's constructed well and pieces aren't easily pulled off. Glued-on pieces can come off easily and pose a choking hazard.

While on a popular online shopping site, I was shocked to see an overwhelming number of negative reviews citing safety concerns about a relatively recently launched cat-toy product line. The manufacturers clearly were focusing on sales, not cat health. Nothing is more important than your cat's safety, so if buying toys online, read reviews, pay attention to safety alerts from other consumers, and use your own common sense.

Whether you purchase a toy online or at your local store, inform the retailer and the manufacturer if the toy has safety issues. Dogs aren't the only pets who require sturdy, well-made toys that can withstand chewing and don't come apart.

Solo Toy Testing. Set up her solo toys so they pique her interest as she wanders through the house, and of course, make sure you've provided toys that appeal to her. You may have to invest a little time and money in a toy-preference test by trying out different types on your cat. It's worth the investment, though, because playtime is very valuable for mental, physical, and emotional health.

Prey Appeal

Because of a cat's limited color vision, the movement, shape, sound, and size of potential prey (or toys) are more important to the cat than the prey's color.

Don't Give Up. I come across many people who simply give up and claim that their cats just don't play. Every cat plays (unless in pain, sick, or in fear). You just have to figure out what's stopping your own cat. Does she live in a tense environment? Maybe she hasn't played in so long that her skills need a little practice . . . or you just haven't gotten the type of toys she prefers. Just as some cats have definite preferences in the mouth feel of their food or the paw feel of their litter, some have toy preferences.

Question:

My cat will play with toys on her own, but whenever I try to get involved in the play, she just runs away. What am I doing wrong?

Pam's Answer:

Playtime with your cat may seem like a no-brainer, but there are actually a few mistakes you can make that can keep the cat from enjoying the game. Some mistakes in your playtime technique can even contribute to behavior problems. That may be surprising, but when you compare the way cats hunt (stealth and stalking) with the frantic counterintuitive way we often ask them to play (constant high-speed motion and frustration), you can see that our methods very likely create more negative reactions than positive. Here are five common mistakes to avoid:

Don't Use Your Hands as Toys. Wiggling fingers are definitely convenient when your cat is nearby and in play mode, but what actually happens is, you send the unintentional message that biting flesh is acceptable behavior. If the cat learns that biting during play is allowed, she'll learn that biting is an acceptable and effective form of communication whenever she wants to get a point across.

The association your cat has with your hands should be only that they're used for gentle petting and holding. If they're also viewed as toys, the cat may decide to playfully bite another unsuspecting family member, with painful results. Don't send mixed messages about biting—even in play.

This Isn't a Wrestling Match. Don't use your hands to pin the cat down or wrestle with her. In addition to the danger that you'll end up injured, doing so changes the tone from play to battle, wherein the cat views you as an opponent. Cats don't wrestle their prey to the ground, and they don't want to be wrestled to the ground by a human. It's not a fair game at that point. If you wrestle your cat and have her on her back, you've put her in the defensive aggressive posture. You may find yourself getting bitten and scratched in earnest.

Be Still and Small. Don't stand over your cat and wave the toy around. You become too much of an imposing presence if you do that, which can take the focus off the toy. Instead, sit in a chair or on the floor so you're not hovering over the cat. This may put your cat more at ease so she can focus on her prey.

Don't Prevent Your Cat from Being Successful. Nobody enjoys playing a game if they never get a chance to win. If you wave the toy all over and keep it out of the cat's reach, you're just creating frustration. Playtime needs to be physically *and* mentally rewarding. If your cat chases, pounces, stalks, leaps, and attacks the toy but never gets to capture it because you've kept it out of her reach, the game becomes just an exhausting exercise in disappointment.

During interactive play sessions, your cat needs as much mental satisfaction as physical activity. She needs opportunities for successful captures throughout the game. Think of the toy as prey that gets caught but manages to wriggle away a few times. Toward the game's end, move the toy slower and eventually let the cat have one final grand capture.

Don't Dangle the Toy in the Cat's Face. No prey in its right mind would go up to the cat and willingly offer itself up as dinner. A cat's prey drive is triggered by movements *across* or *away* in her visual field. Movement coming at her is confusing and can put the cat on the defensive. Movement in her direction turns the toy into a potential threat.

Don't End the Game Abruptly. Imagine you're a cat and you're having a great time, your energy level is just starting to rev up, and then suddenly the toy is whisked away into a closet and you haven't even had time to capture it. No matter how much time you plan on dedicating to the playtime, wind the action down toward the end of the game so the cat can start to relax again and feel that she has successfully done her job.

Question:
Do you recommend using laser light toys for cats?

Pam's Answer:
I think many people who use a laser toy like it because it gets a guaranteed instant reaction from the cat, but unfortunately it can also cause frustration. If you really take time to understand how cats hunt using *all* of their senses, you'll realize that chasing a red beam of light without ever having the satisfaction of capturing it isn't much fun.

I advise my clients not to use those toys for playtime with their cats. If they're absolutely set in their ways about using it, my recommendation is to begin the game with the laser toy and then start shining it on an actual interactive toy, so eventually the cat can go after the toy alone. For laser-obsessed cats, the goal is to eventually shift the focus to the toy, so the cat parents can ultimately cease using laser lights altogether.

Cats Use Their Sense of Touch. Cats are tactile creatures and when they pounce on prey they rely on being able to feel the captured treasure underneath their paws. Cats have carpal whiskers on the undersides of their paws (at the wrist), and they use those whiskers to sense the movement of prey when they have their paw over it. Imagine doing a great job of stalking and pouncing repeatedly but *never* feeling that you've captured your target. Putting a paw over a laser light is an exercise in frustration.

Give Your Cat Time to Use His Brain. When people use the laser lights, they often move them too abruptly, causing the cat to stop playing in a natural feline way and begin just randomly bouncing off the walls in an attempt to get the target. Although this frantic, comical behavior is very amusing for cat parents to watch, and they assume they're giving the cat much-needed exercise, this isn't how cats hunt naturally. Cats are sprinters; they don't hunt by chasing to exhaustion. Cats are ambush predators, relying on stealth to inch closer and closer to their prey. Once within striking distance, they execute a well-timed pounce. Having your cat race around until his sides are heaving doesn't benefit him physically or mentally.

For playtime to be truly beneficial, it must be both mentally and physically satisfying. If you simply focus on physically keeping your cat active and neglect his need for mental satisfaction and confidence, then you're doing him a disservice.

In some cases, chasing laser lights can cause cats to develop a fixation on any flickering light.

Safety of Laser Light Toys. Although manufacturers may claim the laser lights are safe, I'm also concerned about what happens if you accidentally shine the light in the cat's eyes. Not all laser lights are made well, so if you do insist on using one, you must not point the light toward the cat's eyes. During an active play session, it can be hard to control where the light shines—another reason to use regular interactive toys instead of the laser.

Question:

My cat has lost interest in his toys. What do I do now? I can't afford to keep buying new ones.

Pam's Answer:

You may have purchased countless toys for your cat, but if they're left out all day and night, they may lose their appeal. Are those toys doomed to being ignored forever and never played with again? No. It's just time to do a little tweaking in terms of environmental enrichment. Here are some tips for keeping toys interesting and fun:

Rotate Toys. Your cat doesn't need fifty toys all at once. Instead, pick a few to leave out for several days; then put them away, and bring out a few more. Sometimes seeing a toy that hasn't been around for a few days creates renewed interest.

Place Toys in Interesting Locations. Instead of dumping a few toys in his play basket or tossing them on the carpet, strategically place them in areas to spark curiosity. Place a fuzzy fake mouse on one of the perches of a cat tree. Hide a crinkly ball toy inside an open paper bag placed on its side. Roll a Ping-Pong ball along the floor. Place a toy so it's just barely sitting on a window ledge and can easily be knocked off with the swipe of a paw. Use your imagination.

Keep Interactive Toys Special. Interactive toys, which are the ones designed like fishing poles, shouldn't be left around when you aren't conducting a play session. It creates a safety issue because a cat can easily choke or get strangled on any stringed parts. Being left out can also cause them to lose their appeal. The interactive toys should be used for scheduled playtime to maximize activity, bonding, and fun.

Stealth and Patience

Cats are sit-and-wait hunters. They can stay motionless for long periods of time, waiting for prey to move into striking distance. Then . . . pounce!

"Marinate" with Catnip. Not all cats respond to catnip, but if your cat does, place some toys in a container with a little catnip so they can pick up some of the catnip scent. Make sure the container is tightly sealed and placed where your cat can't reach it. Once or twice a week, you can take one of the "marinated" toys out for your cat's enjoyment. When it comes to catnip, though, limit your cat's exposure to no more than twice a week. Giving it too often can cause your kitty to develop an immunity to its wonderful effects.

Question:

I love to play with my cat on the bed, but I think I may have created a bad habit. Shasta now jumps on the bed and bites my toes! Should I stop playing on the bed?

Pam's Answer:

Cats love to play, and they're usually ready for a game at any time. While a pre-bedtime playtime session is a great way to encourage your cat to sleep through the night, the one place you shouldn't conduct that game is on your bed. Consistency is important in training, and if you send the message that it's OK to leap, pounce, and play on the bed, then she may also feel it's OK to jump on your wiggling toes when you're sound asleep in the middle of the night. If she begins to think of the bed as a giant playtime trampoline, then you can't blame her when she sits on your chest in the wee hours of the morning and paws at your face to rouse her favorite playmate.

Making the Bed

To decrease the chances of having your toes under the covers attacked at night, don't entice your cat to pounce when you make the bed in the morning. Keep her on the floor.

Choosing Locations. Playtime location can be an important factor in behavior modification, so use it to your advantage, and don't set your cat up to receive mixed messages. If you want the bed to be a place where you can enjoy cat cuddles, petting, and napping, don't use it as a feline playground. You can also use the opportunity to help your cat associate a particular location with a positive experience, in addition to the typical areas you may choose for playtime, such as the living room or family room. If your cat gets nervous in the front hallway near the door, for example, you can gradually work your way up to playing in that area, so she associates having fun and feeling confident in that spot.

Question:

My cats are littermates and have been together for five years, yet they have distinctly different playtime styles. Charlie will jump in the air after any toy, but Harry likes the toys only when I drag them along the floor. Why would they be so different?

Pam's Answer:

Most cats will play regardless of whether the toy darts along the ground or flies up in the air. Preferences for air play or ground play may be apparent from a young age, or they can change as the cat matures. A cat who once did gravity-defying leaps to capture his fuzzy mouse five feet off the ground may now prefer stalking and pouncing with all four feet close to the floor, now that he's a senior.

Ground Play. There are many opportunities to vary your movements in ground play. Depending upon the toy you choose, it can slither like a snake, skitter like a mouse, or dart around like a cricket. From the beginning, choose several toys, so you can vary the types of movements you do during different play sessions. If, however, your cat shows a strong preference for a particular toy or a particular type of movement, go with it. The point is to make this a fun time for the cat.

Use the Environment. During ground play, your cat will depend on stealth, speed, and accuracy to capture the toy. Don't play just in the middle of the room, where there's no way for your cat to conceal himself. Include objects in the environment that allow your cat to be invisible. Whether a few pillows tossed on the floor, an open paper bag, or a box, your cat will appreciate being able to sneak up to his prey.

A timid cat unsure of his environment may initially prefer ground play and may prefer being able to remain somewhat hidden during play. As he becomes more confident, though, you may discover that he enjoys it when you incorporate more air play into the session.

Air Play. In air play, keep in mind that the toy shouldn't be in motion over the cat's head 100 percent of the time. Even birds have to land at some point. Provide your cat the opportunity to leap in the air, but also periodically let the toy make contact with the ground so he can pounce.

Also, the toy shouldn't be totally out of reach. If you keep the toy too far over your cat's head, he'll end up just sitting and watching it instead of being an active participant in the game.

Regardless of how individual your cats' play preferences are, what's most important is to allow several captures so they enjoy the feeling of success.

Question:
What is catnip and is it really safe to give to my cat?

Pam's Answer:
Catnip is a perennial herb belonging to the mint family. It's a plant native to Europe that was imported to the United States and other countries. The

plant can grow about two to three feet tall and has heart-shaped leaves with blooms that can be lavender, white, or pink.

If grown outdoors, catnip can quickly take over your garden, not to mention the fact that it'll attract the neighborhood cats to your yard.

Catnip products come in many forms—fresh, dried, sprays, catnip-filled toys, catnip-filled chew products, and catnip-scented scratching posts. If you buy the dried form, it's best to look for good quality, organic catnip free from pesticides and fillers, because the quality can vary.

The Catnip Response. Nepetalactone is the chemical in catnip that causes the response. It creates a feeling of euphoria without any addictive or harmful effects. Here's an interesting fact: The catnip response is inherited, and it's estimated that about 30 percent of cats lack this gene. Kittens and elderly cats don't typically respond to catnip, and in fact, young kittens may actually be repelled by it.

> ## Not Just for the Little Guys
> Even big cats, such as tigers, respond to catnip.

The catnip response lasts about ten to fifteen minutes, and it takes an hour or two for the behavior to reset before a cat is capable of reacting to the herb again.

Cats react to catnip through inhalation. They use their vomeronasal organ to analyze the scent. Inhaled catnip has a stimulating and euphoric effect, whereas ingested catnip has a calming effect.

When exposed to catnip, cats tend to sniff, roll, lick, and even eat the herb. All of this is totally normal and harmless.

Unexpected Reactions. There are some cats who become aggressive when exposed to catnip. In a multicat household, test responses by offering the herb to one cat in a separate location so you can gauge reactions. If you find one cat who gets a bit aggressive, offer him catnip in a separate location, and then wait until the effect has totally worn off before reuniting him with his feline companions.

Behavior Modification. Catnip can be used to help entice a sedentary or depressed cat to engage in playtime.

Rub catnip on the scratching post to encourage your cat to rediscover the benefits of scratching in appropriate places.

How to Offer Catnip to Your Cat. Catnip should only be offered a maximum of two or three times a week. If cats are constantly exposed to it, they can permanently lose their ability to respond.

In the herb's dried form, the volatile oil, nepetalactone, needs to be released before offering it to your cat. Rub the dried leaves between your fingers to release it.

You can find cat toys in your local pet supply store with resealable pouches for filling with catnip. This is a better option than buying prefilled toys, which are often filled with poor quality catnip.

Catnip can be offered in toys or rubbed on them, scattered on a paper plate, and rubbed on scratching posts, or you can place some in a knotted sock.

Buying and Storage. Store catnip in a container with a tight-fitting lid kept totally out of a cat's reach to avoid unplanned self-serve catnip parties.

If you grow your own catnip, offer some of the fresh leaves to your cat. You can dry the rest by hanging the harvested plants upside down to dry. Then store the herb in an airtight container. It's best to keep the plant out of the cat's reach if it's in your indoor garden.

When purchasing loose catnip, look for organic brands that don't have filler, and inspect it to make sure there aren't a lot of stems. The more leaves and blossoms, the more potent the catnip.

Chapter 8

Living It Up

*Creating a cat-friendly home you
and your budget can live with*

Question:

I've heard the term environmental enrichment *but am not sure what it
means. Is it something I should be doing for my cat?*

Pam's Answer:

Environment plays a huge role in cat health. Understimulated cats are at
risk of developing boredom-related or stress-relieving behaviors, such as
overgrooming, chewing inappropriate items, picking on companion
pets, retreating into isolation, overeating, self-mutilation, compulsive
behavior, and loss of appetite.

Born to Move. Let's first look at your cat and her amazing skills. Your cat
has fine-tuned senses. Her ears can move independently and hear sounds
humans can't. She can pinpoint sound location with impressive accuracy.

Her binocular vision is excellent in low light and can see in what humans consider total darkness. Then there's a cat's sense of smell. She can detect odors we'd never know were present.

Now let's look at the cat's body. The cat can jump five to seven times her height. She walks on her toes for speed and stealth. She's incredibly flexible and able to make lightning-quick directional changes when running. Her whiskers help her navigate in the dark and help her detect prey, among many other functions. There are many other features of your cat's body that give her incredible speed, stealth, agility, and accuracy of movement—which we call catlike grace.

Imagine having all that equipment and never getting to use it. That's the way it is for many cats. They're brought indoors (and we want them there for safety), but there's nothing to do once there. Cats weren't meant to be sedentary and eat mountains of food. Cats were born to move.

Why an Increase in the Fun Factor Is Beneficial. Pleasurable exercise promotes physical health. If your cat is active, she can stay in good shape. Her muscles get a workout, her bones stay strong, and she develops a normal, healthy appetite.

Let's look at the benefits you may not be aware of. A cat who has positive experiences usually has more confidence. A fun, safe environment makes for a happy, confident cat. A stressful or boring environment equals an unhappy, anxious cat.

If a cat has no stress release, she may come up with a coping mechanism that isn't beneficial. A common stress-relieving behavior is overgrooming. The cat may lick one place so much that bald spots appear. When you provide outlets for energy release, the cat has something to do instead of destructive behaviors.

When a cat hunts, dopamine (a neurotransmitter) is released, creating a feeling of eager anticipation. This release is initially triggered by the nearness of prey. Cats enjoy hunting. In hunting mode, the cat is less depressed or bored. Opportunities to experience eager anticipation and exploration are important. Luckily, you don't have to supply mice and birds so your cat can experience stimulation; you can give a cat similar stimulation with toys and playtime.

Playtime. Cats benefit from several types of play. For interactive play, you control a wand-type toy so your cat can concentrate on being the hunter. Move the toy like prey so she can practice her skills.

Solo play involves furry mice, crinkle balls, and other small toys. Ratchet up the fun factor by placing those toys in objects or locations to inspire curiosity. Place a furry mouse inside an empty tissue box. Cut paw-size holes in a box, tape the flaps closed, and toss in some toys. Drop a Ping-Pong ball inside a paper bag. Have a furry mouse peek out from the top perch of a cat tree.

You can provide food-related environmental enrichment, whether you're home or not, with food-dispensing toys. The concept of working for food is natural for a hunter; she's hardwired to use her senses and physical skill to get prey. Batting a food-dispensing ball around provides much more activity and fun than camping out at an overfilled food bowl. The other benefit of puzzle feeders is that the cat will eat slowly.

It's Healthy, Too. You can have the best environment money can buy, but don't ignore your cat's health. An enriched life for your cat means that the human family has to stay on top of health issues, preventive care, and treatment of pain, illness, and injuries. It also means keeping the cat safe.

Enrichment Without Fear. The environment the cat lives in shouldn't create fear or stress. The cat shouldn't be fearful of other pets or family members or be subjected to punishment. If she's too frightened to come out from under the bed, then she's in desperate need of one of the most basic aspects of environmental enrichment—security. No one should live each day in fear. Address the cause of fear and begin behavior modification. Even if your situation requires you to set up separate areas for cats, your home can still be a secure, happy, and enriched environment. It should never be a prison. If you're unsure where to start, ask your veterinarian for a referral to a qualified behavior expert.

Creating Vertical Space. An elevated location provides security for a cat, especially in a multicat home. The more vertical space, the more territory the cats have to share. If there's tension between cats, one may climb to a high place as a display of status. This can often be the display a cat uses instead of physical confrontation. An elevated spot may also be a refuge for a timid cat. She knows she's safe there because no one can sneak up behind her.

You can create vertical space with a cat tree. Manufacturers make trees in various heights and configurations. Depending on your budget, you can purchase a simple tree or an elaborate one that reaches the ceiling.

Catwalks and shelves can add to vertical territory. You can purchase shelves and walkways, or you can make your own. You can also install cat stairs on the walls for the cats to access various shelves and perches. You can make the setup elaborate or simple. In a multicat home, make two sets of stairs so one cat never blocks another from getting up or down.

Window perches are great middle-ground options. You can install perches that attach to window frames. Some have heating elements—great for winter days when there's a draft coming in but the cat still wants to watch the snow come down. Older cats will appreciate the added warmth.

Secret Hiding Places. Hideaways can be in the form of beds with raised sides, such as a pyramid-style or donut-shaped bed. You can even take a box and turn it on its side to make a bed. Line it with a soft towel for your cat's comfort. For a very timid cat, cut a hole in the box as an entrance, turn the box upside down and your cat has a complete hideaway.

Tunneling for Fun. A tunnel can be a wonderful addition for environmental enrichment. Purchase soft fabric tunnels or make your own using paper bags.

The Dining Room. Your cat needs a secure feeding station that promotes peaceful mealtimes. Give each cat her own food bowl. Community bowls can spark resource guarding and intimidation. Eating in close proximity can be stressful even to cats who are normally very friendly toward each other. In addition, don't use double feeders with food in one side and water in the other. Food particles can get into the water and make the taste unpleasant. Keep food and water bowls clean and replenish the water bowl with fresh water every day.

Environmental enrichment also means making sure your cat receives top-notch nutrition. Your cat needs excellent quality food that's appropriate for her age and health.

Water can be used for enrichment as well. In addition to the regular water bowl, consider using a pet water fountain as well. This is a good option for cats who like to overturn their water bowls in fun. Water should be fresh and the bowls washed daily. If you are using a fountain, it also needs regular cleaning.

The Powder Room. Part of creating a healthy environment involves a litter box setup that's clean, with the right size box in a location that's appealing to the cat. Don't drop the ball when it comes to litter box maintenance.

Scratching Post. If your cat is scratching the furniture, she doesn't have the right post. Scratching is a natural behavior. Supply a tall, sturdy post that's covered in a rough material such as sisal.

Visual Enrichment. There are cat-entertainment DVDs that showcase prey. Many cats become fascinated by the visuals and sound effects. Such videos can be a great way to entertain your cat or jump-start a play session.

Outdoor bird feeders can be very entertaining. Set one up near the window where the cat has a perch or cat tree.

Social Interaction. Cats are social animals, although their social structure differs from that of dogs. Environmental enrichment includes social interaction with members of the family. If you added a cat to your life as a convenience pet because you're never home, then she's living a lonely, boring life. She needs time with you and other family members.

Your cat might also benefit from a cat companion. After a gradual and positive introduction, having a buddy can make a huge difference when it comes to enriching a cat's life.

Enjoying the Outdoors Safely! It is possible to take your cat outside safely, if you are prepared with a completely enclosed space from which there is no escape. There are companies that make such cat enclosures. You can find enclosures that sit in the window, as well as ones that can be installed outdoors. Make sure the enclosure is well constructed and sturdy. The enclosure should also allow the cat immediate access back into the house. Think of it as a feline screen porch.

Bring the outdoors in by creating opportunities for your cat to enjoy novel scents and textures. In the fall, I bring in leaves for my cat to enjoy. She loves the scent, the crackling sound, and the texture. In winter I bring in snowballs, and in spring and summer, I bring in all kinds of interesting things. You can even bring in a log for the cat to scratch on, as long as you don't mind the mess and the occasional spider who may hitch a ride inside.

No More Ho-Hum. Environmental enrichment is a necessity, not a luxury. It's time to increase the fun factor in your cat's life and reevaluate levels of security and stress.

Question:

Help! Marcella climbs on everything in my house. I'm afraid one day I'll find her on the ceiling fan. Why does she have to climb all over?

Pam's Answer:

Being able to safely climb is an important aspect of your cat's daily life. Climbing to an elevated spot enables a cat to watch over her environment. If your cat goes outdoors, the ability to climb is crucial to her survival because it helps her escape predators, and indoors she has the same instinct and need. As always, the solution is to give her safe options that direct her to where you want her to go.

The Benefits of Climbing. Although you understandably don't want your cat scaling your drapes or climbing up unsteady or delicate furniture, it's beneficial to make sure she does have safe climbing opportunities. Climbing is one of the ways kittens learn about their skills and abilities. By climbing they perfect their sense of balance and develop their muscles and flexibility. For an adult cat, first and foremost, climbing is *fun*! It's also good exercise, and it enables your cat to safely reach those elevated areas where she feels more secure.

Climbing Increases Territory. The more vertical areas available to your cat, the larger her territory. This becomes more important in a multicat household. Vertical territory will go a long way toward reducing cat-to-cat conflicts and will provide safety and security for more timid cats.

Safe Climbing. Because climbing is normal behavior for a cat, provide acceptable options for her. A sturdy, tall, multiperch cat tree is a great place to climb. If you have some vacant wall space, consider installing a few cat shelves. A client of mine who lives in a New York City loft chose to wrap one of the support beams with sisal. His cat gets a state-of-the-art scratching post and a great place to climb. There are many ways to create climbing opportunities, whatever the size of your home or apartment.

The Nature of Your Cat. Don't fight what comes naturally to your cat. Instead of shooing her off the furniture or getting angry when she climbs the drapes, provide her with better options. You'll both be happier.

Question:

I'm looking at purchasing a cat tree. How do I know which one is best? Some are very expensive, and I don't want to waste money on one my cat won't use.

Pam's Answer:

When shopping for a cat tree, keep your cat's size and personality in mind. If you have a large cat, don't choose a tree with small, flat perches. The cat has to feel comfortable on the perch and not be worried about a leg hanging over the side. I recommend the U-shaped ones because they allow the cat to feel the perch against his back. Cats like to back up against things when resting so as to feel more secure and less vulnerable to a rear attack.

Cat trees are easy to find at your local pet-product store and online. Prices vary, depending upon whether you want a basic tree or an elaborate one. What matters most to your cat will be the sturdiness, height, and comfort of the tree. Unstable trees won't get used by the cat and are a huge waste of money. The taller the tree, the wider the base should be. Be certain the tree can withstand your cat leaping from the ground to one of the high perches without so much as a wobble. Match the tree to your cat. If he's practically a floor-to-ceiling leaper, then you need to invest in an industrial-strength cat tree. Some cats tend to climb up the tree, but others try to land on the top perch from across the room.

Human Appeal Versus Cat Appeal. There's definitely a trend now toward sleek, visually appealing, and unique cat trees. While it's great that cat trees can now be displayed front and center in the home, there's a downside to be careful about. Some of the trees I see online are clearly meant to make a design statement to other humans. The cat trees may look cool to you, but they don't necessarily look comfortable for a cat, with their slippery, narrow, or small perches. Keep your cat's comfort, size, age, and mobility in mind when shopping for a tree. The sleek, wooden trees may not provide the warmth, softness, and comfort that an older cat needs. Also, some of the designer trees are not multicat-friendly, so you'll need more than one tree if you have more than one cat. I'm all for being stylish, but my first concern is always what's most beneficial for the cat.

Cat Tree Location. Once you've purchased the ideal cat tree, give careful consideration to placement. Typically, a great option is to put the tree by a window, so your cat can watch outdoor activity. If you don't like the look of the cat tree and plan to place it in some unused bedroom or in the basement, it'll just end up gathering dust. The tree needs to be located in a spot your cat will find appealing.

Question:

Murphy seems like a very confident, happy cat, but he also likes to hide quite often. Does that mean he's scared? Should I give him more hiding places or encourage him to stay in the open?

Pam's Answer:

Since the early 1980s, when I first started working with clients on their cats' behavior problems, a big part of my consultations have covered the importance of creating an environment that allows the cat to engage in natural behaviors, provides security, and strengthens the cat-human bond. The umbrella term for this approach is environmental enrichment.

One aspect of environmental enrichment that's often misunderstood or overlooked is the need for the cat to have hiding places. Many people think of feline hiding as a problem. It's true that a cat who's frightened will almost always look for a safe place to seek refuge, and it's important to do behavior modification to help the cat feel more secure, but it's also crucial that hiding places be made available. If a cat doesn't have a place to hide, he'll remain stressed and frightened. Hiding places give the cat time to calm down so he can choose when and how to venture out again. If he doesn't have a place to hide, he'll be unlikely to feel relaxed enough to engage. The cat who feels backed into a corner without any choices is the cat who lashes out or bites. When given the choice, a fearful cat will almost always run and hide. An important part of the behavior modification process with a frightened cat involves offering those hiding places.

Nevertheless, hiding is also a natural part of a well-adjusted cat's life. Even if your cat isn't normally fearful, it's still important to make sure there are adequate hiding places available in your home. There are times when a cat wants to be visible, and there are times when he wants to be invisible. Solo cats, companion cats, confident ones, and less confident ones will all appreciate having secure hiding places. For some cats, the hiding places may just be cozy napping areas out of reach of the family dog or toddler.

When we think of environmental enrichment, the first things that probably come to mind are toys, climbing structures, and opportunities for entertainment. Those things, while extremely important, are only pieces of the overall puzzle. Enrichment involves allowing the cat to engage in normal behaviors, and for an animal who has the unique distinction of being both predator and prey, the ability to hide ranks high on the list.

Cozy Hideaways. Hiding places can be created with things you already have around the house. Your cat may use his hiding places for various reasons, so the purpose should determine the type of setup you create. For example, a hiding place created as a napping area should be comfy and cozy. A pyramid-style or donut-shaped bed works well there. For an inexpensive homemade option, you can take a box, turn it on its side, and line it with a comfy towel. Pay attention to whether your cat prefers to nap up high or on a middle level. That'll help you choose a place for the cozy napping hideaway.

If your cat loves to be on a cat tree but doesn't like to be so exposed, you can attach a hideaway to the top perch or buy a tree that has at least one covered perch.

Typically, cats don't feel as secure on ground level, so napping hideaways should be elevated to some degree. Depending upon your cat's personality and the circumstances within your environment, that elevation can be mid-level, or it may have to be high enough to be out of reach of children or the family dog.

Choice. A huge part of my behavior modification technique has to do with making sure the cat always has a choice. The cat who doesn't have choices is the cat who feels stressed and backed into a corner. The cat who has choices—whether to be seen or remain hidden, whether to sit on his cat perch or on the arm of the sofa, or whether to engage or just observe— is the cat who feels calm. Offering a hiding place or two is just one aspect of creating a secure, comfortable, and safe environment for any cat, but for a fearful cat, it can make a world of difference.

Question:
I would like to get a cat, but I live in a very small apartment. Is that enough space?

Pam's Answer:
For a cat, the quality of the space is much more important than the size of the space.

We live in a horizontal world, but cats live in a vertical world. You have vertical spaces in your apartment that can increase the size of your cat's territory. Look around. I'll bet you can point to various elevated locations where a cat might like to hang out. It might be the top of the refrigerator or maybe on top of a bookcase or tall dresser. There are several reasons why a cat would choose those locations. The higher up she is, the more visual advantage she has.

Vertical territory offers a cat an opportunity to climb and get a little exercise as well. Playing up and down a cat tree is good for those feline muscles.

The ability to hang out in a cat tree or window perch and watch the bird activity outdoors is the feline version of reality television.

So Many Options. Vertical territory can come in many forms. A multi-perch cat tree is a great choice because it offers the cat a chance to climb up and down. The support posts of the tree can double as scratching posts if they're covered in a rough material, such as sisal.

Vertical space not only includes cat trees or window perches but also shelving and hideaways. You can purchase or construct a kitty walk on a wall. Just make sure the shelves are secure and wide enough to safely and comfortably hold a cat. You should also add a nonslip material to the surface. Be sure to install some cat-size stairways leading up to the shelves or stagger the shelves so each one can be used to get to the next higher one.

Even in a small apartment, you can significantly increase the size of a cat's territory by incorporating more vertical space.

Have fun and be creative when "thinking outside the box" for your future cat. Go online and you'll find lots of pictures of how elaborate some people have made the vertical territory. Look for companies that manufacture cat-specific structures. This is a great opportunity to give an indoor cat the ability to exercise, snooze, climb, play, and just watch the world from up above.

Question:

While browsing through a pet-supply catalog, I saw some tunnels intended for cats. How would I use a tunnel that way, and would a cat really be interested in hanging out in a tunnel?

Pam's Answer:

Most cats love to play by hiding in things. Whether it's an open paper bag or a box, your playful cat will find a way to make a game out of jumping into it or will use it as an extra napping place. It's an important part of environmental enrichment to supply those things for your cat's fun and convenience, but those bags and boxes can serve an even more important function in your cat's life as well. They can provide security.

The Value of Cat Tunnels. If you have a cat who spends most of her time under the bed or in the closet because she's too frightened to step out into the open, you can use boxes and paper bags, along with commercially available cat tunnels, to increase her comfort zone. The use of homemade or store-bought tunnels will help a frightened cat feel protected enough to step out from her anchored hiding spot.

A frightened or unsure cat often chooses to remain as invisible as possible when having to navigate around a room. She may walk behind furniture or stay on the perimeter of the room. To walk through the open, more exposed center of a room requires more confidence. If your cat spends so much time in hiding, increase her comfort level by using tunnels so she'll begin to explore more.

Types of Cat Tunnels. You can buy soft-sided cat tunnels at your local pet-product store, or you can make your own. To make a paper-bag tunnel, cut the bottoms off a few bags, and then fully open them. Roll a one-inch cuff on the ends of each bag to increase the sturdiness. This will prevent the bags from collapsing too easily. Then tape the bags end to end to form a tunnel. Don't use plastic bags for this or as any toy.

To make a box tunnel, the easiest thing to do is to find a long box, so you don't have to tape a couple of boxes together. You can either cut the flaps off or tape them so they stay open. If the box is big and your cat is small, you can leave one flap hanging down to provide just enough room for her to enter the tunnel while offering more hiding ability.

In a multicat household, if you decide to use long tunnels, choose ones with additional escape options midway through. This way, a cat has the option to leave if another cat enters the tunnel from the other end. This will prevent a cat from having to back all the way out or try to turn around in such close quarters.

Tunnel Placement. This part is very important. If you have a new cat who is still in her sanctuary room, place the tunnels so they form a path to resources. The tunnels don't have to totally cover the room; they just have to provide a little bit of coverage for the cat, so she'll feel less exposed when she needs to go from under the bed to the litter box or the feeding station. The ability to venture out will help her feel safe enough to check out her new surroundings.

Increase Confidence. No matter how long you've lived with your cat, if she's an under-the-bed or in-the-closet hider, you stand a much greater chance of getting her to risk putting one paw outside of her secure area if she feels protected enough. A well-planned tunnel is just the ticket.

Chapter 9

The Human Element

*We can be a hard species
to live with*

Question:

*We just found out we're expecting a baby. Our cat, George Clooney, has been
our only "baby" for many years. Do you have any suggestions of how to help
him get ready for the fact that he's about to become number two?*

Pam's Answer:

Cats aren't big fans of change. Imagine how confusing it must be when
there's suddenly a new family member brought home. From the cat's point
of view, this event takes place without any warning. Many people incorrectly assume that any negative behavior a cat displays toward the new
baby is based on jealousy, but that's not true. It comes from confusion and
fear caused by this major change in the cat's normal routine and the fact
that much of his environment suddenly becomes unfamiliar. The cat wakes
up one day to discover that a strange-smelling, strange-sounding creature

has just landed in his territory. What's worse is that everyone around the cat suddenly starts acting all panicky, shooing him away or yelling at him if he so much as tries to approach this strange little hairless creature. Add to that the fact that no one seems to have time for the cat anymore.

The earlier you begin to ease your cat through the transition, the better it will be for all concerned. Here are some basics to get you started:

Maintain Your Cat's Normal Schedule. A big mistake many expectant parents make is to shower the cat with an incredible amount of attention *before* the baby's birth because they know they're not going to have much free time later. As a result, your cat gets comfortable with the increased amount of playtime, cuddle time, and attention, but then when the baby comes, his whole world falls apart. Before the baby's birth, create a schedule you'll be able to maintain afterward.

Help Your Cat Get Comfortable with Sounds. Babies cry, and sometimes their cries are ear-shattering. I recommend getting one of the Sounds Good CDs by dog trainer Terry Ryan, the one that focuses on sounds babies make. Start by playing it at a very low volume while George engages in something positive, such as interactive playtime or receiving yummy food. Gradually, in subsequent training sessions, increase the volume.

Babies aren't the only ones able to make uncomfortable sounds. There are countless toys and pieces of equipment designed to entertain and stimulate baby by generating sounds—exersaucers, bouncy swings, musical mobiles, electronic playtime mats, and many others. If you know your cat is jumpy around certain types of noises or if you just want to be extra careful by giving him adequate time to adjust, purchase noise-generating baby equipment far enough in advance so that you can set it up and give the cat time to investigate. Periodically turn certain toys on or jiggle them so your cat gets used to it all.

Preview the Coming Attractions. Do you have friends with babies? If so, invite them over (one at a time) so your cat can adjust to the actual sound, smell, and sight of what will be happening in his future. Don't choose friends with toddlers. You want initially to expose your cat to a child who isn't that mobile.

Respect Your Cat's Nose. Allow your cat to investigate the new items you bring into the house as you prepare for the baby's arrival. He'll want to sniff the crib, changing table, clothing, toys, etc. Let him do a full investigation. If you sense he's getting tense about any object coming into the house, distract him with a play session, or offer a treat when he approaches the object. Clicker training works well here. Click and reward for any calm behavior around baby equipment or furniture. You can also take a clean sock, gently rub your cat around the mouth, and then rub the corners of the baby furniture. Cats have scent glands on their cheeks that release pheromones. The pheromones deposited during cheek-rubbing are "friendly." Cats don't typically cheek-rub objects unless they feel comfortable and secure. If you help your cat by doing some faux cheek-rubbing for him, you may help speed up his feeling of familiarity with the object.

And While We're on the Subject of Your Cat's Nose. Start wearing baby powder and baby lotion. This may help later on because the baby will have a scent similar to yours.

Know the Facts About the Litter Box During Your Pregnancy. If you're pregnant, you have most likely been advised by your doctor not to handle litter box duties. Some poorly informed doctors or relatives may even advise you to get rid of your cat. This is due to the risk to the fetus from toxoplasmosis. While toxoplasmosis is certainly a danger, it's important that you know the facts. You're more at risk of getting toxoplasmosis from handling raw meat and not properly washing your hands, or from using the same cutting board for vegetables that you use for raw meat. You're also at risk from ingesting undercooked pork, lamb, or beef.

Some cats do carry toxoplasmosis, but the ones most at risk are those who are allowed outdoors and eat birds and rodents. Cats on raw-food diets are also more at risk.

The reason pregnant women are advised not to handle litter box duties is that the disease-spreading oocysts are shed in the feces of the cat. The oocysts take one to three days to become infective once they are shed, so you'll greatly reduce your risk if the litter box is scooped on a regular basis. Another family member can handle the duties. If you must be the one to clean the litter, scoop twice a day, wear disposable gloves, and then thoroughly wash your hands *every time*.

You are also at risk of getting toxoplasmosis if you do outdoor gardening. Wear gardening gloves and wash your hands immediately afterward.

If you have questions about toxoplasmosis, talk to your doctor and also your cat's veterinarian about all the precautions you need to take, but there's no reason to get rid of your cat. Common sense and good hygiene are what's needed here.

Playtime Is Valuable. Your cat needs his normal playtime schedule. Engage in at least one or two interactive play sessions a day after the baby comes home. Do play sessions while the cat is in the presence of the baby to help form a positive association. Solo playtime is also important, so the cat can have something fun to do while you feed or interact with the baby. Make the solo playtime fun—don't depend on the basket of toys sitting in the corner. Those are boring! Place a fuzzy mouse in an empty tissue box or put a toy in a paper bag. Make the solo toys more interesting. Incorporate the use of puzzle feeders, because they're a great way to entertain the cat while you're busy with the baby.

Crib Safety. Many new mothers are worried that the cat will jump into the crib. In reality, *nothing* should be in your child's crib, not even a blanket or stuffed toy. If you're concerned about the cat, invest in a sturdy crib tent. In most cases, though, once the cat hears how loud a baby can cry when hungry or wet, he won't want to sleep that close.

If you've set up the crib in advance of baby's arrival and find the cat hanging out in it, go ahead and set up the crib tent now. You can also fill the crib with empty soda cans and bottles. That way, the cat won't feel comfortable in there, and you can hope that he'll be trained to avoid the crib well in advance of baby's arrival.

Question:

My toddler is at the age when he has become fascinated with our cat, Marilou. I want him to enjoy the cat, but I'm afraid he might hurt her. I'm also afraid the cat may scratch Adam. How can I help them become friends?

Pam's Answer:

Your cat and your child can develop a close and wonderful relationship. Your son is at the age when you can demonstrate the correct way to interact with the cat. In addition, provide your cat with areas of safety and refuge. This blossoming relationship can start your child on a lifetime of showing tenderness toward animals.

Pet with an Open Hand. Incorrect petting technique can quash a budding relationship. Show your child how to gently pet with an open hand and to stroke in the direction the fur grows. Some cats have sensitive areas or definite preferences when it comes to certain body locations. Instruct your child on the areas to stay away from. Many young children pet by patting the cat, but most cats don't enjoy that kind of touch. The overall preferred method is to use smooth strokes. The typical place cats enjoy being petted is on the back of the head. Some cats like long strokes down the back, but for other cats, that's either too stimulating or a sensitive area. Know what Marilou likes so you can instruct your child correctly.

Create Special Games. Animals love to play. Children love to play. Children love to play with animals. Help your child pick out a cat toy— preferably a design that resembles a fishing pole—and show him how to conduct a play session with the cat. Teach your child not to poke the cat or point the toy in her face, as well as not to frustrate the cat by keeping the toy out of reach. Never leave your child to play unsupervised with your cat.

Place open paper bags on their sides and have your child try to get the toy in each bag. Both he and the cat will have fun. If you're concerned about your son using a long-wand toy, use something like a peacock feather or a soft snakelike toy, such as the Cat Charmer. Another option is to have your child use a wand to create catnip bubbles. Catnip bubble solution can be purchased at your local pet-product store or online. Just don't let your child blow the bubbles in the cat's face.

Read About Pets. Look for books written for children about pets, or tell stories about cats or dogs. Use story time as an opportunity to help your children develop more compassion and understanding about how animals feel and what they need. One of the things I frequently did during story time was to ask my children how they thought the animal felt when something good or bad happened.

Model the Behavior You Want in Your Child. Your child is learning from watching how you care for and interact with the family pets. Demonstrate that your cat needs proper health care, good nutrition, love, fun, and kindness. If your child sees you reprimanding the cat in an inappropriate way, there's a chance he'll do the same. Even the way you talk about the family cat can influence how your child views the relationship. Calling the cat "stupid" if she does something undesirable will send the wrong message to your child. You hold the key to whether your child and your cat develop a good or bad relationship.

Question:
How can I get my cat to stop hating my new husband?

Pam's Answer:
Life in that rose-covered cottage can quickly turn into *Nightmare on Elm Street* if the cat hates the love of your life. Beginning a new relationship is stressful enough without the cat coming into the room to hiss or growl. Here are a few tips to help you get your cat to see the good side of Mr. Right:

Your Cat Isn't Jealous. This may come as a shock to you, but your cat isn't reacting this way because she's upset that you're spending more time with someone else. It's actually confusion and fear that make her less than hospitable to your husband. Your cat is a territorial creature of habit, and it can be very unsettling and stressful for her to suddenly have someone unfamiliar spending time in the house. It's also confusing to have her normal routine turned upside down. People often make the mistake of trying too hard to get the cat to like the new person. The cat parent may try to force the two together. The cat parent may pick up the cat and physically place her in the new person's arms.

A new person in the home can be an overwhelming territorial invasion from the point of view of some cats. All of a sudden, furniture, clothes, and other belongings with an unfamiliar scent are being hauled into the house. Moving into your husband's house or into a new house can be even more overwhelming, because now the cat has lost everything that was familiar.

Changing Your Cat's Mind About Your Spouse. First of all, you can't rush this process. Cats need to feel that they have some wiggle room. The more you try to force the cat on your spouse, the more she'll back away.

Sock Magic. Let's start with scent. You can help her begin to feel more comfortable if your spouse carries some of the cat's scent. Take a clean sock and gently rub around your cat's mouth to collect some of her facial pheromones. Cats facially rub on objects when they feel comfortable in the environment. Rub that sock on some of your spouse's personal belongings, such as shoes, briefcase, etc. Get more socks and repeat the process (not all at one time—don't wear her cheeks out). You can also rub the pheromone-baited sock on the corners of furniture pieces belonging to your spouse. You can also have your husband wear pheromone-baited socks around the house.

The Way to a Cat's Heart Is Through Her Stomach. Ask your husband if he'd be willing to be the one who prepares the cat's food and serves it. Your cat may not feel comfortable eating with him in the room, but his scent on the food bowl will be a start toward associating good things with his presence.

Treat giving can also be done by your husband. It may initially involve casually tossing a treat so the cat can eat it at some distance from the newcomer. You can also do clicker training with your cat. Click and reward for any positive step toward your husband. In some cases, that positive step may simply be that the cat is willing to walk into the room where your husband is sitting. Regardless of whether you clicker-train or are simply offering treats for desired behaviors, set the bar low enough so the cat is rewarded for the smallest of steps. Let the cat set the pace, and you'll find her becoming more comfortable about getting closer.

The Power of Play. Playtime is a powerful tool in your behavior modification toolbox. When a cat is in play mode, she's having a good time, good brain chemicals are being released, and she's making positive associations with her surroundings. Initially, you may have to conduct the play sessions while your husband sits on the sidelines, but it'll be a way for your cat to see that she can let down her guard and focus on the toy instead of worrying about your husband. Use an interactive toy based on a fishing pole design so you can keep the action going. Don't move the toy too close to your spouse. Keep the action within the cat's comfort zone.

In subsequent sessions, you can sit closer to your husband as you conduct the play session and then eventually hand the toy off to him. Work up to having him initiate games with your cat.

The Environment. Provide your cat with plenty of areas where she can retreat and feel comfortable when your husband is around. If there's no place for her to hide or retreat, she'll feel very vulnerable and end up diving under the bed. There should be at least one cat tree in the environment so she can get up where she'll feel safe. Your husband will need to understand that the cat tree is off-limits and that when the cat's up there, she wants to be left alone. If he respects that refuge, then the cat will begin to feel that she can go to the tree instead of hiding under the bed in another room.

Create hideaways using pyramid-style cat beds, boxes on their sides, or donut beds, so she can feel invisible yet stay in the room.

The Litter Box. If the litter box is currently located in an area where your husband will also be (such as the bedroom or master bathroom), set up an additional box in another area so your cat will always have a choice.

Making Contact. If your cat approaches your husband, let her do a scent investigation without being interrupted. Just because she comes up to sniff his pant leg doesn't mean she wants him reaching down to pet her or pick her up. Even if the cat walks across his lap, let her do so undisturbed. It's better to leave your cat wanting more rather than rushing the process and ending up with her darting away again.

Question:
Why does my cat come up only to my friends who are allergic to cats or don't like them?

Pam's Answer:
Your cat can zero in on the visitors who dislike cats because they make absolutely no attempt to interact. There's no direct eye contact, and you can bet that they won't reach down to pet or hold your cat.

From the Cat's Point of View. Cats are territorial and from their point of view, your home is their territory. When guests come over for a visit, some cats view them with suspicion. After all, these visitors have an unfamiliar scent and move and sound not at all like familiar family members. The cat lovers who visit your home may rush right over to the cat to greet him without paying attention to body language and signals the cat is giving that clearly say, "Back off." The guest who immediately approaches your cat doesn't give him time to do any scent investigation or determine whether the approaching human is friend or foe. The cat haters or the people with cat allergies, however, will ignore the cat, and this gives him all the freedom he needs to check them out at his own pace.

Pam's CatWise Clue

Seven Things That Make Sense to Your Cat but Not to You. You love your cat very much, but there are probably a few behaviors that leave you scratching your head. These are the behaviors that don't seem to make any sense. Even though you may not be able to figure out why your cat displays some odd behaviors, that doesn't mean they aren't functional or don't serve a very logical purpose. Here are seven things that make sense to your cat but not necessarily to you:

1. The Jekyll and Hyde. Your cat jumps into your lap and curls up. He may even rub up against you as if asking to be stroked. You start petting him, he purrs with delight, but then after a few minutes, he hauls off and swats you. What gives? Has your cat turned into Dr. Jekyll and Mr. Hyde? Although this sudden change in attitude seems to come out of nowhere, it's a relatively common behavior in some cats when you exceed their tolerance for being petted. This behavior, known as petting-induced aggression, happens when a cat gets too stimulated from constant petting and his body language signals have gone unnoticed. He feels that the only way to get you to stop is to scratch or bite.

2. The Nibble and Puke. This happens to some cats who are allowed outdoors. Many cats enjoy eating grass and will sit in the grass, doing their best sheep impersonation. After a few minutes of munching the greenery, you hear that familiar sound of a cat about to vomit. Many cat parents grow some kitty greens for their indoor cats' munching pleasure, and in most cases, they must do a little vomit cleanup afterward. Why do cats like to eat something that almost always causes them to puke? There are several theories among experts, but no one really knows for sure. One theory is that a cat uses grass to address an upset stomach. Some cats may also munch on grass to help them vomit up hairballs that aren't passing through the stomach.

3. The Paw Dip. Why does your cat dip his paw into the water bowl and then lick the water off instead of just drinking the normal way? It doesn't seem to make sense to humans, but it's a very practical behavior from a cat's point of view. In some cases, the cat chooses the paw method if the water bowl is too deep or too narrow. Cats have long whiskers, and they don't like getting them squished. Dipping the paw makes it more comfortable. A cat in a multicat household may resort to paw dipping as a matter of safety. He may not feel comfortable enough to lower his head into the bowl, which will obstruct his view. If he needs to keep an eye on any opponents, then dipping his paw is a better method. Finally, if you don't keep a consistent water level, your cat may develop the habit of paw dipping if he has trouble determining where the water line is.

4. The Rear View. For many cat parents, this seems very insulting behavior. The cat jumps up on your lap to sit but then faces away from you. He may even curl up next to you with his backside facing you. It may seem that wherever the cat decides to sit, whether it's on the coffee table in front of you or on your desk as you check your e-mail, you always get the backside view. There's a simple reason for this. He's not being insulting; he's actually displaying immense trust. Because a cat is both predator and prey, he wants to position himself in the safest place. If he turns his back on you as he settles down, he's showing that he trusts you and maybe even that he's going to watch the environment for both of you. It certainly makes sense to keep a keen eye on his surroundings in case a wayward mouse happens to scurry across the floor.

5. The Crazy Cat Dance. Your cat suddenly, without any obvious reason, bolts through the house as if chasing an imaginary mouse. He dances around, he pounces, and he may even take a flying leap onto his cat tree. You look all around but can't find evidence of any mouse, spider, or even a dust bunny. What gets into some cats when they get the "cat crazies" and almost slam into the walls? Chances are, your cat is either chasing a shadow or a light or he has simply had such a buildup of energy that he needs to get it out. Cats, being hunters, are built for movement. If your cat has been sleeping too much and hasn't been offered adequate playtime to work off some of that energy, he may just take it upon himself to chase some dancing light. Keep in mind, as well, that cats have fine-tuned senses, so your kitty may hear, smell, or see something that goes totally undetected by you.

6. The Paperweight. No matter how many toys you leave out for your cat or how interesting the environment may be, he will most likely choose to sit on the one piece of paper you're trying to read. If there's a piece of paper on the floor, your cat may opt to plant himself right on top of it instead of any of the other, more comfortable spots in the room. It doesn't make sense, right? It does to your cat. When it comes to sitting on papers or magazines you're reading, your smart cat knows exactly where your focus is. If he wants attention, the obvious place to be is right where your eyes are directed—the paper. As for a piece of paper on the floor or desk that no one is paying attention to, it may have to do with the cat's natural desire to be on something elevated. If he wants to be on floor level or on a desk but also wants to be just a bit higher, he may feel that the paper, because it's different from the rest of the surface, gives him a little lift.

7. The Cover-Up. You put a dish of food down for your cat, and he takes a few nibbles but then paws at the floor in front of the dish in the same way he does when covering his waste in the litter box. Is your cat saying the food stinks? Is this the feline equivalent of a restaurant patron who sends bad food back to the kitchen? Is kitty comparing his meal to a pile of cat poo? Actually, it's a normal behavior and is based on a cat's survival instinct as both a predator and prey animal. If your cat doesn't finish his meal, pawing at the floor is his attempt to cover the food so as not to attract predators. It also prevents potential prey from being alerted to the fact that a predator is in the vicinity. Even indoor cats who never go outside to hunt retain those survival instincts.

Question:

How can I help my cat, Benny, be more comfortable when I have guests over?

Pam's Answer:

First, you'll need to do some preliminary work with Benny. Get a fishing pole–type toy and conduct some interactive play sessions. Do these sessions in various parts of the home, but make sure you do a good number of them in the room where company would normally enter. The more play sessions you do, the more Benny may begin to have positive associations with all rooms in the home.

You'll need a volunteer for the next part of the training. Ask a friend to visit. The purpose of this visit is to show your cat that a visitor to the home is not a threat in any way. Ask your friend to come in and sit down without making any eye contact with Benny. He also shouldn't touch or interact with him in any way.

The Scaredy Cat. If your cat runs and hides, casually go to him and conduct a low-intensity play session. Don't drag him out from under the bed or poke the toy in his direction. If he's under the bed, just sit on the floor nearby and casually move the toy in an enticing way. The message you want to convey is that everything is fine and there's no need to be afraid. Your cat may peek out to play, or he may stay hidden. It doesn't matter. The message will reach him. If he does come out, play with him. If he peeks his head out from under the bed, that's perfectly fine. If not, don't worry, because he may make progress in future sessions. Any baby steps should be rewarded. After your brief visit with Benny, go back to your guest.

If your cat ventures out of the bedroom and makes an appearance in the room where your visitor is located, you're making good progress. Have the interactive toy nearby and conduct a casual little play session. Keep the toy a good distance from the visitor, though, so your cat can stay within his comfort zone.

If you do this exercise a few times a week, Benny may begin to realize that visitors aren't threatening. Just make sure guests don't attempt to interact with him or directly make eye contact with him.

The Watch Cat. If Benny takes an aggressive approach with visitors, you can use the same technique. Make sure the visitor makes absolutely no attempt to interact. Conduct a low-intensity play session with the cat or offer treats when he's in the room with the visitor. You can even feed him a meal while the visitor is there. Just be sure Benny is far enough away so he feels safe and secure.

"Go to Mat." Target training can be beneficial here, and you can use it to train your cat to go to specific locations. I use a soft place mat as a mobile location that can be put anywhere in a room. Target training can help you create a place that the cat will associate with being calm. For more on target training, see Chapter 2.

A Place of His Own. Regardless of whether Benny is a scaredy cat or a watch cat, he'll appreciate having a hiding place. To keep him in the room instead of having him disappear into a far-off bedroom, provide an A-frame or donut-shaped bed so he can feel protected and hidden. If you already have a cat tree in the room and your cat doesn't feel secure enough, place the A-frame bed on one of the perches. That way he'll feel secure because he's on a high perch but also hidden inside the cozy bed.

The Invisible Cat

Something as simple as a box can provide security for a cat. It's a way to peek out and observe the environment while feeling hidden. The ability to remain invisible can help reduce anxiety.

I'd also recommend some additional environmental modification in the form of cat shelves. A few strategically placed, comfy shelves may offer your cat an elevated "cats only" location to cautiously observe the activity in the room.

Question:
Is it true that cats are aloof?

Pam's Answer:
When I began doing cat-behavior consulting, it was very common to hear people referring to one myth or another about cats. Many people were resigned to living with a cat who had behavior problems. Many didn't feel it was worth putting much time and effort into interacting, because everyone knew cats were aloof, independent, not affectionate, and certainly untrainable. While I never agreed with those myths, I did understand why people believed them: There wasn't much accurate information out there about cats. What surprises me these days is that there's so much more information available. All you have to do is watch an Internet video featuring cats to see that they're social, trainable, and most definitely not aloof. People routinely misjudge cats as being solitary, so they never try to provide companionship for them, no matter how lonely they may be. The problem with our perception is that we keep comparing cats with dogs and trying to show that one species is better than the other. The truth is, they're just different.

No Aloofness Here. Cats are very tuned in to their environment because they're hardwired as predators. Their keen senses are on high alert for the sight, sound, or smell of potential prey. What you may interpret as aloofness is this exquisite animal being ready for anything. Just because a cat may not jump to immediate attention when a cat parent calls her name doesn't mean she's aloof. She's focused.

Affection. Cats show affection in many ways, and you might not even notice some of the more subtle ones. A cat doesn't have to be a lap cat to be affectionate. She may enjoy sitting next to you or maybe even several inches away, but that doesn't mean she's not affectionate. Most cats enjoy being petted, as well, but not necessarily in the same way you'd pet a dog. No belly rubs for the cat, please, because you'll very likely trigger a defensive response. Some cats may also have preferences when it comes to where on the body they like being petted or for how long. Some cats will enjoy a massage for extended periods, but some prefer only a drive-by stroke or two. A cat spends a great deal of effort getting to know you as a companion—your routines, what you like, what you don't, etc. If you do the same, you increase your chances of having the relationship you've always wanted with her.

Independence. While it's true that, in general, cats can be left home alone for longer periods than dogs, they're still dependent on us and are not low-maintenance companions. The misconception that cats are independent and require little or no care causes many of them to suffer needlessly, both physically and emotionally.

Cats need your companionship, and in fact some will go through separation anxiety if left alone too often or for too long—something most people associate only with their canine counterparts. A cat may not display separation anxiety as plainly as dogs do, so it can be easy to overlook the signs that a cat is concerned and confused.

Solitary or Social? Cats are constantly called solitary creatures, but that's not true. Cats are social animals. Their social structure is different from that of dogs. The misconception may come from the fact that because they're small predators, they often hunt alone because they go after prey that'll supply only enough food for one. Cats are also unique in that they're predators but are also prey.

I believe the other factor causing people to become confused about a cat's social structure is that they're territorial, so intercat relationships must go through the delicate process of identifying and negotiating turf issues. A dog may instantly become friends with another dog he meets, so it may seem frustrating when you realize that cat introductions won't ever be accomplished that quickly. I've often said there's a reason there are no cat parks in the world. Cat introductions require finesse and territorial negotiations. One cat isn't going to happily bring a ball to the park in the hope that she'll find another cat to play with.

If you just look at a cat's world from her point of view, you'll see a wonderful companion who's ready to offer you so much love. Don't compare cats with dogs; see them for the gorgeous cats they are. Dogs are great at being dogs. Cats are great at being cats. Plain and simple.

Question:

Why does my cat bite me when I try to pet her stomach?

Pam's Answer:

With a dog, a popular position for petting is often the belly rub. To most dogs, nothing feels as enjoyable as when you endlessly scratch and rub that tender tummy. As you've witnessed when you try that with your cat, however, you end up with a scratched hand and a few bite marks.

Vulnerability. The last thing a cat wants is for a larger predator or opponent to have access to her most vulnerable area, where her vital organs are located. The typical response for a cat who has her stomach touched is to spring into defensive mode. She may grab your hands with her paws and then maybe even bite. She isn't being mean to you; it's a natural protection reflex.

Exposing the Belly. Why would a cat expose her belly? That depends on the immediate circumstances in which she finds herself. If she's in a face-off with another cat, rolling over onto her side or back to expose her belly isn't a sign of submission. It's the ultimate defensive reaction, which communicates to the opponent that the gloves are off: All weapons (teeth and all claws) will be used if the fight is to become physical.

If a cat is stretched out on her back in a sunny spot in a room of your house and looking peaceful and relaxed, she feels very comfortable and not threatened. She's secure enough in her immediate environment to enjoy the warmth of the sun on her stomach. Don't ruin that moment by thinking it's OK to pet her in such a vulnerable spot. For many cats, having their bellies rubbed automatically triggers that defensive reaction. Don't take it personally or think your cat has suddenly taken to viewing you as the enemy. It's a reflex, and your cat is just reacting in a normal way.

Chapter 10

Animal House

Keeping peace when it's reigning cats and dogs

Question:

I would like to add a second cat to the family. How do I know what type of cat to choose?

Pam's Answer:

How can you be sure you'll bring home a cat who'll be a good match for your resident cat? There's no way to guarantee that the choice you make will result in a harmonious household, but I do have a few tips to help you increase your chances of a successful match.

Don't try to match up an elderly resident cat with a kitten. Kittens have very little respect for territory and boundaries. The revved-up kitten's attempts at playfulness and curiosity may end up being too stressful to the senior feline. If your elderly cat is ill, has limited mobility, or is impaired in any way, then it's not a good idea to add a second cat. The last thing your elderly cat needs is more stress.

If your adult resident cat is playful, healthy, sociable, and energetic, then a kitten might be a good choice.

Complementary Personalities. Think about your resident cat's personality in general. Is she outgoing? Assertive? Is she a take-no-prisoners type of cat? If so, then look for a second cat who won't compete with that personality. If you choose another take-no-prisoners type of cat, you'll probably end up with lots of nose-to-nose confrontations as each cat tries to take charge. On the other hand, you also don't want to choose a cat from the opposite end of the scale. A very timid, shy cat would not do well with a very assertive cat. Choose a cat with a complementary personality, one who is outgoing and friendly but not on either extreme of the personality chart.

> ## Don't Add Fuel to the Fire
>
> In a household that currently has multiple cats, you must first address any stress-related behavior problems before attempting to add yet another cat.

Male or Female? As for whether to get a male or female, many people have believed for years you should get a cat of the opposite sex. I have never accepted that theory, and in all my years of doing professional behavior consulting, I've found that making good personality and temperament matches has been far more important than whether the cat is male or female.

Don't Rush. Take your time when choosing a second cat. You'll be bringing in a companion who you hope will become a lifelong buddy for your resident cat, so don't rush the decision.

Question:
We'll soon be adopting a second cat as a companion for Merle, my six-year-old Persian. Someone suggested that we just put them together and let them work it out, but I'm nervous about that. Is there a special way to introduce cats?

Pam's Answer:

Many cats benefit from having feline companions. That said, cats are also territorial, so the introduction process requires some finesse and patience. If you just toss the cats together with a "they'll work it out themselves" mentality, you'll put a tremendous amount of stress on both cats and risk physical injury to them. An incorrect or hurried introduction can set the cats up to become bitter enemies. On the other hand, the correct introduction can open the door to a lifelong feline friendship. The more cats, the more resources and resource locations are needed and the more hiding places and escape routes are needed. It's crucial to make sure you have an environment that can support healthy, secure, happy, and enriched coexistence.

As you go through the introduction process, keep this in mind: The cats have been given no choice in picking their companions or territorial restrictions. We ask a lot from cats when we present them with a companion. We get to choose *our* partners in life. It's something to remind yourself of, especially if you lose patience or become frustrated during the process.

Cats in High-Alert Mode. You may know some people who used the old-fashioned (and not well-thought-out) method of simply putting the cats together and letting nature take its course. Some of these people may have had successful outcomes, but at what cost? How stressful were the introductions? And did the cats really become friends, or did they merely divide up the territory and draw a line in the sand? Just because the cat parents don't see overt aggression doesn't mean that these cats aren't living under constantly stressful conditions. The "let them work it out" method is risky, ineffective, and inhumane. Why would you want to use a technique that puts all cats involved at risk?

Do It the Right Way. The proper new-cat introduction technique must address the emotional and physical needs of both cats. From the resident cat's perspective, there's an intruder in his territory. From the newcomer's point of view, she has just been dropped on hostile turf. Both cats need to have security. If they feel there's no safe place for them, they'll revert to survival mode, and you'll see panic, fighting, and perhaps spraying. If, however, they feel they can remain in their comfort zones while checking out the situation, you can usually keep a lid on the panic. Both cats need safe areas to decompress during this life-changing event. Your resident cat doesn't understand why he no longer has the entire territory to himself. The newcomer must get to know an unfamiliar territory, unfamiliar humans, *and* an unfamiliar cat. Talk about stressful!

Step One: Set Up a Sanctuary Room

Set up a room to be used as a safe place for the newcomer, a place that's hers alone. This gives her time to get somewhat familiar with her new surroundings in a more secure way. It's stressful enough for a cat to move to an unfamiliar environment, so before you introduce her to your resident cat, let her get her bearings and have time to herself in a sanctuary room. You don't want to even try an introduction with a reactive newcomer, so the sanctuary gives her a place to get herself back to normal functioning level. The more relaxed each cat is, the better the chances of a successful introduction.

The sanctuary room can be any room you can close off. It should contain a litter box, food and water, a few cozy hiding places, a scratching post, and toys. If you use a carrier to bring the cat into the house, leave the carrier in the room with its door open, so the cat can stay in there if she chooses, before venturing out into the rest of the room. If the newcomer cat is timid or fearful, being able to stay in the carrier containing her own familiar scent may provide much-needed comfort in the beginning.

For a fearful cat, set up some paper-bag tunnels inside the sanctuary room as safe routes for her to get to the litter box or food without feeling too exposed. Put other hiding places around the room for her as well, such as upside-down boxes with entrance holes cut in them. This may help her feel that she doesn't have to remain hidden under the bed or in the closet. If she spends her days cowering under the bed or wedged behind your suitcase in the closet, she'll be too frightened and reactive, and that'll lead to an unsuccessful and extremely stressful introduction.

I Know You're in There! Even though your resident cat won't be able to see the newcomer, he's going to be aware that she's on the other side of the door. This is normal, but by having the newcomer in the sanctuary, you're letting your resident cat know that only a portion of his territory has been invaded, not the entire home. That's important so as not to overwhelm him.

Cat-Appeasing Pheromone Therapy. The use of the cat-appeasing pheromone product Feliway Multicat, in diffuser form, may help during the
intro. The analogs of pheromones in this particular product are related to
easing tension and increasing social engagement. The diffuser doesn't
have a scent detectable to humans.

Step Two: Mealtime Is Training Time

The key to a successful new-cat introduction is to *give the cats a reason to
like each other*. You can't just separate them for a long time and then open
the door expecting them to magically form a bond. They'll need to see
good things happen when they're in the presence of each other, and,
later, within sight of each other. The best way to do this is with food and
treats. Food is a powerful motivator!

Feed the cats by placing food bowls on either side of the closed sanctuary door. How far from the door will be determined by the reactivity
level of each cat. If your resident cat won't come within six feet of the
door, then place his food bowl well within his comfort zone. In subsequent sessions, you'll gradually move the bowls closer to the door.

Be mindful, though, of just how close is too close. In general, cats feel
safer eating alone, so don't push the issue by asking two unfamiliar cats to
share a small space when eating. Even after the introduction is complete,
the cats may still prefer to have a good distance between them during
mealtime.

Minute Minder

Start out by keeping interactions very brief. Less than
three minutes for each session is more than enough.

If one cat eats faster than the other, you can give that cat a bowl with
some obstacles in it (like the type of bowl used for dogs who eat too
quickly). If feeding moist food, you can push the food against the bottom
and sides of the bowl rather than placing a heaping mound of food in the
center, so the cat has to spend more time licking at it.

Don't offer too much food during each training session. It's better to
do frequent, short sessions that end on a positive note.

Step Three: Let the Nose Do the Talking

The Sock Exchange. I came up with this method many, many years ago, and it has been very successful in new-cat introductions. It's simple and starts with a pair of clean socks.

Place a clean sock on your hand and gently rub the newcomer along the sides of the mouth to collect some facial pheromones. The pheromones around the cat's face are "friendly" pheromones. Cats rub their faces on things where they feel comfortable. Using the sock, we're going to simulate a cat producing lots of friendly pheromones.

Place the scented sock in your resident cat's area. This will give him a chance to do his own initial investigation of the new cat's scent. If you have Feliway spray, you can give a quick spritz on the bottom part of the sock (not near where you rubbed the new cat's real pheromones). Feliway, as opposed to Feliway Multicat, contains the F3 fraction of facial pheromones, the ones associated with self-identification, territory, and familiarity. In theory, when a cat smells the synthetic pheromones, he'll consider them his own. Using the pheromone spray is optional, but if it's in the budget, it can't hurt and may increase your odds of success. If you decide to use Feliway products, use the spray on the sock and the Feliway Multicat in the diffuser. That way, you'll maximize the effects of both.

Let your cat do his own investigation. I use clicker training with introductions; I click and reward any positive move the resident cat makes toward the sock. I click and reward for merely walking toward the sock. I click for anything I would like to see the cat do again, and I ignore any undesirable behavior. For example, if the cat sniffs the sock, I click and reward. If he walks by the sock without giving it a second look, I click and reward.

I use the sock because it gives the cat time to get to know the other cat's scent in a safe and controlled way. The cat doing the sniffing can safely approach, and I can do behavior modification without worrying that one or both cats will get injured.

Take the mate to that sock and rub the resident cat to collect the facial pheromones. Place that sock in the newcomer's sanctuary room.

You can do the sock exchange as often as needed. You also don't have to use clicker training. If you prefer not to use it, then offer a treat to the cat for any behavior you want to encourage. If you don't want to give treats, then you can use a portion of his food. This method will work only if you feed on a schedule rather than having food available all the time. If you've always kept food down for free-choice feeding, this might be the time to consider going to scheduled meals. Food is a powerful tool for behavior modification, but it won't work if the cat is never hungry.

When rewarding the cat's behavior as he comes upon the sock, keep in mind that the behavior doesn't have to be over-the-top great; it can be a very neutral behavior, such as simply walking by the sock. He doesn't have to roll all over it in order for this to be a positive behavior. We're looking for any sign of relaxation or acceptance.

Use the sock to rub objects in the environment as well. This will help the newcomer get a leg up on establishing a sense of familiarity when she starts exploring beyond her sanctuary room.

Now it's time for the newcomer to investigate, to explore her new territory and spread her scent around the environment. This has to be done safely, so your resident cat will need to be placed in a separate room. Then open the door to the sanctuary room and let the newcomer check things out. As she walks around, she'll be distributing her scent. Do this exercise a couple of times a day.

Depending upon how reactive your resident cat is, you can also let him do some exploration of the sanctuary room. Put the newcomer in another room so she can explore safely (or place her in her carrier, and then put the carrier in another room). Then open the door to the sanctuary room so your resident cat can check things out. Keep toys and treats handy for distraction. Whether to let your resident cat into the sanctuary room depends on how reactive he is, so you'll have to be the judge here. For some cats, the sanctuary room of an unfamiliar cat is too over-the-top. For other cats, it's a chance to do a more in-depth scent investigation in a safe way. Use caution.

Step Four: Peekaboo

The next step involves opening the sanctuary room door just a crack during the feeding sessions. Feed the cats within sight of each other but far enough apart so they don't feel threatened. Do short sessions in which you offer a tiny amount of food and then close the sanctuary room door. It's better to do several short sessions a day that end on a positive note rather than attempt one long session in which someone's tolerance is tested and a fight breaks out. If one cat routinely tries to bolt through the door, use a doorstop to prevent the door from fully opening. You can also place a hook-and-eye closure on the door temporarily.

Step Five: Fully Opened Door

When do you move on to this step? That's determined by your individual situation. There's no set time limit on how long you should stay in one phase before entering the next. If your cats aren't comfortable enough yet with eating on either side of the door when it's cracked open, then you aren't ready to move to the fully opened door. Cat introductions shouldn't be rushed. Take each phase slowly, and watch your cats' reactions to determine whether to move on. It can take days or weeks, and they might progress, then regress a bit.

If you think it's time to open the sanctuary room door, but you're worried that one cat may charge through, or if one or both cats have already tried to do so, then you can take an interim step. Put two or three baby gates stacked on top of each other across the entrance (to forestall leaping), or install a temporary screen door (with secure pet screening). This will allow the cats to see each other without being able to charge. When the short feeding session is over, close the actual sanctuary room door again. You can even use just one baby gate during the feeding sessions if you stand by the door, ready to close it in case the worst happens. Even though the cats could easily hop over the gate, it can be just enough of a barrier to relax the cats so they'll be comfortable to eat.

Keep doing sessions in which the cats see each other while eating or getting treats. Gradually increase the exposure time.

True Friends or Just a Truce?

Although the desired outcome is for the cats to become the best of friends, they may never get beyond just peaceful coexistence.

Continue the Clicker Training. As you gradually increase the time the cats are exposed to each other, use clicker training; click and reward for any positive move. I tell my clients to click for any absence of an unwanted behavior. For example, if one cat breaks a stare or walks by the other cat without hissing or swatting, that deserves a reward. Again, even if you don't use clicker training, offer a food treat or verbal praise for any positive sign.

Use Playtime. Use interactive playtime as a way to help the cats have more positive experiences with each other. Do parallel play by holding a fishing pole–type toy in each hand or by enlisting the help of another family member. This way, each cat will have a toy. You don't want the cats competing for one toy or risk having one cat intimidated by the other cat. When you use two toys, each gets to enjoy the game while seeing the other cat in peripheral vision.

Final Step: The Cats' Environment

Set up the environment to encourage security and fun, with plenty of territory for everyone. This will be very important when the cats spend more time together and are no longer separated. Use cat trees, perches, and hideaways to create low, medium, and high levels. If you increase the elevated territory in the environment, you greatly increase the cats' perception of the amount of territory they have. Vertical territory helps a cat feel safe because he knows he can't get stalked from behind and is able to better survey the environment. Some cats also use vertical territory as a way to display status, thus often avoiding a physical confrontation.

Increase environmental enrichment to give the cats ways to redirect their focus, release energy, and have fun! Set up food-dispensing toys, puzzle toys, and other opportunities for solo playtime. A bird feeder outside the window or some cat shelves for climbing and playing may divert their attention from each other and ease tension.

Have more than one litter box and more than one scratching post in the shared environment. The litter boxes and scratching posts shouldn't be in the same room, because you don't want one cat to have no other choice but to cross the other cat's path. Place resources in each cat's preferred area to give the cats more choice and help them attain peaceful coexistence.

Continue to do the mealtime training, letting the cats eat in each other's presence but never out of the same bowl. It's a good idea to feed in separate bowls because doing so will train them for the future possibility of one cat having to be on a special nutritional program. Using separate bowls also limits the stress of having to eat so close to each other, something cats don't typically enjoy.

> ### Yours, Mine, and Ours
>
> When you decide to have a multicat household, whether large or small, you must ensure that each cat has safe, secure, and convenient access to all resources. Then continue to closely monitor.

Remember: Don't Rush. I always advise clients to go at the pace of the most stressed-out of the cats. If one cat is ready and willing to make friends but the other cat isn't, you have to go at the pace of the unhappy cat. New-cat introductions take time, but it's worth it to increase the odds of helping these two cats develop a good relationship.

Question:

Our two cats have one chair in the bonus room that they frequently fight over at certain times of the day. At night, Yoshi, my two-year-old cat, doesn't care about it at all, but if Moody Blue even tries to get up there during the day, there's a huge battle. Why do they fight over it only in the afternoon?

Pam's Answer:

Nobody does time-sharing better than the cat. I'm not referring to a cat's ability to pick out a condo on the beach, but rather the ability to coexist with other cats. Cats try hard to work out a schedule for sharing territory or particular spots in the house during certain hours. If you have a multicat household where there are no disputes, then your cats have more than likely worked out a time-sharing schedule.

If one cat chases another off a chair or sits on the bed and prevents a companion cat from using that same space, then the time-sharing arrangements in your house haven't been agreed upon yet.

The Mechanics of Time-Sharing. How does time-sharing work? As with your cats, one may prefer a certain chair or perch during a specific time of day. Although a particular cat can predictably be found in that spot during daylight hours, he may have another favorite location during the evening.

Time-sharing problems occur when there aren't enough prime areas for each cat to claim or when one cat challenges another in an attempt to take over that spot. These challenges may happen when a higher-ranking cat wants to flex his muscles and make a lower-ranking cat move. Challenges can also occur when the cat parent is around. For example, the cat parent's bed may be used by a lower-ranking cat during the day, but when it's bedtime, another cat may claim that spot, even to the point of showing aggression toward any cat who tries to jump up.

Watch How Your Cats Interact. Observe how your cats time-share, and make sure there are plenty of prime areas for everyone. If the cats fight because each one wants to claim the chair, then set up a window perch, a heated donut-shaped cat bed, or a cat tree in the room. This may be enough to create an appealing alternative.

Act Your Age

Cats reach social maturity between two and four years of age. This is the time some will start to challenge their cat companions. Cats who previously got along may start to squabble.

Enough Resources for Everyone. If there's the least bit of tension in your multicat home, don't add fuel to the fire by asking the cats to share resources (see answer below).

Look around your home to see if there's anything you can do to help with time-sharing issues by increasing the number and location of resources. Very often, it just takes a little environmental tweaking on your part to reduce the tension between your cats.

Question:

Thomas is the youngest of my four cats. He's eight months old, and he's starting to intimidate my other cats whenever it's dinnertime. I wonder whether he's doing it at the litter box as well. How can I stop what appears to be bullying?

Pam's Answer:

Bullying means something very different in the cat world than in the human one, so I think of it in a different way. The bully is really protecting something, not picking on someone. In some multicat homes, resource guarding is very obvious. In other homes, it can be very hard to detect, due to how subtle the behavior may be. The cats may seem to get along, and in most aspects of their lives together, they may not have any issues. There might be one or more situations, though, that do cause one cat to become protective of something.

Guarding Food. Probably the most common resource-guarding behavior happens at the feeding station. Sometimes the sweetest cat can turn into a tiger when preventing his feline companions from coming close to the food. He may guard just his own bowl, or he may patrol all of the bowls. If you feed out of one common food bowl, he may guard the entrance to the kitchen. The guarding cat may push the other cats out of the way in order to eat first. If one cat has been repeatedly bullied at the food bowl, he may learn to just wait until the intimidator has finished eating. The intimidated cat may sit off to the side or may have learned not to enter the kitchen at all in order to avoid a physical confrontation.

Dealing with Resource Guarding at the Food Bowl. The key to heading off resource guarding is to offer more resources. When a cat has a choice, he's less likely to become stressed and feel he needs to defend something.

In the case of the feeding station, set up food bowls in more than one location. If you leave food out for free-choice feeding, divide up the food into several dishes and spread them out. The resource-guarding cat can't be in all places at once. If the resource guarding was triggered by the cat having to share a bowl with another cat, then setting out more bowls in one location may be enough. If the behavior is more severe and the intimidated cat won't eat while the guarding cat is in the same room, set up additional feeding stations around the house, placing one in each cat's preferred area. Choose locations where intimidated cats naturally feel more comfortable. Place bowls on various vertical levels to help intimidated cats feel more secure because they can watch for any sign of another cat entering the room.

Use puzzle feeders during the day to give your cats something to do in order to earn food rewards. Hunting puts cats in a good frame of mind. Provide opportunities to work for food and earn a reward to help relieve boredom, ease tension, avoid potential aggressive encounters, and prevent the cats from getting too hungry. Just make sure you set up a good number of puzzle feeders throughout the house so everyone gets a chance to enjoy them.

Guarding the Litter Box. Litter box guarding can be extremely subtle. The cat may appear to lounge in the middle of the hallway leading to the room where the litter box is located. He may look relaxed, but in reality he might be protecting the path to the litter box. Other cats would have to walk past the guard to eliminate.

As with the feeding station, choice plays a very important role here. Don't put your cats in a tense situation by forcing them to share one box. Even if you've set up more than one box, if you put them all in the same room, you still let one cat guard them. Place boxes in several locations around the house so every cat has a comfortable and secure option. When deciding where boxes should be located, choose areas where one cat won't be forced to enter another cat's territory. Moreover, when you know you have a cat who tends to guard, don't place resources where other cats have to walk past a narrow opening, such as a long hallway, if you can avoid it.

Resource Guarding Can Happen in Many Situations. Always provide choice, and don't put your cats in a situation where they're forced to share something. You may have a cat who grabs a toy during an interactive play session and intimidates the other cats into staying in the background. To avoid this, do your interactive sessions individually, or use more than one toy.

Always set your cats up to succeed, and they won't disappoint you.

Question:

I live in a large house, and yet my two cats have never been able to get along. Is there anything I can do?

Pam's Answer:

Cats can be very happy in small apartments; an expanse of real estate isn't as important to them as to us. What counts more is how you've arranged things in the rooms. There's a very long list of potential reasons why the cats in your home may not get along, including lack of socialization, poorly done socialization, medical issues, personality conflicts, and so much more. From what I see during many of my in-home visits, though, the two most common reasons are how the environment is set up and the cat parent's lack of awareness regarding subtle signs of conflict.

Conflict Bubbling Below the Surface. Even though cats are social animals, it's their nature to hunt alone. They don't hunt in packs, and the prey they pursue is very small—enough for one meal. Even if your indoor cat doesn't engage in outdoor hunting, he's hardwired to be protective of his resources, and some cats are more concerned with their resources than others.

The social interaction between your cats goes smoothly when no one feels the need to compete for food, safe places to eliminate, safe napping areas, and the attention of the cat parent. In many households, however, I see cats in environments where there's ongoing competition for resources. The tension and conflict may be so subtle that the cat parents don't even notice, or they may misinterpret it until one cat starts hiding or all-out war is declared, with fur flying and banshee screams. You may not have been watching at mealtime, when one cat consistently backs off when the other one enters the room. You may not have paid much attention during playtime to the fact that one cat is the main participant when you get out a single interactive toy for both cats. Or maybe you've just gotten used to the fact that one cat claims your bed at night and won't let the other one up there.

A timid cat might take to living under the bed or skulking around the house to access resources when the coast is clear. He may even begin to display sickness behaviors from the ongoing stress. A more assertive cat may engage in resource guarding. He might frighten another cat away from the feeding station, favored sleeping areas, and toys. He may lounge on the path to the litter box to keep another cat from it. This behavior could be so subtle that you don't see it, or could be so blatant that there's growling, hissing, body-language signals, or actual fighting between the cats. The overt aggression is the one cat parents notice, but sadly, conflict bubbling just under the surface can go on for years without being addressed.

Tension between your cats can also occur if more attention is paid to one cat than the other, if it seems that one cat is favored. Cats don't misbehave out of spite, but when a cat parent interprets it that way and spanks, yells, or squirts water at one cat for a perceived infraction, it doesn't help the feline relationships. A cat intimidated by another cat may resort to eliminating outside the litter box due to fear. A cat parent who yells or punishes the cat for the "misbehavior" escalates an already stressful situation for the cat.

A Cat's-Eye View of Her Environment. Cat parents want their cats to live as part of a happy family, but many times they don't consider how the cat's nature plays into the need for resource security. You may want your cats to share one community food bowl in the kitchen or share one big litter box in the laundry room, but one or both of those things may be what's triggering conflict. Much of a cat's social interaction with other cats has to do with resource availability. Cats live together cooperatively when there are adequate resources for everyone. Competition and conflict occur when there isn't enough to go around, no matter how many rooms there are in your house. Here, size doesn't matter; number does. Even though you're sure you've put enough food in the bowl for both cats, one of the cats may not feel that way or may not feel safe eating from the same bowl. Even though you've set up a litter box that's big enough for two cats, a cat of lower status may not feel comfortable entering the territory of the higher-ranking cat.

Include sources of cat-appeasing pheromones in the environment. They may foster more positive social contact.

Make Sure There's Enough for Everyone. Watch for subtle signs of tension you may have previously overlooked. The solution, in many cases, is simply to increase the number of resources. Your cats may feel more secure if you increase the number of feeding stations. In some cases, that may involve just giving each cat a separate bowl, or you may have to set up feeding stations in multiple locations. Instead of having one toilet area, set up boxes in multiple locations. Unless your cats play cooperatively, sharing equally in the game, engage in individual interactive play therapy. If doing group play, have another family member focus on the other cat, or if you're by yourself, hold a fishing-pole toy in each hand, so two cats don't have to compete.

Divide your attention equally among the cats. Even if you're mad at one cat for "bullying" or peeing on the carpet, don't show favorites. Your attention and love are also cherished resources to your cats, and they shouldn't have to compete for those.

Cats Can Be Subtle

People who are used to the signs of dog aggression can miss signs of cat aggression, because it may be covert.

Vertical Territory. We live in a horizontal world, but cats live in a multi-level vertical world. The more vertical territory you can create in the home, the better for everyone. A cat of high status typically prefers to perch in the highest location. A timid cat may also choose an elevated spot for safety and for maximum visual warning time to see approaching opponents. If you don't have vertical territory, cats may compete for the spot on top of your refrigerator or bookcase. Provide cat trees, window perches, and if possible, a few cat shelves to increase vertical territory. It's a great way to increase the size of your feline environment within your home. Just the addition of some safe cat shelving may calm the waters.

When creating cat shelves, provide more than one escape route so no one ever feels trapped. Conflict happens when cats feel backed into a corner with no way out. When confronted with a potential threat and the choice of fight or flight, cats much prefer escape over doing battle.

Disagreements between your cats are bound to happen from time to time, but if you set up the environment with more resource availability and security, you'll greatly reduce the chances of competition and conflict.

Question:

Help me, Pam! My cats don't get along. They don't actually fight much, but I can tell they really don't like each other. Should I give up and just find one of them another home?

Pam's Answer:

It's good that you're aware of those subtle signs indicating your cats aren't getting along. In my consultations, I've found that many cat parents don't recognize the fact that their cats aren't getting along with each other because there are no overt signs of aggression. The cats aren't engaging in an outright battle with fur flying and bloodshed, so they miss the subtle signs of tension. Cats generally prefer *not* to fight; that's why they do such elaborate posturing. Each cat hopes that his puffed-up "I'm a really bad dude, so don't mess with me" posture convinces his opponent to back off. There can also be some intimidation going on that's just under the radar; one cat may guard the path to the litter box or nose another cat out of the food bowl. Not all companion cats are going to get along 100 percent of the time; just as among people, there are bound to be some misunderstandings and miscommunication. If you notice a pattern of intimidation, though, there may be more animosity between your cats than you thought.

Find the Cause. In order to eliminate the aggression between your cats, you have to find out what's causing it. If the aggression is sudden and uncharacteristic, then there could be an underlying medical cause, so your cat should be examined by the veterinarian. One cat might be experiencing pain, and that may be causing the aggression toward the other cat.

If the cats had previously gotten along but have suddenly become enemies, redirected aggression is a possible cause. One cat may have spotted an unfamiliar animal outside and redirected his aggression toward a companion cat. If one cat visited the veterinarian and then was attacked by his feline companion upon returning home, the attacker might be displaying nonrecognition aggression. There are different types of aggression and many causes, so you need to sharpen your detective skills in order to uncover the trigger.

Make Some Changes. When the relationship between the cats is tense but doesn't seem serious or dangerous, you may be able to begin a behavior modification program to help them feel more at ease with each other. Create an environment inspiring security. Just wishing the cats will get along or punishing them for reacting to each other will do nothing but continue the downward spiral. It's time to make some changes in the environment and create positive associations.

Sharing Isn't Always a Good Thing. Look at the cats' living environment and see what you can do to create more separate safe zones and security. For example, perhaps the cats have been sharing one food bowl and you notice they tend to compete for access. Give each cat his own bowl in that case. Another thing to look at is the litter box. The rule of thumb is N+1. It might be time to place another litter box in the home.

Vertical Territory. You have some prime real estate within your home that isn't being used, real estate that may make a difference in whether you have a happy cat household or an unhappy one. Just look up. Vertical territory gives the cats some safe places to perch and oversee their territory.

You can increase vertical territory in many ways. If the budget allows, you can go over the top and create amazing vertical space, or you can do very cost-effective changes. Your cats will appreciate any vertical enhancements, as long as they're safe, secure, and comfortable.

Make Positive Associations. The behavior modification here starts with giving the cats a reason to like each other. Show them that good things happen when they're in the presence of each other. Offer treats only when they're together and relaxed.

Give equal amounts of attention so one cat isn't favored over the other. You may be upset with the one cat who you feel is initiating the aggression, but it's important to show each cat the same amount of attention.

Cat-Appeasing Pheromones. If it's in the budget, it might be worth trying the Feliway Multicat diffuser in the environment to help increase calm, social behavior. You'll still need to incorporate appropriate behavior modification.

Playtime Is a Valuable Tool. Use playtime as a behavior modification tool. Conduct individual interactive play-therapy sessions so each cat has chances during the day to focus exclusively on being a hunter and can enjoy the game. Do these sessions separately, so the cats don't have to worry about each other. In addition, conduct parallel playtime sessions so the cats can play "together" but not have to compete for one toy. If possible, have another family member play with one cat while you play with the other. The cats will see that they're in the room together but no one is doing any intimidation. If you don't have another family member to help, you can still do parallel play by holding a fishing pole–type toy in each hand. It's awkward at first, but you'll get more adept at it with practice. If cats have something to focus their attention on other than each other, they may relax.

Be Calm. The way *you* behave can influence your cats' reactions to each other. If you're tense when they're together because you anticipate something awful happening, they'll pick up on that. Punishing one cat for reacting to his companion cat will do nothing to help them find a reason to like each other. Be calm, so your furry little emotional cat sponges will be more relaxed.

When Things Go Horribly Wrong. What do you do if the relationship between your cats is so bad that there's a risk of someone getting injured? What if they can't even be in the same room together for one second without a battle erupting? Then it's time to do a reintroduction. There are times when the best way to heal the relationship is to start from scratch. Instead of continuing to go down the current road, which clearly isn't working, it's better to separate the cats completely and introduce them again as if they had never met (see below).

Things Won't Change Overnight. Be patient. Helping your cats change their association with each other will take time.

Question:

When I got married, I tried to introduce my cat to my husband's cat. Three years later, they still fight constantly. My husband is sick of the growling, hissing, and fighting. He says one of the cats will have to go, but I love them both. Is there any hope that we could get them to agree to a truce?

Pam's Answer:

When you have cats who aren't getting along and all your attempts at behavior modification have failed, it's time to do a reintroduction. If the aggression between your cats is so severe that they can't even be within sight of each other without an immediate brawl taking place, then a reintroduction is your best bet.

What Is a Reintroduction? In a reintroduction, you separate the cats and introduce them in the same way you would if they'd never met. This gives each cat time to get back to normal and not be so anxious, so you can help them gradually get comfortable with each other.

Trying to keep a lid on serious intercat aggression when the cats are constantly in each other's sight can be very counterproductive, because both cats remain at a high level of reactivity. There's also a good chance of injury to one or both. A reintroduction gives you more control. It lets you keep the interaction between the cats at a level that doesn't spark extreme reactions.

How Long Does a Reintroduction Take? The time needed will be determined by how serious the aggression has been, how much time you can dedicate to doing the behavior modification, and how receptive the cats are. In other words, I wish I could give you a set timeline, but you have to go at the cats' pace. Every situation is unique.

The Reintroduction Method. The first step is to separate the cats by creating a sanctuary room for one of them. If your house is set up in such a way that you can divide it up so each cat has her own territory, that will do as well. If you're setting up a sanctuary room, you just need a separate room that can be closed off. The room needs to be equipped with all the necessities—food, water, litter box, scratching posts, toys, and some cozy napping places.

If you're wondering which cat to put in the sanctuary room and which cat to let have the run of the rest of the house, here's how I typically make the decision. If one cat is clearly displaying ongoing offensive aggression, I usually put that one in the sanctuary room. Then the aggressive cat can't think she ran the other cat off and is the mighty victor holding the prime territory. However, if the cat who's the "victim" is too stressed or nervous about having the run of the house, put him in the sanctuary room to give him more security. You have to make the decision based on the dynamics between the cats and their individual personalities. The most important thing is that the cats get separated.

During the Separation. The separation is mainly to allow the cats to relax again and to prevent further injury or aggression. It's important, though, that this time of separation not be viewed by them as a prison sentence. Spend time with the cat in the sanctuary room; do some interactive play and some quiet petting to make this experience as enjoyable as possible.

Behavior Modification Through Mealtime. Just as in a new-cat introduction, the main purpose of the reintroduction is to *give the cats a reason to like each other.* You can't just separate the cats for an extended period of time and then open the door expecting them to have forgotten they've been archenemies for the last few years. The behavior modification you do when the cats are once again exposed to each other is what makes the difference. They need to see good things happen in each other's presence but experience those rewards gradually enough to stay in their comfort zones. This way, the chances of their aggression boiling over again will be decreased. During the exposure time, you'll use a very valuable behavior modification tool: *food.* Remember the old adage, "The way to a man's heart is through his stomach"? That applies double to cats! Food can accelerate the acceptance process.

Feed the cats by placing food bowls on either side of the closed sanctuary door. How far from the door will be determined by how reactive the cats appear. In subsequent sessions, you'll gradually move the bowls closer but never too close. Cats generally prefer to eat alone, so don't push it. Even the best of feline friends may become nervous if asked to eat next to each other.

Set the Scent Mood. Pheromone therapy can contribute to an atmosphere of calm and help keep a lid on aggression and tension as you do the reintro. Don't view it as a quick fix to avoid behavior modification, but rather a little assist to keep the cats comfortable enough to consider some degree of social interaction, even if they keep far apart at first.

Scent Swapping. Scent is a very important means of communication among cats. While your cats are separated, it's important to make sure their scents stay distributed around the house. You want the scents to stay fresh, so doing a room swap will help. The cat who had the run of the house has been freely distributing her scent, but we have to make sure the cat in the sanctuary can do that too. Periodically do a scent swap by letting the cat in the sanctuary room out into the house to distribute his scent. Before doing this, place the other cat in a separate room temporarily; it can even be the bathroom, because it's just for a little while. Then you can move that cat into the sanctuary so she can distribute her scent there.

During the scent swap, keep a casual eye on each cat (don't hover or else you risk making them nervous) so you can distract a cat with an interactive toy should tension start to rise. You don't want the scent swap to create anxiety; the point of the exercise is to remind each cat—gently, not overwhelmingly—that the other cat is still around.

You may not have to do the scent swap for very long. The duration will depend on how reactive your cats are and how serious the aggression between them has been in the past.

Social Dining. Now it's time to open the sanctuary room door a bit when feeding the cats. Have the cats eat within sight of each other but far enough apart so nobody feels threatened. Keep these feeding sessions brief by offering a small amount of food. It's more productive to do brief sessions that end on a positive note than to try a long one and risk pushing the cats' limits.

Wide Open Door. Move to this phase when you feel the cats are comfortable with the previous one. Don't rush the process. If in doubt whether it's time to move on, stay at the current stage a bit longer. There's no time schedule here. You want the cats to return to a friendly or at least neutral relationship.

If the thought of the fully opened sanctuary room door is scaring you because you're afraid one cat is going to charge, stack two or three baby gates on top of each other across the entrance. Another option is to install a temporary screen door. The cats will be able to see each other but won't be able to fight. If you choose this interim step, make sure you close the actual sanctuary room door again when the feeding session is done.

As you progress with the feeding sessions, gradually increase the exposure time and start to let them wander around more.

Clicker Training. As you increase the time the cats are exposed to each other, use clicker training. Click and reward for any positive move, however small. Click for any absence of an unwanted behavior. For example, if one cat breaks a stare or walks by the other without hissing or swatting, that cat deserves a reward. If you choose not to clicker-train, offer a food treat or verbal praise for any positive sign.

Use Playtime. Use interactive playtime as a way to help the cats associate positive experiences with being together. Do parallel play by having a fishing pole–type toy in each hand, or if you can, enlist the aid of another family member. The cats shouldn't compete for one toy, lest one be intimidated by the other. When you use two toys, each gets to enjoy the game while seeing the other in peripheral vision.

Tweak the Environment. This is the time to take a new look at your cat environment to see if there's anything you can do to improve enrichment and sense of security. The more interior territory you can create, the easier it'll be for each cat to find enough personal space. Indoors, cats have to overlap most of their personal territory; the more you can help them do this, the better. Use cat trees, perches, and hideaways to create low, medium, and high levels. If you increase the elevated territory in the environment, you increase the cats' perception of the amount of territory they actually have. Vertical territory also helps a cat's sense of safety and security, because he knows it'll be harder for an opponent to sneak up on him from behind. In all directions, the vertical territory makes it easier to see an approaching opponent. The ability to scope out the territory is a big plus from a cat's perspective.

There are many small ways to divert their attention and help them release energy and have fun! Set up food-dispensing toys, puzzle toys, and other opportunities for solo play, like a bird feeder outside the window or some cat shelves for climbing.

If the previous setup included just one litter box and one scratching post, you should increase those numbers. During the time the cats were separated, you already had to increase the number of resources, so keep that up once the cats are together again. The less the cats have to share and/or compete, the less likely they'll fight.

For meals, provide separate bowls for the cats even after they're reunited. This'll lessen the chance of competition and bullying. In some cases, depending on your specific situation, the best way to create peaceful coexistence during mealtime is to feed the cats in separate locations.

Remember the Importance of Choice. A cat who doesn't feel she has a choice is a cat who feels threatened. The cat who feels backed into a corner is the one who'll lash out or display unwanted behavior. As you go through the reintroduction, keep in mind how important *choice* is to a cat, and provide that crucial necessity at each stage.

Question:
What's the best way to introduce dogs and cats?

Pam's Answer:
To keep the cat and dog safe, you must do your homework first, soberly assessing the personality of both the resident animal and the proposed addition to the household. Prepare in advance to try for a compatible match. Once you've picked a companion, you need to do an appropriate introduction. If you simply put a cat and dog together to "work it out," you create a dangerous and potentially deadly situation.

Make a Good Match. Consider the personality and disposition of your current pet. If you have a dog who has been allowed to chase squirrels, cats, birds, or rabbits and has a high prey drive, then adding a cat to the household would probably not be wise. If you know from past experience that your dog has been aggressive toward cats, that's also a sign getting a cat would be too dangerous. If your cat has been aggressive toward dogs in the past, or very afraid of them, adding a dog might add too much stress to her life. If you have a large dog or one who has been allowed to play on the rough side, then consider adding an adult cat to the home and not a small kitten.

Try to match complementary personalities. Don't get a timid cat for a rambunctious dog. Don't match a nervous dog with a revved-up kitten. Look for personalities and dispositions that will go together nicely, rather than opposites.

The Introduction. Before you begin introducing the two pets, clip your cat's nails to reduce any potential damage should the unthinkable occur. Take your dog for a good walk or engage in playtime, so he'll be relaxed, not revved up.

Now for the actual intro: Put your dog on a leash. Don't attempt to do an introduction if your dog isn't leash trained; you need that extra measure of control. Place the cat in a room with a baby gate to prevent the dog from gaining access if he slips out of your grasp. Sit outside the room with your dog and reward him with treats and praise when he focuses on you and not on the cat. You can have toys for him as well. Clicker training is a great tool to use in this situation, so you can click and treat the dog for a relaxed body posture or for turning his attention to you. If the dog gets tense and starts staring at the cat, divert his attention. When he breaks the stare, click and reward.

If the dog isn't comfortable, move farther away from the cat's safe room. As the dog gets more comfortable, you can move closer, a few inches at a time. Stay at a distance that's comfortable for the animal who is most stressed out.

Walk the dog back and forth in front of the safe room and reward him when he focuses on you and follows your cues. If he lunges at the baby gate, growls, barks, or stops walking to stare at the cat, walk him away from the gate until he relaxes. He'll learn that calm behavior lets him stay closer to the baby gate but rambunctious behavior causes him to have to leave the area. Don't yell at your dog or jerk on the leash during this process; simply walk him away from the area and allow him to try again. If he gets reactive, walk away again. He'll eventually get the idea that calmness is the best option.

Making Progress. During the introduction sessions (and it'll take multiple training sessions), if at any time the dog tries to aggressively go after the cat, or if the cat appears dangerously aggressive, then this isn't a safe match. If you feel uncertain as to whether the situation might improve, contact a certified behavior expert to work with you.

During the introduction phase, keep the cat and dog separated unless you're there to supervise. Keep the dog on a leash until you're absolutely sure each animal is comfortable with the other. Never leave the cat and dog unsupervised—even for a few seconds—if you're not sure they have established a safe relationship. This may take days or even weeks.

> ## No Sharing
>
> Cats need more protein and fat in their diet than dogs do. Your dog may want to steal a little of Fluffy's food because of the appealing taste, but it's dangerous to let a dog eat cat food. Establish separate feeding stations.

Environmental modifications should be made to ensure ongoing safety, even after the cat and dog are allowed to be loose. Provide plenty of escape options for the cat, such as a tall, sturdy cat tree or other elevated areas where she can go if the dog chases her. Even after the pets have become friends, a cat may find a dog's play-solicitation attempts disconcerting. The option to escape to higher ground must always be available.

Question:
How can I keep my dog out of the cat's litter box?

Pam's Answer:
It's totally gross to us. Why in the world would the family dog want to sneak into the cat's litter box and steal a few munchies? Yet it happens in homes every day. Many dogs just love to eat cat poop!

Understanding the Behavior. There have been many theories as to why dogs engage in this behavior—coprophagy, or the eating of feces—and they include compulsive behavior, boredom, and nutritive value. It is a common behavior in many dogs. It's seen more in puppies, but some dogs never grow out of it.

If your dog engages in this behavior, contact your veterinarian to make sure there isn't a nutritional issue going on and also to discuss the possibility of any behavior problem as the underlying cause, especially if your dog is also eating his own feces or the feces of other dogs. Your veterinarian may give you a taste deterrent product and/or offer some dog training guidance or give you a referral to a behavior expert.

How This Affects Your Cat. The litter box is a sacred place from your cat's perspective. If she finds shreds of feces strewn across the carpet or, worse, finds the dog with his head in the box, the cat won't have a comforting feeling. The litter box could feel unsafe to her if the dog shoves his nose in there whenever he pleases. He may begin to follow your cat to the box in the hope of receiving a fresh snack. If you have a covered litter box, the cat may feel trapped inside if the dog stands right at the entrance.

Create a Dog-Free Litter Box Zone. While you're figuring out the cause and doing necessary training with the dog, it's time to tweak the litter box setup. If the dog can't get to the cat's poop, then he can't eat it. Simple as that. The litter box must be convenient for the cat but inconvenient for the dog.

The easiest way to keep the dog out of the box is to place the litter box in a place he can't get to. If the dog is bigger than the cat, place a hinged baby gate in the doorway to a room but raise it up a few inches from the floor so the cat can easily go underneath. You can also cut a little entrance in the middle of the gate so the cat can slip through but the dog can't. If using a gate with a mesh-type center, cut a square out that'll easily accommodate your cat and then secure a wooden frame around it so there's no jagged mesh exposed.

If the dog is small and could fit under the gate, put the baby gate at normal height, but place a box, stool, or other object just inside the room, on the other side of the gate, so the cat can get over and will have something to land on.

If the cat doesn't have any difficulty climbing or making a small jump, then there's another option. If you have a small dog, you may be able to simply put the box on some kind of platform.

If the litter box is elevated and you have a cat who needs a little help getting to it, place a cat tree nearby so she can easily climb up and over to reach the box. The carpeted perches on the cat tree will make it easier for her to grip. If using the option of putting a cat tree near the box, make sure you also provide an additional cat tree away from the box so she has a safe elevated resting area that isn't near her toileting spot. No one likes to sleep in the bathroom. Monitor your cat's ability to get to the box as well. As mobility decreases, you need to create a setup that's easier to navigate without any climbing.

What Not to Do. Don't resort to using a covered litter box or stick the box in a closet with a pet door. Cats do like some privacy but not covered boxes or ones hidden in closets. Those boxes limit escape potential. When a cat has only one way in and out of the box, she can be ambushed by another companion animal. Many covered boxes also can make cats feel cramped when taking care of personal business.

Question:

My son wants to get a gerbil. How can I train my cat to stay away from it?

Pam's Answer:

While there are certainly multispecies households, I would strongly advise not asking predators and prey to live together. One bite or scratch from a cat could easily maim or kill a bird, gerbil, mouse, or other tiny pet.

Mixed Messages. I think it sends a confusing and frustrating message to the cat that she can chase, pounce, and attack birdlike toys or even be let outdoors to hunt but then must live with prey but not be able to hunt it.

The Stress Factor. Even if you manage to train the cat to stay away from the prey, imagine the stress that the bird, gerbil, or other pet lives with daily. That animal doesn't know he's safe; all the little pet knows is that he can see, smell, and hear a predator nearby. A bird in his cage high above the cat or the mouse in his habitat still experiences all of the extreme stress of being in the presence of a predator.

Chapter 11

Fraidy Cat

*Convincing your cat to
come out of hiding*

Question:
Should I worry about how often my cat gets stressed?

Pam's Answer:
When I talk to some people about how stress affects their cats, I sometimes get very strange looks. When I first started my cat behavior consulting business, the idea of understanding stress in cats was pretty much unheard of. I even remember being laughed at when I started talking to my clients about cat stress. Cats experiencing stress? What nonsense! These days, the veterinary world is doing more and more to educate clients about stress in cats, and veterinarians work hard to minimize stress in the clinic. For some cat parents, though, even with more information available about how stress affects cats, the idea that their

pampered pet could have anything to feel stressed about is a ridiculous one. Is it really ridiculous? Absolutely not. All animals react to stress, and it can be dangerous, so it's important to learn the signs and evaluate your cat's situation to see if there's anything that can be done to keep stress levels to a minimum.

Understanding Cat Stress. No one, not even your cat, can escape a certain amount of stress in life. In fact, some stress is necessary for survival. If your cat perceives an immediate threat, it's the acute stress response that triggers the release of hormones responsible for the fight-or-flight (or freeze) response. The fear from the impending threat and the stress response it triggers is what prepares the cat to fight it out or retreat. This acute stress response is short-lived, and once the threat is over, the cat's physiological systems return to normal.

Cat parents are likely to recognize acute stress. The cat's ears are usually laid back flat, the pupils dilated, and the body crouched; the cat often hisses or growls. Just think about how most cats look on the exam table at the vet's office or when one outdoor cat comes face-to-face with an unfamiliar cat.

Chronic Stress. Chronic stress is easily missed by cat parents. Chronic stress occurs when the cat is left in a state of uncertainty over a long period of time, not because of a single event. Think of a cat forced to live every day with another cat who displays constant hostility, or a cat living in an environment where the litter box is dirty and unappealing. What about the cat confined to a cage in a shelter for months? What about the indoor/outdoor cat who has moved to a new neighborhood and is put outside every day with no safe retreat back to the security of his home? These are just a couple of examples, but there are so many other situations that could create chronic stress. It's important to look at your cat's world from his point of view. Use your CatWise skills to see what might be the stress culprit. Pay attention to your cat's movements and behavior. Your cat is a marvelous communicator. His behavior patterns and body language provide volumes of information. The problem is, many times we're too busy to notice, or we fall into the pattern of assuming cats are low maintenance or unsociable, so we brush off those behavior changes.

The cat's body is equipped to handle short-term stress. It's the chronic, long-term stress that can cause behavior problems and even disease. The body wasn't designed to handle ongoing, relentless stress.

Signs of chronic stress can be very easy for cat parents to miss. The cat may start hiding more often or might have a decrease in appetite. Maybe the cat has started being inconsistent in using the litter box. Because most of the behaviors happen slowly over time, they can be easily overlooked or attributed to something else.

Some Cats Handle Stress Better Than Others. There's a genetic component to how well your cat handles stress. How she was socialized also plays a significant role. A cat who was exposed to a variety of sights, sounds, and people as a kitten stands a better chance of coping with stress than the cat who didn't receive this training. Stress felt by the queen can also be transmitted to the kittens. The other big factor is the environment, a cause that I find many people miss. A person may bring a cat indoors, provide complete safety and the best health care, but not realize that neglecting environmental enrichment may create stress. Maybe the cat parent is unaware that the noisy, chaotic home environment is frightening to the cat and on a day-to-day basis it's contributing to continued stress. Even the most loving cat parent may be unaware that insistent, inappropriate attempts at interaction with the newly acquired, frightened shelter cat may appear threatening. With no relief from the forced physical contact, the cat becomes chronically stressed.

Individuality

Don't assume that all the cats in a household can handle the same level of stress or will display stress-related behavior the same way.

How Do You Help a Stressed-Out Cat? The first step is to figure out the stress trigger. You can provide a loving, warm, wonderful home for your cat, but if he feels he's living in hostile territory because your other cat relentlessly ambushes him, then that environment, no matter how cushy, is stressful. Look at your cat's environment through his eyes. Imagine how it would be if you felt your home wasn't safe. Imagine having to worry about being attacked every time you walked into the kitchen or bathroom. How stressed would you be if someone bullied you during meals and made you so afraid that you had to sneak into the kitchen to eat when no one was around? Or what if you were forced to use a filthy bathroom day after day? Look at your world from your cat's point of view and you'll be surprised how many stress triggers you'll see—many of which can be modified or eliminated. No, you won't be able to take away all of your cat's stress, but if you start considering his point of view, you'll discover many little (and some big) adjustments that'll make a huge difference.

Here Are Some Suggestions to Get You Started:

- Help your cat get comfortable with the cat carrier so car travel won't be so frightening.
- Take your cat to a veterinary clinic that has worked to create a cat-friendly practice.
- Address multicat tension issues now, before they get any worse.
- Make sure there are adequate resources for each cat, to reduce competition and guarding.
- Maintain good litter box hygiene.
- Create environmental enrichment in the home.
- Socialize your cat by gradually and gently exposing him to novel stimuli.
- Ease your cat through life transitions rather than making abrupt changes.
- Maintain your cat's veterinary care.
- Engage your cat in daily interactive play sessions.
- Do gradual, positive new-pet introductions.
- Provide good quality nutrition.
- Provide cozy hiding options for napping.
- Increase vertical territory.
- Educate family members about what the cat needs.
- Be consistent in training.
- Provide choice.

Each situation is unique. This list gives you just an idea of what your cat might need. What's most important is to look at your cat's circumstances and figure out what might be causing the ongoing stress. In some cases, all that will be needed are some minor tweaks to help him feel more secure. In more serious cases, the ongoing stress response is causing harm to him emotionally and physically. If you feel the cat is too stressed, talk to your veterinarian about a referral to a qualified behavior expert.

Pam's CatWise Clue

What Causes Stress in Cats? Just like some people, some cats are more easily stressed than others. You may have a cat who is normally timid and fearful, whom even small stress triggers leave vulnerable. Things that you may assume are so minor that your cat shouldn't even notice can create stress, such as:

- having new carpet installed
- loud music being played
- dirty litter box conditions
- a change in food brand
- a change in litter brand or type
- travel
- new furniture
- being denied access to particular hiding places
- appearance of a strange cat in the yard
- a barking dog
- visitors in the home
- repairs being done in the home

Big stress triggers are easier to identify because they're usually things that would affect *our* stress level as well, such as:

- divorce
- death in the family
- moving to a new home
- major renovation
- new baby
- illness
- abuse
- addition of a cat or dog to the home

- natural disaster
- injury

Sometimes, though, we get caught up in dealing with our own stress crisis and fail to see how it's also affecting the cat.

Question:

When I was a child my parents had a golden retriever who had separation anxiety. I now have a cat, and I'm sure she has the same thing. Is it possible for cats to experience this? I always thought cats didn't mind being alone.

Pam's Answer:

Many people have an inaccurate image of cats being solitary creatures who don't need companionship, but they actually are social and do form very strong bonds to their human family members and animal companions. They can be lonely and anxious when left alone for too long.

Causes of Separation Anxiety. Cats who were orphaned may be prone to separation anxiety. Too-early weaning can also be a factor. It's my opinion that providing confidence-building interaction with your cat and a cat-friendly environment play critical roles as well. If your cat has no other activities and no ways to build confidence without being attached to you at the hip, there's a good chance of separation anxiety. I believe many cat parents reinforce the separation anxiety by rewarding the cat for clingy, needy behavior, but don't provide proper socialization.

Your cat may go along just fine and have no problem with your coming and going on a daily basis, but then something, such as a change in work schedule, a vacation, or a divorce, could trigger separation anxiety.

Signs of Separation Anxiety in Cats. When the cat parent leaves, the cat may meow excessively. Elimination outside of the litter box might also occur. The cat may urinate or defecate on the cat parent's bed or on clothing belonging to the absent human family member. It's easy to misread this behavior as spite, but it's actually a way for the cat to self-soothe by mixing his scent with yours and to communicate his concern over your absence. The cat may also be trying to help you find your way home.

Other signs of separation anxiety may include excessive grooming, eating too fast, or not eating at all when the cat parent is absent.

Treating Separation Anxiety. Before concluding that your cat has separation anxiety, it's important that he be examined by the veterinarian. His behavior may have an underlying medical cause. Once your cat is diagnosed with separation anxiety, behavior modification techniques can be used to reduce his stress and increase stimulation in your absence.

Increase the environmental enrichment. If you want your cat to feel satisfied, entertained, and secure when you aren't around, then the environment in which he lives has to make him feel that way. Use environmental enrichment to spruce up his indoor surroundings. Incorporate puzzle feeders, puzzle boxes, playtime, elevated areas, hideaways, and more to encourage him to find ways to trigger and satisfy his prey drive. The more enriched and secure the environment is, the better your cat will feel when he's by himself. For enrichment to work effectively, though, don't just toss the puzzle feeders and toys on the floor right before you leave. You first have to incorporate these activities into your cat's life when you're home. Make them a part of his daily schedule so he's totally comfortable with them and even looks forward to their appearance. That way, you'll have a much better chance of success when you set them out before you walk out the door for work.

The Cat Who Misses You Too Much

If puzzle feeders are left untouched upon your return home, that may mean your cat is too distressed to eat. Keep in mind that toys, puzzle feeders, and environmental structures are not replacements for cat parent interaction and proper socialization. Cats are social animals.

A cat tree is a great piece of real estate for a cat. It serves as a place to nap, play, climb, and scratch, and if placed near a window, it will provide a front-row seat for bird-watching. As long as there's no threat of other cats coming into the yard, consider putting a bird feeder outdoors so your cat will have some first-rate entertainment while perched on his cat tree.

Modify *Your* Behavior as Well as His. *Inspire confidence when you interact with your cat.* Don't reward your cat with attention when he's meowing and being insistent. Instead, reward him with petting, treats, praise, and attention when he's acting the way you *want* him to act. Reward him when he's quiet. Reward him when he does something to entertain himself. Reward the behavior you want to see again, and don't reinforce the unwanted behavior.

Engage your cat in interactive play sessions every day. Twice a day would actually be even better. Interactive playtime allows your cat to simply enjoy being the mighty hunter. For a cat, being able to engage the prey drive and enjoy a successful capture is the ultimate in joy and satisfaction.

Don't make a big production about leaving. If you anticipate that your cat is going to suffer separation anxiety, you just make it worse if you overdo the good-bye. Your cat will think you're leaving for a month instead of just eight hours. Make your good-byes very casual. Cats easily pick up on the emotions of their human family members. If you're upset, your cat may get upset.

Practice coming and going. If your cat starts to get tense whenever he hears you pick up your keys or sees you reach for your purse or coat, then practice doing those things several times a day without actually leaving. Pick up your keys and put them back down. Do this multiple times. Later in the day, walk to the door and then back. Do that several times. Now put the two together—pick up your keys, walk to the door and then back. Later in the day, put on your coat and then take it off. Then do all three—put on your coat, get your keys, and walk to the door. Work up to actually walking out the door and then immediately returning. Each time you walk back into the room, greet your cat casually or engage in a little play session. Vary the times you do these training sessions throughout the day or evening. Gradually increase the time spent outside of the home.

TV and Music. There are cat entertainment DVDs available showcasing birds and other interesting little critters. You can have one playing when you're set to walk out the door. Put the TV on a timer so it'll go off after the DVD ends. For music, set the radio to a classical or soft-music station. Just having the music in the background may serve as a buffer for any outside noises that might trigger anxiety. *Through a Cat's Ear* is another option to try. This is a CD of psychoacoustic music designed to create a feeling of calm. It's available online.

If Medication Is Needed. There are some cases in which medication may be needed in conjunction with behavior modification. Your veterinarian or a veterinary behaviorist will advise based on the specifics of the cat's case. If medication is prescribed, it *must* be used with appropriate behavior modification. It shouldn't be viewed as a substitute for doing the behavior work needed to relieve the cat's anxiety.

Question:
How can I help my cat not be so afraid of things? I have the poster-child fraidy cat.

Pam's Answer:
Many things can cause a cat to become fearful, such as:

- Lack of socialization as a kitten
- Being the target of aggression by other animals
- Pain and illness
- Being the target of abuse
- Stressful living conditions (too many cats, dirty conditions, tense family environment, etc.)
- A move to an unfamiliar environment (new home, being relinquished to shelter or being rehomed)
- Change in family (new cat parent, death, divorce, or new baby)
- Excessive ongoing noise

Here are some ideas to help create more security for a fearful cat:

Hideaways. A fearful cat feels more secure if he knows he can't be seen. Ironically, having a secure place to hide periodically may soothe him into coming out more often. There should be hiding places set up for him in all the rooms he frequents. If you want to encourage your cat to venture out from under the bed, you need to set up cozy alternatives for him. A-frame cat beds are great hideaways because the cat can peer out if he wishes, but he knows he won't be attacked from behind. High-sided donut beds are also good. Cats love being able to curl up into a tight little ball and feel the sides of the bed surrounding them.

Create homemade hideaways with cardboard boxes. Place the box on its side and let one of the flaps hang down so the opening is partially covered. Line the box with a towel or cat bed.

A cat tree is a great piece of real estate for a cat, but if he's fearful, he may not be secure enough being so exposed on a perch. If that's the case, choose a cat tree that has at least one semi-enclosed perch, or you can place an A-frame bed on one of the perches. Some fearful kitties actually like being on an open perch up high, because it gives them a visibility advantage. They have more warning time to see someone approaching. Being on the top perch of the cat tree also keeps the fearful cat from being attacked from behind.

Interact at the Cat's Pace. If you think you'll be able to help your cat to get over his fear by forcibly holding him in your arms or insisting that he interact with family members, you're very mistaken. All you'll do is severely set back the trust-building process.

What a fearful cat needs is choice. If he feels he has the choice whether or not to move closer and check things out or interact with you, then he'll be more relaxed about it. A cat who feels he has no choice will always feel backed in a corner and will look for the first opportunity to bolt for cover.

Because some fearful cats choose to freeze rather than flee or fight, you can easily misinterpret this behavior as calmness. Before you assume that the cat is relaxed, carefully evaluate the body language and immediate environment. Airplane ears, dilated pupils, lowered head, crouching, and tense body position aren't signs that your cat is merely chilling out.

Offer Incentive. Keep treats on hand, and whenever your cat makes even the smallest positive step, reward him with something yummy. Clicker training works well in this type of situation. You can click and reward for any behavior you'd like to see again, such as walking into the room or poking his head out from under the bed.

If your fearful cat won't take the treat from your hand, then gently toss it closer to him. If the treat consists of wet food, place a little on a chopstick in order to put a distance between you and the cat. Many times for fearful cats I've taped soft-tipped baby spoons to the end of a chopstick in order to give the cat a larger amount of wet food without getting too close.

Peace and Quiet

Place your cat's food bowl in an area that provides security. Don't place the feeding station near a window or sliding glass door. The appearance of outdoor animals may cause your cat to feel threatened.

Playtime. Use a fishing-pole toy to encourage your fearful cat to play. The pole puts a distance between you and the cat, so he'll be able to stay in his comfort zone. If he's more comfortable being partially hidden under the bed or behind a chair, you can still offer playtime opportunities with the fishing pole. The movement you do should not be frantic or over-the-top, though. A fearful cat doesn't want to view the toy as an opponent. Make your motions low-key, and make it easy for him to conquer his prey. And sit on the floor or in a chair when playing, so you don't hover over the cat.

Choose your interactive toy based on your cat's personality. If he's extremely frightened, you may need to start with something like a feather and gradually work up to more challenging toys.

Resources. If you want your cat to feel comfortable venturing out from under the bed, create secure paths to resources, such as the litter box, scratching post, and feeding station. If he doesn't feel safe, you'll never see him during the day, because he'll wander out to eat or use the litter box only in the middle of the night when the family is asleep. Locate resources so the cat doesn't have to walk across the house to reach them. You can even create little tunnels along the way so he remains partially hidden. You can use soft-sided fabric tunnels (available at your local pet-product store and online), or you can make your own by connecting several paper bags that have the bottoms cut out. You can also use boxes or even large cardboard tubing.

Body Language. Observe and respect your fearful cat's body language. Respect his communication signals. If his body language is saying, "Please don't come closer," and you continue to move toward him, he'll soon learn to dart away whenever you approach. A fearful cat will typically crouch low.

Environmental Enrichment. In addition to the hideaways, the cat tree, and interactive playtime, pique his curiosity and trigger his desire to play by creating a more interesting environment overall. Put out some puzzle feeders and distribute interesting little toys for him to bat around during solo playtime. They will help him form positive associations with his surroundings.

Question:

My cat is afraid of thunderstorms. Is there anything I can do to help him?

Pam's Answer:

Thunderstorms can be very unsettling. Dogs are typically the ones who start shaking, crying, or hiding when Mother Nature gives a sound-and-light show, but cats can also become nervous. If thunderstorms cause your cat anxiety, here are six tips to help you maintain calm during the storm:

1. Be Aware of Your Body Language. If the storm makes *you* nervous, your cat is likely to pick up on that anxiety. Cats are masters at reading body language, and they know when we aren't behaving and moving as we usually do. I have always referred to cats as little emotional sponges, so make sure you aren't giving off visible nervous behavior that might be soaked up by any feline family members. Do your best to assume a calm demeanor.

2. Provide Cozy Hideaways. Probably the most comforting way for your cat to ride out the storm is to be curled up and hidden. Provide several cozy hideaways for him so he doesn't have to hunker down under the bed or in a corner of the closet. A pyramid-style bed may provide added security for an anxious cat. If you have some hideaways in places where you spend the most time, they might encourage your cat to stay in the room with you rather than duck under the bed in a room by himself. If your cat prefers to be alone, consider setting up a sanctuary room where he can have hiding options and necessary resources.

3. Comfort, but Don't Reinforce Fear. You can pet and comfort your cat, but do so in a way that sends a calming signal. If you coddle too much, you may send a reinforcement signal conveying that he's right to be scared. You don't want to reinforce the fearful behavior or reward it, and this is a surprisingly easy mistake to make.

4. Pheromone Therapy. The commercial pheromone product Feliway mimics the calming natural facial pheromones cats have. You can buy the pheromone product at your local pet-product store, at a veterinary clinic, or online. Just give a little spritz to objects in the room, or use it in the diffuser version. If you know a thunderstorm is predicted, plug in the diffuser in advance. If using the spray version, spray the corners of objects where cats would normally facially rub. Keep the cat out of the room for about thirty minutes to allow the alcohol in the product to dry. Once dried, there's no scent detectable by humans. The spray is good for specific targeting, and the diffuser is good for general coverage of an area.

5. Antianxiety Wraps. There is a pressure wrap called the Thundershirt, which works by applying gentle pressure that provides the same calming effect that swaddling has on infants. As with pheromone therapy, some cat parents report that the wrap works well, but others say it has no effect. The wrap comes with a full set of instructions, and it's very important that you follow them. Take your cat's measurements so you'll buy the right size. Sizing is based on weight and chest size.

The problem with the anxiety wrap is the cat may simply freeze; while he may look calm, he might actually still be anxious. You know your cat best, so if you use the wrap, make sure the cat really does appear calm. I've seen immediate positive results with the Thundershirt in some cases but no effect in others. If your cat is very frightened by storms, it's worth a try.

6. Sound Therapy. You can slowly desensitize your cat with thunderstorm CDs. Play one at very low volume while engaging your cat in interactive play. Gradually increase the volume during the training sessions. Terry Ryan sells a series of sound-effects CDs called Sounds Good, created to help dogs overcome sound-related fears, but they're just as effective for cats. There's one of thunderstorm sounds.

One thing I did with my cats, and also my children when they were small, was to play New Age music CDs that had rain and thunderstorm sounds in the background. The music was calming for all of us, and they got used to hearing thunder. While the music was playing, I would engage everyone in playtime, or we'd have snacks.

Question:

Maddie gets so worked up at the animal hospital. What can I do to reduce her stress?

Pam's Answer:

It doesn't take a rocket scientist to figure out that going to the vet is not high on a cat's list of favorite places to visit. Without any warning, the cat is shoved into a carrier, put in a car, and whisked off to a place that smells, looks, and sounds scary. In the exam room, she's removed from the carrier, placed on a cold exam table, and then poked and prodded. It makes perfect sense to fight with all her might to make sure she never has to go back there.

Because it certainly isn't a good idea to avoid taking your cat to the veterinarian, you need to have a plan. If your current plan consists of chasing the cat through the house, cornering her, and then battling to shove her into the carrier without becoming the victim of a furry slasher, then it's time to come up with Plan B, because Plan A stinks. There's a better way. Here's my list of dos and don'ts.

Do Look for a Feline-Friendly Veterinary Clinic. Look for a clinic that has separate waiting areas for cats and a separate feline-only exam room. There are even cat-exclusive veterinary clinics.

Don't Choose a Clinic Based on Convenience. Tour the clinic and meet the veterinarian(s) beforehand to make certain that it's the right place for your cat.

Do Pay Attention to How Your Cat Is Treated. Does the veterinarian take time to greet the cat and try to get her comfortable? Is restraint used immediately without first seeing if a "less is more" technique will be more effective and less stressful to your cat? Does the veterinarian communicate clearly to you?

Don't Take the Carrier Out Only When It's Time to Go to the Vet. This is sure to cause panic in your cat as she learns to associate its appearance with something unpleasant. Leave the carrier out all the time so it becomes a neutral object in the environment.

Do Train Your Cat to Be Comfortable in the Carrier. Offer treats and feed your cat near the carrier and then eventually inside the carrier, so she associates it with positive experiences.

Don't Try to Grab Your Cat at the Last Minute. Dragging the cat out from under the bed is guaranteed to create stress. Plan ahead so you can do this in a relaxed way and won't have to keep a large supply of bandages in the medicine cabinet. Spray Feliway in the carrier, or use the towelette version twenty to thirty minutes before putting your cat inside.

Do Take the Time to Desensitize Your Cat to Car Travel. Put the cat in the carrier and then place the carrier in the car for a few minutes. In subsequent sessions, work up to starting the engine, and then take short drives around the block. To help a cat relax during car travel, the trip shouldn't always end at the veterinary clinic.

Don't Forgo Your Cat's Medical Care Because of the Way She Acts at the Clinic. Routine veterinarian exams are crucial to your cat's health.

Do Handle the Carrier Gently When the Cat Is Inside. Be mindful of holding it steady and not swinging it around or bumping into things. When driving, try to make smooth turns and stops. The last thing your cat needs is for you to focus on her so much that you come up to a stoplight too fast and have to slam on the brakes.

Don't Spook Your Cat with Baby Talk. You'll only make your cat more nervous by talking in a high-pitched voice or baby talk. And don't stick your fingers into the carrier to pet her. Let her settle down and have this time to be invisible. If your cat gets very panicky, play the *Through a Cat's Ear* CD during the ride.

Do Schedule Periodic Visits to the Clinic just to get your cat comfortable with being in the environment. Quick visits in which the cat gets greeted and petted by a staff member may help reduce fear during future visits. This is especially beneficial if you're training a kitten.

Don't Schedule Your Appointment for the Doctor's Busiest Time. Unless you have no other option, avoid Saturday appointments.

Do Cover the Carrier. Draping a towel over it means your cat won't feel so exposed. Bring a couple of extras, so you can place one on the exam table and one over your cat. The scent of something familiar, combined with being able to remain somewhat hidden, may provide more comfort.

Don't Let Other People or Dogs Come up to the Carrier. Politely inform approaching children that your cat is nervous and needs her space.

Do Bring Treats. Snacks, an interesting toy, or even some catnip will help calm and distract your cat during the appointment.

Don't Pull the Cat out of the Carrier. Don't tilt it or hold it in the air to shake the cat out, either. Instead, open the door and give the cat the option to explore and venture out without being yanked out.

Do Give the Cat the Option of Remaining in the Carrier for as Much of the Exam as Possible. If you use a kennel-type carrier, remove the top and let the cat remain in the bottom half. Place a towel over her, as well, so she can feel invisible.

Don't Yell at the Cat. Don't yell or scold her for hissing, growling, or even scratching. If your cat reacts negatively because she's very frightened, punishing only heightens her fear.

Do Learn Your Window of Opportunity as to when your cat reaches her tolerance limit. Don't keep the cat on the exam table after the examination while you and the veterinarian talk. Let her go back into her carrier rather than risk her fidgeting and getting more stressed.

Don't Assume That There's Only One Way. For the physical exam, some cats do better in the cat parent's lap than on the table.

Do Move the Carrier out of Sight. If the cat's exam takes place on the table, she won't struggle to bolt back into the carrier while the veterinarian is trying to do the physical exam.

Don't Place a Cat on a Slippery, Cold Exam Table. First put down a towel, fleece pad, or some other padding. You can also put a rubber mat on the table first to prevent the towel from sliding all over. Feeling that she has something to grip will give your cat a little more security.

Do as Much Advance Preparation as Possible. Write down any questions or concerns you have about your cat's health problem or behavior.

You may even want to take some video on your smartphone if that's the best way to demonstrate a particular behavior or issue.

Don't Expect Your Cat to Be Sociable Immediately. After your return home, she may need time to groom herself and get comfortable in her environment again.

Do Give Your Cat Time by Herself. Scent is a major form of communication between cats, and it's normal for the cats who stayed home to feel threatened by the vet clinic scents on their feline companion. If you have a multicat home, give the returning cat some alone time.

Don't Spread the Vet Scent. Wash the carrier and towels before putting them back in your cat's environment. The last thing your cat wants when she's back home is the lingering scent of the clinic.

The Value of a Life

Many cats are acquired by rescue or adoption without cost or are impulsively acquired when one discovers a mother cat and her kittens under one's porch. Nevertheless, they need the same lifelong veterinary care as the most expensive purebred purchased from a breeder.

Your cat needs good veterinary care throughout her life. It's important for cats to have yearly exams and for geriatric cats to have twice-yearly exams. In addition to the routine wellness exams, it's also crucial to have your cat receive veterinary care at the first sign of a potential medical problem. You may not ever be able to completely reduce the stress a cat may feel during the veterinary visit or even during the trip to the clinic, but you can reduce some of that fear, and every little bit counts.

Mobile Veterinary Care. If it's simply impossible to get your cat to the veterinary clinic, look into mobile veterinary services. There may be a mobile veterinarian in your area who can come directly to your home.

Pam's CatWise Clue

Eight Tips on How to Be a Good Veterinary Client

1. Turn Your Cell Phone Off. While in the exam room, don't take phone calls or text. Focus your full attention on your cat and what the doctor is saying and doing. In addition to being rude, you stand a good chance of missing important information your veterinarian may be trying to convey.

2. Prepare Ahead of Time. Write down any questions you have for the veterinarian. It's easy to forget something once you get inside the exam room. If you have a question about a particular behavior problem, it might be very helpful for your veterinarian to actually see it, so if possible, capture the behavior on your smartphone.

3. Be on Time. Respect the veterinarian's time and the time of other clients. Do your part by showing up on time. Your veterinarian may run late due to an emergency, so be tolerant of delays.

4. Transport Your Cat in a Carrier. A carrier, whether it's a hard plastic kennel type or a soft-sided luggage type, will greatly reduce your cat's stress and ensure her safety. Unrestrained animals in a vehicle pose a serious danger to the driver. Unrestrained animals in the clinic become very stressed and add to the anxiety of other animals around them. The safest way for your cat to be transported to the clinic (or anywhere else, for that matter) is in a carrier.

5. Don't Complain to the Receptionist About How Much Services Cost. First of all, the receptionist doesn't set the price. Moreover, animals are living longer because of advancements in veterinary care, but that comes with a price. The latest technology and medication does cost more. If you can't afford the proposed treatment, talk to your veterinarian about a payment plan. If you think you're being ripped off, discuss it with the clinic manager or veterinarian, and if you're still unsatisfied, then look for another clinic. Veterinarians aren't getting rich off their clients. The advanced technology needed for clinics to stay up-to-date comes at a price. You have a right to question fees, but do so in the same way you'd like to be addressed. Standing at the front desk and loudly complaining is unpleasant for everyone in the clinic.

6. Take Notes. If you're being told a list of instructions from the veterinarian, ask for written instructions or take your own notes. You can also record the instructions. You don't want to have to call the clinic with a problem because you forgot something.

7. Follow the Veterinarian's Instructions. Compliance is a huge factor in whether your cat responds to home care. Whether it has to do with specific feeding instructions, physical exercise, cage rest, behavior modification, or medication, be sure to comply with instructions.

8. Communicate. If you're unhappy with service, talk with the veterinarian to give him or her a chance to correct the problem. Your veterinarian may be unaware of something going on in the clinic in terms of how your cat was treated or how a staff member interacted with you. On the other hand, it's also important to let the veterinarian know when you're pleased with service. If a staff member in the clinic has gone above and beyond, be sure you let that person and the veterinarian know how much that thoughtfulness is valued.

Question:
Why is my cat grooming himself so much? He has created bald patches on his body.

Pam's Answer:
Psychogenic alopecia is the formal name for this condition, in which the cat engages in excessive grooming that becomes an OCD-type behavior. This goes beyond the normal fastidious grooming a cat would do. It begins as a displacement behavior used for stress reduction. Sometimes the excessive licking eventually turns into actually pulling out clumps of hair or even chewing on the skin.

Any number of things could trigger the need for the behavior. Here are a few possibilities:

- The addition of another cat
- Move to a new home
- Renovation in the home
- Addition of a new family member
- Death or divorce
- Living in a chaotic environment

- Lack of environmental stimulation
- Boredom
- Depression
- Confinement (such as hospitalization or boarding)
- Litter box problems
- Change in litter box setup or location
- Change in food
- Unhealthy living conditions

When it comes to the stressors that could potentially lead to psychogenic alopecia, keep in mind that they're different for each cat. One cat may handle a major change in the environment while another cat may feel the need for a displacement behavior if you so much as rearrange the furniture. Things you don't view as stressful could actually cause your cat a large amount of stress. Each cat has a unique tolerance threshold.

Understanding Displacement Behavior. A certain amount of displacement behavior like excess grooming is normal in a cat's world. It helps reduce the anxiety a cat feels in a particular situation. The problem occurs when there's no relief from that anxiety, so the cat continues the displacement behavior in order to self-soothe. Ongoing situations that produce anxiety without relief may lead the cat to require the displacement behavior to a point where it becomes obsessive.

Other Causes of Excessive Grooming. Before labeling the condition as psychogenic alopecia, it's important to rule out other potential causes for excessive grooming such as:

- Skin conditions
- Pain
- External parasites
- Allergies
- Hyperthyroidism
- Cystitis or other urinary tract problem

Your cat must be seen by the veterinarian to rule out any potential underlying medical condition causing the behavior. In addition to diagnostic testing, clues to the cause of the behavior may be revealed by the body location the cat is licking. If the diagnosis is psychogenic alopecia, your veterinarian may refer you to a veterinary behaviorist or other certified behavior expert.

Treatment for Psychogenic Alopecia. There are three major components to helping a cat with psychogenic alopecia:

- Reduce stress.
- Create security.
- Increase environmental enrichment (i.e., make life fun again!).

Carefully evaluate your cat's living conditions so you can discover the possible cause(s) of his anxiety. Cats don't like change, so if you've been inconsistent with the feeding schedule or less than diligent about litter box maintenance, that could be a source of anxiety. If your work schedule has changed or you've entered into a new relationship that causes your cat to be alone for longer periods, that sudden change and increased solitary time could be the root of the problem.

Multipet environments can provide wonderful companionship for cats, but they can also be an ongoing source of stress or fear. If your overgrooming cat shares his home with other pets, it's time to look at the relationships and see whether there's hostility or intimidation. Perhaps the cat feels afraid to cross another cat's preferred area to gain access to resources.

If you have no clue as to the source of stress, consider setting up a nanny cam so you can catch potential triggers as they happen during the day or night when you aren't around.

An enriched and interesting environment is another important aspect of feline life. Cats are predators. They were born to explore, hunt, and use their senses. Psychogenic alopecia may be the result of your cat simply having absolutely nothing to do. Set up puzzle feeders, puzzle boxes, and other solo activities to keep your cat engaged during the day. Make sure there are adequate climbing opportunities in the form of a cat tree, cat shelving, or window perches. Rotate toys to prevent boredom, and when you place them out, hide them around the house so your cat can go on treasure hunts.

Engage in interactive playtime at least twice a day to help provide exercise, fun, and bonding time with you.

Medication. If your cat isn't responding enough to behavior modification, your veterinarian or veterinary behaviorist may recommend adding medication. If so, it should be used in conjunction with behavior modification, so if it's prescribed, don't drop the ball when it comes to the hands-on work the human family members need to do to help the cat recover.

Chapter 12

Don't Do That

Training your cat to stop doing those things that really annoy you

Question:
I love my cat, Midnight, very much, but I just don't understand why he misbehaves so much. Do cats do things because they're mad at you?

Pam's Answer:
In tackling behavior problems, we fail from the get-go when we assume the cat's motivation is spite, anger, or stupidity. I promise you, your cat isn't off in a corner plotting to ruin your life. A cat "misbehaving" is actually a cat trying to solve a problem.

Misbehavior or Misunderstood Behavior? Every behavior a cat displays serves a function, or it wouldn't be repeated. Animals aren't stupid. The key to successful behavior modification is to figure out what triggers the repeated behavior and what the cat gets from it so you can change the conditions. To change the outcome you have to change the setup.

Effective behavior modification gives the cat an alternative behavior of the same or more value than the unwanted behavior. Force-free training sets the cat up to succeed because it provides the things he needs and allows him to make the choice. The animal who doesn't have any choices is the one who reacts out of fear. Many cats are relinquished to shelters, banished to the outdoors, abandoned, or even euthanized for behavior problems that are correctable.

Be CatWise and realize that the unwanted behaviors are not abnormal. You may not like them, but the cat isn't crazy or spiteful. He's responding to what his instincts tell him. If he scratches the furniture, he isn't intentionally shredding your favorite chair. He has a natural need to scratch and will seek out the most effective object for that function. If the scratching post doesn't meet his needs, then his intelligent brain directs him to something that works better.

The Four Steps to Correct Unwanted Behavior. Caught up in wrong assumptions about a cat's motivation, cat parents often accept bad advice from unqualified people. That's a shame, because much of behavior correction comes down to common sense:

- Discover the underlying cause.
- Identify what the cat is getting from the behavior (the payoff).
- Provide an alternative as good as or better than the current behavior.
- Reward the cat for the desired behavior.

Why Punishment Doesn't Work. Many people reprimand the cat for "misbehavior." Instead of focusing on what the cat needs and how to help him succeed, these cat parents, out of frustration, choose punishment. Imagine the stress the cat endures when he's punished for a behavior that's actually normal and needed in the feline world.

Let's examine litter box problems, for example. The cat stops using the litter box and starts urinating on the carpet in the dining room. The cat parent who punishes—rubs the cat's nose in the mess, hits, yells, sends the cat into time-out, or shoves the cat into the litter box—has succeeded only in elevating the cat's fear and stress to an emotionally and physically unhealthy level. What if the cat was eliminating outside of the box because he was in pain due to a urinary tract problem and associated the box with his pain? Because he'll now associate punishment with the need to eliminate, he's not only in pain from the medical condition, but he's afraid and unsure about where to pee or poop. As a cat parent, you intended to convey the message that the cat's choice for elimination was wrong, but the actual message he received was *urination is bad and will result in punishment and fear*. Because urination will have to occur again at some point when his bladder gets full, he'll become stressed and may try to retain urine as long as possible. That's not physically healthy. He may also attempt to find a more secretive place for elimination to avoid your punishment. Either option causes even more stress to an already stressed-out cat.

Cats Aren't Dogs or Fur-Covered Children. Many behavior problems could be corrected or avoided in the first place if people stopped viewing their cats as child or dog substitutes. Cats should be loved and cherished, but when you forget that they're *cats*, with specific, normal feline needs and an inability to scheme on human terms, you're setting yourself up for failure. When you adopt a cat but expect him to act like a dog and then are disappointed because he doesn't interact with you the way dogs do, you create a lose-lose situation. See cats as the beautiful, intelligent, playful, social creatures that they are, and you might just be surprised by what you can learn. You have an opportunity to have an amazing relationship with the cat in your life if you take the time to look at his world the way he does and stop expecting him to be another species.

Question:
My cat loves to chew on my indoor plants. Is there any way to stop the behavior?

Pam's Answer:
Many houseplants are poisonous to cats. The effects can range from minor irritation to death. Hanging plants create even more enticement, as the kitten or cat bats the plant in play and then bites down. Some cats who don't have enough environmental enrichment can get into the habit of playing with and nibbling on houseplants just out of boredom.

What Plants Are Poisonous? For a list of poisonous plants, visit the ASPCA Web site. The site contains many pictures for identification. Here's the ASPCA list of the seventeen plants most poisonous to cats:

- Lilies
- Marijuana
- Sago Palm
- Tulip/Narcissus Bulb
- Azalea/Rhododendron
- Oleander
- Castor Bean
- Cyclamen
- Kalanchoe
- Yew
- Amaryllis
- Autumn Crocus
- Chrysanthemum
- English Ivy
- Peace Ivy
- Pothos
- Schefflera

There are some common plants, such as dieffenbachia, that can cause intense burning and swelling of the tongue after just a few small bites. This can lead to difficulty in breathing. I see these plants included in many gift arrangements.

It's important to make sure all potentially dangerous plants are kept completely out of reach. Some plants can cause immediate death no matter how quickly you get help, so know the plants you have and remove the ones that are dangerous.

Signs of Plant Poisoning. Many of the signs will depend on the type of plant ingested. Some signs may include:

- Excessive salivation
- Vomiting
- Difficulty in breathing
- Diarrhea
- Fever

- Abdominal pain
- Mouth and throat ulcers
- Trembling
- Irregular heartbeat
- Red, itchy skin around the mouth

Treatment for Plant Poisoning. If you think your cat has chewed on a poisonous plant, contact your veterinarian immediately. If it's after hours and there isn't an animal emergency clinic in your area, call the ASPCA Poison Control Hotline. The treatment will depend on the type of plant ingested. If you can't identify the plant, take it or a piece of it to the veterinary emergency clinic with you, because they may be able to identify it. Your veterinarian isn't necessarily a plant and garden expert, but you stand a much better chance of helping your cat if you bring the plant with you so they can attempt identification.

Keep Your Cat Safe. In our house, we've decided it's not worth the risk, so we don't keep live plants indoors. If you decide to keep plants or have chosen to keep only the ones that aren't deadly, make sure you coat them with a bitter anti-chew spray. Spray the plants, including the undersides of the leaves, being careful not to get any on your hands. I recommend wearing disposable gloves because the spray *really* tastes awful. If you spray the plant indoors, protect your floors and carpets by putting newspaper down around the plant first. In some cases you may have to do a repeat spray in a couple of weeks.

Keep hanging plants cut short to reduce temptation. Keep in mind that cats love to sun themselves at a window and watch the birds. To reduce temptation, make sure your cat has several safe, plant-free window-lounging locations. Put a window perch at your cat's favorite window or locate a cat tree nearby.

Redirect your cat's interest to more interesting things. If the plant nibbling is happening out of boredom, step up the environmental enrichment. Here are some examples:

- Conduct interactive play therapy sessions at least twice a day.
- Incorporate the use of food-dispensing toys and puzzles.
- Rotate toys to keep them interesting.
- Put out some boxes or open paper bags with toys inside.
- Get a sturdy cat tree and place it by a window.

- Keep a lid on the stress level in the home.
- Provide cat-safe chewing options (such as cat dental chew products).

Grow Safe Greenery for Your Cat's Nibbling Pleasure. If you have a hardcore plant nibbler, try redirecting that instinct by growing some safe kitty greens. You can buy these kits online or at your local pet product store. Squares of rye, wheat, or oat grass are available at local organic grocery stores. You can also grow your own from seeds. Don't use grass from the lawn because of the chemical fertilizers, weed killers, and pesticides it may contain.

Question:
When I'm on the computer, my cat always bites me, but not hard, or knocks things off the desk. Is she trying to tell me to pay attention to her?

Pam's Answer:
In two words: probably yes. In general, a cat trying to get your attention will resort to whatever works. Typical behaviors include:

- Meowing
- Pawing
- Jumping up to be at your level
- Walking around and between your legs
- Stealing objects
- Knocking things off tables
- Biting (usually an inhibited bite that doesn't break skin)

Causes of Attention-Seeking Behavior. This behavior can occur as part of another primary behavior problem, as a medical problem, or simply as a ploy to gain your attention. Cats who suffer from separation anxiety or cognitive issues also often engage in attention-seeking behavior. If the behavior is due to an underlying medical issue, the cat may be seeking your attention as a source of relief from her pain. It can also be because she's confused by her discomfort.

To Correct Attention-Seeking Behavior. Here's the hard part: most cat parents reinforce the very behavior they don't like because they acknowledge the cat for displaying it. When the cat jumps on the table and starts meowing, the cat parent will almost always look at, talk to, or pet the cat.

Even if you reprimand the cat, you're offering attention—just what the cat wanted.

Correcting attention-seeking behavior involves three steps:

- Ignore the behavior you don't want.
- Provide other outlets for the cat's energy and attention.
- Give attention to the cat when she's quiet or acting appropriately.

If the attention-seeking behavior is due to boredom or separation anxiety, make sure your cat has adequate environmental enrichment. Here are some examples:

- A cat tree by the window for climbing and watching the birds
- Puzzle feeders and puzzle toys for reward-based object play
- Elevated areas for play and resting
- Scratching posts for scratching
- Adequate climbing opportunities
- A consistent schedule for mealtimes
- A consistent schedule of litter box maintenance
- A daily schedule of interactive play therapy
- Affection (customized to what the cat enjoys) and interaction from you
- Consistency, security, and stimulation

If you aren't consistent in the cat's feeding schedule, litter box cleaning, playtime, training, or even in the time when you come home at the end of the day, your cat won't know when to expect what and so will ask for things more randomly than you'd like. Provide a consistent and reliable schedule, and she probably won't have to resort to the undesirable attention-seeking behavior. If you play with her using an interactive toy but only every few days, then it's understandable why she'd try to get your attention. Cats are hunters who are equipped with sharp senses. They need appropriate energy outlets. They're also creatures of habit who rely on consistency in their daily lives. Combine the security of being consistent with the fun of daily reward-based activities.

Question:
What is wool sucking, and do all cats do this?

Pam's Answer:

I know it probably sounds like a very weird and unappealing thing for a cat (or any other being) to do—sucking on sweaters, shoelaces, and even bathmats and carpets. The commonest items, though, are blankets and sweaters. In some cases, one cat suckles on another cat's tail or other body part.

Some cats even begin chewing on and ingesting the material; that's when wool sucking transitions into pica behavior (the eating of nonfood items). Pica can lead to intestinal problems.

Wool sucking is usually seen in cats under one year of age. Typically, a cat eventually will outgrow the behavior, but some do continue wool sucking if there is no behavior modification or environmental change made.

Here are some factors contributing to wool sucking:

Abrupt or Too-Early Weaning. Wool sucking seems to be a carryover from nursing. There are several theories as to why a cat may continue it as she matures. One contributing factor may be abrupt or too-early weaning of a kitten from the mother. Ideally, kittens should be allowed to stay with the mother until they're twelve weeks old. Many times though, kittens are removed at the frighteningly early age of six weeks just because they're able to eat solid food. Unfortunately, they aren't physically or emotionally ready to be separated from the mother or littermates. Weaning should also be done gradually even when the kittens can eat solid food. There are also social lessons kittens learn during those weeks that are important as they mature. Unfortunately, though, it does happen, whether at the hands of uninformed humans or due to a tragedy in which kittens are orphaned.

If you adopt or rescue a kitten under eight weeks of age, she may exhibit some wool sucking behavior, especially when in a comfortable position, such as on your lap or in your arms. Just because she's capable of eating solid food doesn't mean she feels ready to let go of that comforting feeling of suckling on her mother (or in this case, your sweater). The soft, warm feeling of a blanket or sweater becomes a second choice since mom is no longer available.

Separation Anxiety or Stress. Stress or sudden changes, such as the arrival of a new baby, the sudden absence of a family member, a move to a new home, a too-dense cat population, or unclean living conditions, can result in wool sucking behavior.

Breed Connection. Wool sucking has been found to be more common in Oriental breeds.

Other Factors. Other factors can include lack of environmental stimulation, nutritional deficiencies, lack of dietary fiber, and underlying medical conditions.

Techniques for Discouraging Wool Sucking Behavior. The first and easiest step in the process is to remove or at least reduce access to the tempting material. If the sweater isn't available, the cat can't suck on it. A good excuse to tidy up your room!

Have your cat examined by the veterinarian to rule out any medical cause for the behavior. Talk about your cat's diet in case the veterinarian feels there's a dietary correlation.

Divert your cat's attention by offering her other activities—especially ones that encourage confidence. Playtime is the perfect choice. When you notice your cat getting in the position that usually precedes wool sucking, distract her with a confidence-building activity, such as interactive play. You can also use solo playtime by providing puzzle feeders and solo activity toys.

Increase environmental enrichment by providing places for her to climb, scratch, play, and nap. A cat tree that overlooks an outdoor bird feeder or something else the cat finds interesting would be ideal. Provide sisal scratching posts so she has appealing places to displace anxiety or emotion by scratching on a rough surface. If she likes watching television, get one of the cat entertainment DVDs that showcase prey and other cat-appealing critters.

Reduce anxiety and stress. Make sure the cat's litter box setup is clean, appealing, and in a location where she feels safe and secure. Address any multicat issues so everyone feels more secure.

If separation anxiety is the issue, that must be addressed through appropriate behavior modification (see Chapter 11).

Question:

My cat is a thief! He steals anything small enough to carry in his mouth. How can I stop this behavior?

Pam's Answer:

You're not alone. Many people share their lives with cats who seem to have very sticky paws.

Stealing Food. Cats are predators, and most are extremely food-motivated. So many enticing food aromas pass in front of your cat's nose several times a day that it can be hard for a hungry cat to resist. This is especially true if your cat is on a special diet and not particularly pleased with it.

Food stealing may result from being fed from the dinner table. If you've offered your cat pieces of your own meal as you eat or if you've rewarded her with food when she begs during the family meals, you may have put the notion in her head that she doesn't really have to wait for someone to give food to her—she can just help herself. Offering food from the table can also create an interest in a food she may not have otherwise been attracted to, such as sugary tidbits.

Stealing food can also occur if it's left out on an unattended counter or table. If you know you have a feline food thief, remove temptation by making sure leftovers aren't kept out.

To reduce or eliminate food stealing, incorporate food-dispensing toys into your cat's mealtime routine. Whether you feed wet or dry food, you can buy or construct puzzle feeders to encourage your cat to eat slowly and enjoy some added playtime while eating. For a cat, working for food is natural, and a puzzle feeder is an easy way to get her to do that.

If you feed on a schedule but there's a huge chunk of time between meals, hunger could be motivating food theft. Cats have small stomachs; outdoors they would probably hunt and enjoy several small meals per day. If you feed only once or twice a day, your cat may be getting too hungry. Divide the food into three or four meals a day. Don't increase the amount, just the number of portions.

If you think you may not be feeding enough food to your cat, get your veterinarian's guidance. The labels on pet food packages are meant to be general guidelines. Your veterinarian can help you determine the amount to feed your cat based on her current weight, age, health, and activity level.

Stealing for Play. Some cats steal things just to play with them. Some objects are so light and easily moved with the slightest touch of a paw that it's impossible for a playful cat to pass up a chance for a little game. Before you know it, rubber bands, paper clips, and bottle caps collect under the sofa and the desk.

Unfortunately, many of the objects your cat may steal for play can be potentially harmful. If your cat plays with a rubber band, earring, or other small object and decides to chew on it, it could get swallowed. Cats have backward-facing barbs on their tongues, which make it hard for them to spit out some things once they're in the mouth.

The best solution for a cat who steals objects for play is to put tempting items away and offer safer alternatives. These should come in two forms. First, make sure you engage your cat in a couple of interactive play sessions per day. Interactive play therapy is a great way for you to control the action and give your cat the opportunity to really shine as the mighty hunter. Next, increase the fun factor in your home by stepping up the environmental enrichment. Give your cat something to do during the day while you're at work so she won't feel the need to steal in order to relieve her boredom. I know you have a bunch of solo toys for your cat, but they're probably just scattered around the house gathering dust. Instead, try staging the environment so it'll be more interesting:

- Put a fuzzy mouse inside an empty tissue box.
- Leave out some open paper bags with toys or treats inside.
- Place toys on cat trees.
- Put some furry mice (fake ones, of course) under furniture so just their tails peek out.
- Use food-dispensing toys and other puzzle feeders.
- Place a cat tree near a window.
- Set up some cat tunnels (or make some with open paper bags).
- Install some cat shelves.
- Get a great sisal-covered scratching post.
- Put a bird feeder outside the window for your cat's viewing pleasure.
- Rotate toys weekly to keep them interesting.
- Use catnip once a week.
- Set up a pet water fountain.
- Play a cat-entertainment video that showcases prey.

Stealing for Attention. Some cats steal for attention. Cat parents may reinforce this behavior by their reactions. Even a reprimand is a form of attention. If you've watched the cat play with the object or even participated in the game before taking it away, you've also reinforced the behavior. If your cat learns that stealing results in receiving attention, she'll do it often.

If you think your cat is stealing as an attention-getting behavior, be sure you don't interact with her when you retrieve the object. Instead, incorporate the behavior modification mentioned previously about playtime. Give your cat an acceptable alternative to attention-seeking behavior in the form of appropriate and adequate play opportunities.

Stealing for Stress Relief. Your cat may be stealing particular objects because they provide some comfort to her if she's feeling stressed. Some cats engage in wool sucking for self-soothing, so the stolen goods may include socks or other cloth items. Your cat may also steal something to self-soothe because it holds a family member's scent. Texture may also play a role in which objects your cat steals for self-soothing. She may be particularly attracted by a certain feel the object has when she touches it with her paws or when it's in her mouth.

If you suspect the behavior is stress related, talk to your veterinarian to first make sure there isn't an underlying medical condition, especially if your cat is engaging in wool-sucking behavior. Then work on figuring out the cause of the stress. Keep in mind that stress triggers for a cat can seem very minor from the human's perspective. Even something like a change in your work schedule or the fact that your oldest child started an after-school job could be a potential trigger. Work on relieving the stress and increasing the fun factor to give your cat appropriate alternatives for her behavior. Playtime and environmental enrichment are confidence builders because they allow the cat to engage in natural, normal behaviors, such as hunting, climbing, jumping, stalking, and running. The more enriched a cat's environment, the more constructive outlets she has for her energy and the more positive associations she makes with her surroundings.

Predatory Behavior. A cat may steal objects and carry them around like prey. She may growl while walking through the house with them and even guard them. If your cat displays aggression toward a family member or another companion animal because of her obsession with objects, talk to your veterinarian about a referral to a certified behavior expert.

Pam's CatWise Clue

The Must-Have Checklist for Solving Your Cat's Behavior Problem. Nobody adopts, rescues, or purchases a cat with the hope of behavior problems developing. The dream you have of life with your new cat is one of companionship, good behavior, and many long years together. Unfortunately, though, things can go wrong, and you may find yourself living with a cat who has now developed one or more unwanted behaviors. It's frustrating, to say the least, for everyone concerned—especially the cat.

When it comes to behavior problems, some pet parents make assumptions, overcomplicate, or underevaluate. In other words, we tend to think we know why the cat is misbehaving. The problem is, it's easy to misread behavior, and as a result, the "solution" doesn't work or makes things worse. This happens when a cat parent assumes that the cat's mad about something and trying to get even. To think that a nonhuman animal can plan punitive action creates a break in the human-pet bond. The relationship starts to change, as the cat parent now views the cat as an adversary.

At the other extreme, the cat parent goes overboard trying to make it up to the "ticked-off" cat and win back his love. All the while, the cat parent misses the actual cause of the behavior problem and uses up valuable time that could be better spent looking for the right solution.

The specific causes and details of a behavior problem in your cat cannot be evaluated here, because each situation develops from your cat's unique circumstances. However, the commonest and most troublesome behavior problems in cats are:

- Litter box avoidance
- Urine marking
- Furniture scratching
- Aggression toward people
- Intercat aggression
- Stress
- Fear

1. Time to See the Veterinarian. Regardless of how sure you are that the problem is behavioral or the cat is acting out of anger or spite, the first call you should make is to your veterinarian. The unwanted behavior may have a medical cause. For example:

- A cat may be aggressive toward you when you pet him because he's in physical pain.
- A cat may be eliminating outside the litter box due to a urinary tract issue.
- A cat may have become fearful of people because of vision problems.
- The overgrooming cat might be suffering from hyperthyroidism.

Once the cat gets a clean bill of health, evaluate the problem based on what a cat needs. Does the situation encourage the cat to engage in natural behavior, or does it create stress? Here are some other examples to get you thinking in the right direction:

- A cat may stop using the litter box because another cat has ambushed him there.
- Litter box avoidance might be the result of too many cats and not enough boxes.
- A cat may spray because a new cat was abruptly introduced into the household.
- A cat may show aggression toward visitors because he wasn't properly socialized to people.
- A cat may hide in fear because the family dog wasn't properly and safely introduced.
- A cat may scratch the sofa because there's no appealing scratching post.
- A cat may unexpectedly attack a companion cat because he just returned from the veterinarian and smells different.

2. Act Early. Don't wait on a behavior problem, hoping it'll resolve itself. If you have two cats who aren't getting along and you're thinking they'll "work it out," you may set them up for lifelong tension. If your cat has peed on the carpet and you assume this is a one-time event, you may miss the fact that the cat has already peed in a number of undetected places. Don't wait. The earlier you address the problem, the greater the chance of success.

3. Be a Detective. You won't be able to solve the behavior problem unless you know what's causing it. If your cat pees outside of the litter box, the problem may have less to do with the box than with a companion cat who ambushes him when he walks down the hall toward it. In that case, you'd now have the information you need, so start a behavior modification plan that would include not only adding more litter boxes in secure locations, but also addressing the cat-to-cat relationship. To work on a behavior problem, you must first uncover the cause (as best as you can) to create a customized plan or make appropriate environmental modifications.

4. Never Punish. Any type of punishment—whether it's spanking, shaking, scruffing, squirting with water, electronic correction, rubbing the cat's nose in his mess, or yelling—serves only to raise your cat's stress level. It doesn't tell the cat that his behavior was unwanted; it tells him he should fear you because of the threat of physical pain. This method of problem correction will damage the bond you share with your cat, increase his fear, and could even lead to a more serious problem, such as aggression. If he's now unsure whether the hand coming toward him is going to stroke him or strike him, he may lash out in defense.

5. Create a Road Map. Rather than punish your cat for what *not* to do, create a plan to clearly define what *to* do. This doesn't mean just placing a scratching post in the room to magically get your cat to stop clawing the furniture. It means creating an effective CatWise road map. The scratching post you put out must meet the cat's needs so as to make the furniture less appealing. If your cat is eliminating outside the litter box because the box isn't clean, swatting the cat won't solve the problem. Cleaning the litter box is the answer. Set the cat up to succeed by providing a better option to elicit the behavior you want. How would you feel if your employer kept telling you what *not* to do and focused on what you do wrong but never showed you what *to* do or encouraged you by acknowledging what you do right?

6. Regain Trust. If you've punished your cat or if he has experienced stress and anxiety due to the behavior issue, this is the time to work on rebuilding the bond of trust. You may not feel like playing with him, creating fun games, petting him, or doing things to instill calmness and security, but that's exactly what you should do. Believe it or not, any behavior problem he's experiencing is already causing him lots of stress. He needs to know you're a source of security and comfort.

7. Stay Calm. Even if your cat has just urinated on your extremely expensive sofa, don't panic. Your little furry emotional sponge will pick up on your stress. If he's stressed out enough about something to pee on the sofa and then he sees you acting like a raging maniac, your reaction will only confirm in his head that the bottom has really fallen out of the world as he knows it. His anxiety level will rise, and I can pretty much guarantee even more behavior problems. And anger won't get the stain out.

8. Remember to Praise. Let your cat know when he has done something right. It comes down to creating that effective road map. No matter how small a step he may make, if it's a step in the right direction, reward him with something he values, such as praise, petting, playtime, or a treat.

9. Know When You Need Help. Some behavior problems are beyond the cat parent's ability. If the problem is too serious, dangerous, or mysterious for you, seek qualified professional help. There are many people on the Internet who claim to be experts, but some lack the ethics, education, and professional experience needed. An unqualified person could make the problem worse. If in doubt, ask your veterinarian for a referral to a qualified cat behavior expert.

10. Don't Give Up. Your cat is a member of the family and deserves your time and attention on the problem that's bothering him. There's no magical overnight fix. The solution will require a commitment on your part, but the payoff is well worth it. Too many cats end up in shelters because families don't realize that behavior modification can solve behavioral problems. When we bring cats into our lives, we make a commitment to provide what those precious animals need to thrive and be happy. Fortunately, you're not alone on this journey. There are many resources available, and the number of qualified behavior professionals throughout the world continues to increase.

Question:
How can I keep my cat from jumping onto the kitchen counter?

Pam's Answer:
There are effective and ineffective ways to keep your cat off the kitchen counter. The ineffective way is to squirt her with water, yell at her, smack her, or grab her. All those methods will just make her afraid of you. She'll

also quickly catch on to the fact that the counter is off-limits only when you're around. She'll wait until you walk out the door and then she'll get back up there. There's a much better way to train without you having to be the bad guy in the process.

The first step is to understand what attracts your cat to the counter because that'll play a role in creating the solution.

Yummy Food and Enticing Scents. There are so many good scents coming from the counter, and depending upon the time of day, there's an array of tasty food just waiting for a hungry feline to enjoy an impromptu buffet.

A Bird's-Eye View. In many homes, the view out the kitchen window is very interesting, especially if you've installed a bird feeder right there or if the window overlooks outdoor activity, such as kids playing on the swing set.

Visual Advantage for Safety. The higher up your cat is, the greater her visual advantage in seeing a feline adversary enter the room. This is especially important in multipet households where relationships are tense. A cat doesn't want to be ambushed.

Attention-Seeking Behavior. Sometimes the cat will jump on the counter to get your attention. Typically, it works because you probably shoo her down or talk to her. From the cat's point of view, this method is effective even though the attention she receives is negative.

The Effective Alternatives. There are two aspects to this program: making the counter unappealing and providing a more appealing alternative. If your cat is attracted to the food on the counter, remove temptation by making sure all leftovers are put away. To entertain her, set up food-dispensing toys so she gets some playtime in during mealtime. If you think she's on the counter to look out the window, set up a cat tree or window perch at another window.

In a multipet home, if your cat is trying to achieve a visual advantage, create an alternative for her. Set up a multiperch cat tree. If you have more than two cats, consider a second cat tree as well, so there will be plenty of space for everyone.

Elevation plays a key role in safety, and cat trees are a wonderful option. Place the tree in an appealing location. Don't hide the tree in a far-off room if the location your cat prefers is in the family room or near a particular window. You can also create safety by putting out some cozy cat beds in high places.

If the counter cruising is an attention-seeking behavior, then when she's up there isn't the time to make eye contact with her or engage in any type of conversation or petting. If she's on the counter and you need to remove her, just pick her up and place her on the floor without any other communication. Pay attention to her when she's on the floor or on allowable elevated areas. This will show her that the attention she wants will only be gotten when she's where she's supposed to be.

The other part of training involves making your counter a less-than-appealing place for feline lounging or cruising. Go to your local hardware store and purchase a roll of plastic carpet protector. If you can, get the kind that has the pointy little feet on one side. Unroll the plastic and cut it into several pieces that will conform to your counter. This also makes it easier to keep the counter protected on one side when you're working on the other side.

Place the protector pieces on the counter with the pointy-feet side up. Your cat will find that the counter isn't an appealing area to walk on. This remote form of training will also prevent you from being associated with this unpleasant turn of events.

If your cat still goes onto the counter despite the carpet protectors, try place mats with double-sided tape. Place strips of the double-sided tape on the place mats, and then scatter them along the counter.

Keep the carpet-protector pieces or sticky place mats in place whenever the counter isn't being used. For this to be truly successful, though, you have to provide her with alternative locations. Cats live in a vertical world, so elevation is very important to them. If you aren't going to allow your cat on specific elevated areas you have to provide her with something more appealing.

Question:
Is there any way to train my cat to stop waking me up at three A.M.?

Pam's Answer:
Wake up, wake up! It's time to play! Well, it's time to play if you're a cat, but if you're a sleeping human, play is last on your list. So why does this pattern repeat itself every night? Why does your cat routinely bite your toes, paw your face, or systematically push stuff off the bedside table in the wee hours of the morning? You may not like this answer, but it's actually very normal behavior under the circumstances. Cats are naturally most active between

dusk and dawn. For most of us, the end of the day is when we're winding down. We come home from work, eat dinner, check our e-mail, relax with family, cuddle with the cat, and then head off to bed. Poor cat has been sleeping all day; when you walk through the door at six P.M., he's ready for the fun to begin. If there hasn't been adequate stimulation during the day from an enriched environment and you haven't played with your cat in the evening, then at some point you're going to get a reminder in the form of eight furry pounds sitting on your chest hours before the alarm clock is set to go off.

Shifting Schedules (His, Not Yours). If your cat wakes you up in the middle of the night or at the crack of dawn, there are a couple of things you can do to help "reset" that little fuzzy alarm clock. First on the list, though, is absolutely the most difficult of all—you have to ignore him when he engages in the unwanted behavior. If you've gotten up to put food in his bowl in an effort to shut him up, then you've only succeeded in reinforcing that behavior. If you've given attention to a cat engaging in attention-seeking behavior, he now knows that that method worked, and he'll repeat it night after night. Even if you've yelled at your cat, he's still receiving some form of attention for the behavior. Instead of showing any reaction, pretend to be asleep. I know this may seem like a strange thing to do, but keep your eyes closed, don't move, and completely ignore your cat. He needs to see that his method gets no reaction.

The Activity Cycle. The second part of this process is easy. It's based on the typical activity cycle a cat goes through as a natural predator: hunt, feast, groom, sleep.

The activity cycle is the basis of a cat's survival in the wild, and simulating it for the indoor cat will help him feel satisfied. He'll enjoy stimulation, activity, and the food reward in a way that follows his natural behavior. It'll make sense to him, and as a result, you'll get that much-needed sleep you've been missing. Here's how the four phases work:

First, a cat expends energy in physical activity hunting prey. In the outdoors, you won't find prey offering itself up on a platter, so the cat has to hunt, stalk, and then pounce—repeatedly if the animal escapes. Cats are not scavengers, so they must constantly seek fresh prey. Hunting benefits a cat physically and mentally.

Second, the cat feasts on his capture. A full stomach is the reward for a job well done.

When finished, the feline hunter grooms himself to remove traces of the prey from his fur. This is important, because a hunter doesn't want to alert other prey to his presence, nor does he want to risk becoming prey to a larger predator. Because of their size, cats wear both hats—prey and predator.

Digestion is next on the list, and since the cat has a full stomach, that usually means he can afford to take a nap to recharge for the next hunt.

Pam's CatWise Technique

Here's how you'll use this behavior cycle to your advantage: Just before bedtime, engage your cat in an interactive play session using a fishing pole–type toy. Technique is important here. Don't wave the wand frantically around so the cat never gets to capture anything. Creating a frustrated cat isn't the goal. Instead, move the toy like prey unaware of an ambush and allow opportunities to stalk, pounce, and capture. The game should last about fifteen minutes, but you can adjust that based on your cat. Customize the game to your cat's physical ability, age, and health. Remember that playtime is as much mental as physical, so give him plenty of chances to capture his treasure. Wind the action down at the end of the game, so your cat is left relaxed, not all revved up. The wind-down at the end of the game is really important, so the cat feels satisfied, much as he would if he had actually killed his prey.

Once the play-hunt is over, it's time to feast. If you feed your cat on a schedule, divide his normal daily portion so you can offer him a postgame snack. If you free-feed, take up the food earlier in the evening and then refresh the food in the bowl after the play session.

After the meal, your cat will most likely engage in a grooming session and then be ready to snooze.

Provide Nighttime Toys. If you find your cat still wants interaction or isn't relaxed enough, then after the game you can set out special toys that make an appearance only in the evening. These can be food-dispensing toys, other puzzle toys, or whatever safe toys your cat enjoys for solo playtime.

Does Your Cat Dream?

Cats experience REM (rapid-eye-movement) sleep just as we do. It's during REM sleep that humans dream, so there's a good chance cats do as well. What do they dream about? The cats aren't telling, but I'd guess there's a fair number of mice and birds in their dreams.

Spruce Up the Environment. In addition to the four-part behavior cycle, set up the cat's environment so there are activities available for him if he wanders around the house at night looking for more stimulation. Hide treats in puzzle feeders or in boxes (such as empty tissue boxes). You can even make homemade puzzle feeders with plastic water bottles or the cardboard inserts from toilet paper or paper towels.

Provide a cat tree, window shelf, hammock bed, or some other resting area for the cat to watch evening activities taking place outdoors. Depending upon where you live, perhaps you can leave the drapes open at one window.

Cat shelves attached to the walls, cat skyways, and other additions for climbing and perching can be added to the interior environment. Depending on your budget, you can purchase sturdy walkways or construct some of your own. Cats love elevation, so increase vertical territory to give yours more opportunities to climb and play.

Another option for a cat who seems uncomfortable with the sudden stillness of the house at night is to leave a radio playing, use nightlights, or put lights on timers.

Remember, your cat naturally seeks stimulation and activity, so make sure he gets adequate environmental enrichment, and don't skimp on your daily interactive play therapy sessions.

The bottom line is to ignore the behavior you don't want but also set your cat up to succeed by recognizing his natural, normal needs and creating opportunities for him to satisfy them.

Question:
Other than keeping the bathroom door closed, is there any way to stop our cat, Fishstick, from unrolling all the toilet paper?

Pam's Answer:
Fishstick walks into the bathroom and spots something too hard to resist . . . the toilet paper hanging next to the toilet. As he reaches up to touch it with his paw, he discovers a great new activity: toilet paper unrolling and shredding. Within minutes your bathroom looks as if a snowstorm had gone through it. Did I pretty much capture the picture?

What You Can Do. What are your options for outwitting a feline shredding machine? Here are some tips:

Before placing the new roll on the holder, squeeze it so the cardboard center isn't perfectly round. That way, when the cat tries to unroll it, it won't spin around so freely.

Position the paper roll so it unrolls from the bottom and not up over the top. That way Fishstick can't unroll it by grabbing the roll with his claws and pulling down.

There are childproof toilet paper holders you can purchase to prevent your cat from having access to the paper roll at all. You can find these in the child safety section of stores as well as online. Some are made so the paper can be dispensed only when the cover is lifted. Others allow the paper to be unrolled only a few sheets at a time.

Increase the Fun Factor. If Fishstick is bored, increase the fun factor in the environment so there'll be other, acceptable activities. Set out puzzle feeders, other activity toys, open paper bags, and other fun things, so the cat keeps busy without getting destructive. Engage your cat in daily interactive play sessions as well.

Question:
Marcus is an indoor-only cat, but he keeps trying to dash out the door when-ever we open it. We're worried he's going to end up getting lost or hit by a car. Can he be trained to stay away from the door?

Pam's Answer:
Door darting is a potentially dangerous behavior. For a cat who lives indoors exclusively, escaping through the door to the outside can result in instant tragedy. Even for a cat allowed access to the outside, being able to just zip out the front door whenever it's opened can have very bad consequences.

The Allure of Door Darting. From the cat's point of view, door darting is the one opportunity to escape to where all the excitement is. When the front door opens, a whole bunch of enticing scents enter the house. For an indoor/outdoor cat, being in charge of his own in-and-out schedule is very appealing. The door is open and there's nothing to do indoors, so the cat takes his chance to head outside for some bird or chipmunk hunting.

Cats who aren't used to being outdoors are at serious risk of being hit by cars, attacked by other animals, becoming lost, or ingesting poison, among many other dangers. Even if your cat darts out the door and usu-ally just sits on the front porch or stays in the front yard, he's in danger.

Types of Door Darters. Some cats are very obvious and insistent about their plan to bolt. They sit and wait for any opportunity—whether it's a visitor entering or leaving, the cat parent entering with an armload of groceries, or a child heading off to school. The obvious door darter makes his intentions known, and although you do everything you can to block his access, he knows there will be one time you're not paying attention and he can zip out behind you.

Then there are the covert door darters. They can be the most dangerous, because cat parents often don't realize the cat is even missing. He hides somewhere in the room, ready to slip out without anyone noticing. It isn't until dinner time that you may become alarmed because the cat isn't meowing in the kitchen the way he always does when you pop open the can.

Hello, My Name Is . . .

Have your cat microchipped to increase the chances of his being identified should he dart outside and get lost.

How to Retrain a Door Darter. First, make sure you don't give him any attention at the door. It's very natural to bend down and greet your cat when you come through the door. Chances are, he's right there waiting for you as soon as he hears your key in the lock. You now have to make the door a place where you completely ignore him. All meet-and-greets need to take place away from the entrance.

Set up an official hello–and–good-bye spot on the other side of the room. This can be a cat tree, window perch, chair, or any place where your cat would enjoy sitting. Start by training him to go to that spot. You can call his name and then reward him with a treat when he goes there. If your cat likes to be petted, call him to that spot and pet him as soon as he lands there. If you do clicker training, target train him to that location. Make sure any treat you offer is so tasty, it's irresistible. When it comes to choosing between darting out the door and munching on a special treat, there should be no doubt in his mind that the treat is of higher value.

When you come in the door at the end of the day, don't look at your cat or greet him until you walk over to that official greeting spot. That's where you can lavish him with attention.

Another option is to offer puzzle feeders before you head out the door. A puzzle feeder will provide your cat with entertainment and give him a food reward for his efforts. Divide up his daily meal portion so you set out a couple of puzzle feeders right before you head off to work in the morning.

Question:
What would cause a cat to want to eat socks? He's making holes in my son's good school socks.

Pam's Answer:
Pica is the term used for the behavior of eating nonfood material. The most common material associated with pica is wool—blankets, sweaters, socks, and jackets—but some cats will nibble on just about anything from plastic grocery bags to litter.

What Causes Pica? There are many possible reasons for pica:

- *Deficiencies in the diet.* Some veterinarians and behavior experts believe inadequate amounts of fat or fiber in the diet may lead a cat to crave these nutrients from inedible sources. Some cats who are anemic may try to eat litter.
- *Boredom or stress.* Cats living in a stressful environment may try to self-soothe with pica. A bored cat not receiving adequate mental and physical stimulation might begin munching on nonfood items just for something to do.
- *Underlying medical problems.* Certain diseases or brain disorders may be associated with pica behavior.
- *Genetics.* Some Oriental breeds are predisposed to wool-sucking behavior, and that can advance to pica.

Discouraging Pica. Have your cat examined by the veterinarian. If there's an underlying medical problem, it needs to be diagnosed and addressed.

- *Dietary adjustments.* Your veterinarian may make a recommendation for supplementing your cat's food with increased fiber. Don't make any dietary adjustments without consulting with your veterinarian. An inappropriate amount of fiber added to the diet can cause major intestinal distress.

■ *Remove temptation.* If the cat is munching on socks or clothing, make sure temptation is removed by keeping those items in drawers, in closets, or in hampers with lids. If your cat chews on plants, remove them from the indoor environment. Do your best to keep items of temptation out of your cat's reach.

■ *Provide mental and physical stimulation.* A bored cat will look for something to do, and that something might include chewing on something inedible. Increase environmental enrichment by providing puzzle feeders, activity toys, scratching posts, cat trees, and other forms of stimulation. If you think your cat would enjoy some exposure to the outdoors, consider purchasing or constructing a safe outdoor enclosure. Some of them are just small enclosures that can be installed in windows; others are more elaborate and have walkways for the cat.

■ *Interactive play therapy.* Engage your cat in a couple of interactive play therapy sessions per day. When you use a fishing pole–type toy, you can control the movements so your cat is able to truly benefit both mentally and physically. She gets to be the mighty hunter and enjoy stalking, pouncing, and capturing.

■ *Safe alternatives for chewing.* In addition to puzzle-feeder toys, try growing some safe kitty greens or catnip for your cat. You can find kitty-greens kits in your local pet-product store. You can also buy squares of sprouted grass from many organic food stores.

■ *Reduce stress.* Use your detective skills to determine the cause of stress in her life. Is there another companion cat causing tension? Is there stress in the family? Have you made changes to your cat's environment? Stress triggers can be big and obvious, or they can be small and easy for humans to overlook. Create a more secure and comforting environment for your cat. Make sure she has cozy little hideaways for napping, elevated areas so she can survey her environment, a secure feeding station, and an appealing litter box area.

■ *Get professional help.* If you can't figure out what might be triggering the pica or have been unable to redirect your cat away from the behavior, ask your veterinarian for a referral to a certified behavior professional.

Question:

Why does my cat grab on to my ankles and bite or scratch me?

Pam's Answer:

Your cat latches on to your ankles because they're moving targets. If there's no other option for play or stimulation, your cat focuses on what's available. The prey drive is triggered by objects moving across or away from the cat's visual field. If your cat isn't getting enough stimulation and playtime, she's going to take it upon herself to find a substitute. Unfortunately in your case, it's a painful one.

Constructive Forms of Stimulation. In order to stop the ankle attacks, provide the cat with a better option—playtime with appropriate interactive toys. Engage in play sessions at least twice a day. Increase the fun in the environment, as well. Strategically set out interesting solo toys and puzzle feeders so your cat has opportunities to work off that energy.

How to Handle an Ankle Attack. If your cat has her paws wrapped around your ankle and her teeth are sinking into your skin, don't pull away or run. Instead, confuse your cat. Gently push toward her mouth, and then stand still. This movement confuses her, and she'll release her grasp. Once the cat releases her grip, stay still and ignore her. She'll soon learn that biting flesh results in an immediate end to the fun.

Question:

I have a nine-month-old cat, and he climbs my Christmas tree and knocks the ornaments to the floor. How can I train him to stay away from it?

Pam's Answer:

Your cat probably thinks you're the absolute best cat parent in the whole world because you just created the max in environmental enrichment. You set up the ultimate cat playground!

Let's Start with What Not to Do. I've seen people try to keep their cats away from the Christmas tree by putting foil around it or by encircling it in a folding dog exercise pen. Although many cats may not enjoy walking over aluminum foil, they'll think nothing of it when it's the only barrier between them and the impossible-to-resist tree. Exercise pen fences may keep a small dog from bothering your tree but will slow your cat down by only seconds before you see his happy head poking out from among the branches.

The other thing I notice cat parents do is to set up electronic deterrents around the tree. Whether it's a sound-generating device or a shock mat, you might keep your cat away from the tree but you'll also distress him. I especially hate these devices in multipet environments. The sound-generating device can upset a cat or dog who isn't even the one trying to approach the tree. Either deterrent device may cause a cat to then react negatively by lashing out at a companion cat. There's no place in your home for either of them.

Keeping the Tree Upright. Your plan starts with choosing the best location for the tree. You may decide that the best option is a room to which the cat won't have access. If possible, locate the tree in a room that can be closed off from the cat. If not, place it near something to which you can anchor it. For example, if there's a large picture on the wall, remove it and put the tree in that spot. Secure the tree to the wall with fishing line and an eyebolt. This will make it harder to knock down. When Christmas is over, put the picture back. Any extra holes you had to put in the wall will be hidden by the picture after Christmas.

You can use the same technique if you have plants hanging from an eyebolt in the ceiling. Secure the top of the tree to the plant hook with wire or fishing line. If this arrangement doesn't seem sturdy enough, you can add extra support by securing the trunk with wire or cord to an eyebolt in the baseboard. You'll just have to cover the small hole with a piece of furniture afterward.

When choosing a location for the tree, a corner is a safer choice. Look around, though, and make sure there isn't a table or piece of furniture too close that your cat might use as a springboard to launch himself onto the tree.

Tree Branches. Before decorating the tree, deter your cat from nibbling on branches by spraying a bitter anti-chew product on the tree. This is especially important if you have a live tree, because you certainly don't want your cat chewing on the needles. You don't know whether fire retardants, preservatives, or pesticides were sprayed on the tree.

Water Reservoir. If you have a live tree, cover the water reservoir to prevent your cat from drinking there. Tree sap is toxic, and so are any tree preservatives you may add to the water. Aspirin is something people commonly use in the water to keep the tree fresh, and that's highly toxic to cats. Use netting or Sticky Paws for Plants over the reservoir. If you use Sticky Paws, place the strips in a crisscross pattern so you can still water the tree but the cat won't be able to get his face in there. Some tree stands have covers that go around the reservoir.

Think Fake. Although I absolutely love the scent of a real live Christmas tree, we have had nothing but artificial ones in our house from the time we brought home our first cat. Although there's still a risk of choking or toxins being released in the body if a cat ingests part of an artificial tree branch, the chances are much less that he'd be interested enough to do so. You can also coat the artificial branches with a bitter anti-chew product to make it even less appealing. If you buy a tree with shiny artificial branches, your cat may be more enticed by the light reflection, so when shopping, opt for the artificial trees made to look like live ones.

Tree Lights. Coat tree light wires with a bitter anti-chew cream before placing them on the tree. I recommend wearing disposable gloves when handling the wires. This way, you don't have to worry about accidentally getting the nasty-tasting product on your fingers and then touching your mouth before you have a chance to wash your hands. The gloves act as a reminder that you're handling icky-tasting stuff.

When placing the lights on the tree, wrap them tightly around the branches so as not to leave any wires dangling. This will make the tree less enticing to your cat.

Don't leave the tree lights on all night or when you're not at home. It's best to completely unplug them when not in use.

Cover the electrical light cords leading from the tree to the outlet. Use pre-slit tubing to prevent your cat from gaining access to the electrical cord.

Routinely check any exposed electrical cord for signs of teeth marks or breaks in the insulation. In addition, routinely examine your cat, especially if he's a kitten or has shown interest in the tree. Check his mouth for signs of burns. Look for singed hair or whiskers. Watch his behavior, as well; check for a lack of appetite, change in breathing, needing to stand up in order to breathe, coughing, or anything that doesn't seem right. If you suspect your cat has chewed on the Christmas tree lights, get to the veterinarian or veterinary emergency clinic immediately. Some internal damage may have occurred that isn't visually obvious to you.

Ornaments and Decorations. These shiny, swaying objects can seem like toys just begging to be swatted by a cat. Breakable ornaments pose a double risk because small pieces can be ingested, and your cat may also injure a paw stepping on the shards. Your best bet is unbreakable ornaments. Save delicate or breakable ones for next year, when your kitty's interest in Christmas decorations has decreased. When (or if) that time comes, secure any breakable ornaments tightly to the branches well in toward the trunk, not hanging at the tips. To limit temptation, don't put ornaments on the bottom branches.

Edible decorations, such as strings of popcorn, cookie ornaments, cranberries, etc., are beautiful to look at but dangerous for your cat. It's just too hard for a pet to resist all those tempting aromas coming from the tree.

Be careful about using metal ornament hooks because they can easily fall from the tree with the ornament if the cat swipes hard enough. If your cat is determined to play with ornaments, use green twist ties so you can tightly secure the ornament to the branch. No matter how much swatting the cat does, the chances of the ornament staying put are much better.

If you have a kitten or a hard-core tree climber, consider making this the year you decorate with totally unappealing decorations (from a cat's point of view). Ornaments and garlands of paper and wood can look beautiful, can evoke nostalgia, and will probably be of little interest to a cat.

Tinsel and Garland. Don't use tinsel at all. It's lightweight, easily falls from the tree, and can cause intestinal blockage if swallowed by your cat. If you use garland, spray it with a bitter anti-chew product before placing it around the tree.

Offer Something Better to Do. Cats just want to have fun, and now that you've done all this preventive work, the other half of the job involves giving your cat something better to do. I know it's a busy time of year, and it might even be the time you often skip a few play sessions with your cat, but he really needs them now. Engage in interactive play sessions at least twice a day to help your cat work off that energy and hopefully tone down his fascination with the Christmas tree. Between play sessions, give your cat some early Christmas presents in the form of fun puzzle feeders or other environmental enrichment toys. Even a few paper-bag tunnels with safe toys inside may interest your cat enough for her to stay away from the tree.

Because cats love to climb, make sure your Christmas tree isn't the only option in the house. If you don't already have a sturdy cat tree, I would certainly suggest you do a little extra Christmas shopping and invest in one.

Growing Up. Typically, it's the kittens and younger cats who show an interest in Christmas trees. You should be able to ease this strict security and tree prep after the first year or two. Some cats, though, never give up on the challenge.

Question:
My cat chews on electrical cords. I know it's dangerous, so how can I get him to stop?

Pam's Answer
Animals experience much of their world through their mouths. For kittens, chewing is a form of play or teething relief. For adult cats, it can be something to do out of boredom or a way to relieve some tooth pain. Make sure you have your cat's teeth checked by the veterinarian. While some things they chew are harmless, many of the objects they focus on are dangerous.

To a playful cat, a dangling cord is just asking to be batted around. Unfortunately, an electrical cord is one of the most dangerous objects for a cat to chew. The cat's sharp teeth can easily puncture the protective insulation and reach the live wires inside.

You can buy cord covers online, at your local home improvement center, or at an office supply store. These cord covers are made of flexible tubing and come pre-slit. You can even try flexible loom tubing, which is very inexpensive. For hardcore chewers, though, your best bet may be something sturdier.

I don't recommend purchasing any covers advertised as coming pre-scented with a citrus smell as a deterrent. Many of my clients themselves have also been deterred by the strong artificial scent.

Bundle cords that aren't housed in tubing together, using clips. This'll make them less appealing and not as apt to move as your kitten brushes up against them. Secure to furniture legs any electrical cords dangling from lamps or phones. For cords running along baseboards, buy plastic cord covers made specifically for those locations.

Use a bitter-tasting deterrent on any exposed cords. These deterrents come in cream, gel, and spray forms and are available at pet supply retailers or through your veterinarian. The creams or gels are better for use on cords because they'll cause less mess to the surrounding area. If you decide to use the spray, cover whatever you don't want sprayed with paper or plastic during application.

Periodically go around and physically check for signs of chewing on any uncovered cords.

Chapter 13

Bad Moods

How to deal with feline aggression

Question:

My cat is aggressive, and I'm not sure what causes it. How do you deal with cat aggression?

Pam's Answer:

Aggression can be scary—not only for the victim (whether human or animal) but even for the aggressive cat. Cats generally do everything they can to avoid an out-and-out fight. The cat who feels backed into a corner with no other option is the one who may lash out with tooth and nail. In general, a cat's first choice is to take the escape route. In order to avoid actual physical encounters, cats do lots of posturing and use their bodies to communicate either that they're big, bad cats who shouldn't be messed with or that they're not a threat. When the body language or other communication signals fail and there's no way to retreat, then cats may resort to aggressive behavior.

I'm Big, and I'm Bad

The "Halloween cat" posture with arched back signals that the cat is ready to engage in battle but is used to give the opponent the chance to back off. The posture can be offensive or defensive, depending upon other accompanying body signals.

Communication. A cat may display aggressive behavior in particular circumstances, but that doesn't mean he's an aggressive cat. People are often too quick to label a cat as aggressive when in reality the cat may merely feel that all escape has been cut off and body-posture signals have failed. Very often, the reason human family members get bitten by the cat is because they either misinterpreted the cat's body language or chose to ignore the clear signals being sent. The key is to identify when your cat is starting to become fearful and aroused so you can defuse the situation before it erupts in aggression.

Sometimes in multicat environments, cat parents may not actually witness the aggression of certain cats toward others. There could be lots of intimidation, stare-downs, and even spraying. Aggression doesn't have to be overt to be classified as aggression.

Aggressive behavior could be due to fear; the cat may feel threatened. He may fear being hurt or restrained, or he may think his resources are in danger, or a mother cat may be protecting her kittens. A cat may feel a territorial threat from an unfamiliar cat or a stranger in the environment. Aggression can be the result of pain, punishment, cognitive dysfunction, hyperthyroidism, arthritis, or several other medical conditions. It could also be redirected toward someone who isn't even the intended target. Aggressive behavior can be the cat's way of reacting due to impaired senses. There are numerous possible causes when a cat feels the need to attack.

Dealing with Aggressive Behavior. Specific behavior modification techniques will depend on the type of aggression exhibited. Cats aren't aggressive just for the sake of being aggressive. It's crucial that the underlying reason for the behavior be accurately identified.

Your cat needs to have a full workup done by the veterinarian in order to rule out underlying medical causes.

After identification of the cause, the way to deal with aggression is to change the circumstances as best you can so the cat doesn't feel threatened. Be aware of behavior triggers or cues that cause your cat to become reactive. If possible, alter the circumstances to allow your cat to feel that he always has a choice. Never punish him for aggression, as that will only heighten his fear and will be counterproductive to any training attempts. Punishment, whether physical or verbal, can cause the situation to rapidly deteriorate and worsen the cat's behavior.

Chill Out

Cats can stay reactive for quite a while after an aggressive episode and should be given time to calm down on their own. Attempts to calm and comfort the cat by stroking or cuddling will only serve to reinforce the behavior.

Because aggression is scary and potentially dangerous, your veterinarian may also offer a referral to a qualified behavior expert. If you do decide to seek professional help, be sure you choose someone who's truly qualified to work in the cat behavior field, such as a veterinary behaviorist, certified applied behaviorist, or certified cat behavior consultant.

Watch for Clues. Cats often give some visual or vocal signals indicating impending aggression. If you learn to watch for these, you can reduce your chances of being injured. Backing off when you see or hear those warning signals will reduce your cat's stress level at that point as well.

Aggression may be offensive or defensive. If offensive, the cat is communicating that he's about to attack his opponent. In defensive aggression, he's showing that he'll defend himself but would rather not fight. Warning signs preceding a potential aggressive strike may include:

- A direct stare
- Ears flattened against head

- Whiskers flattened against side of face
- Whiskers fanned out stiffly
- Dilated pupils
- Constricted pupils
- Exposure of claws
- Piloerection of fur
- Growling
- Body stiffness
- Lashing tail
- Stiff, straight-legged stance
- Hissing or spitting
- Yowling
- Crouched body posture with tail tucked in close

Even though you may be able to avoid an aggressive episode by defusing a situation, you still have to determine the cause. For example, does your cat guard specific areas or even block access to them? If you have more than one cat, does the aggressor stare at him, block his access to resources, or even pursue him although the victim has already retreated? Does the aggression occur when the cat is aroused by something outside or after he has come in from the outdoors? Does the cat get aggressive when visitors are at the house or after they leave? Are you perpetuating the aggression by how you play with your cat? Look for patterns. A veterinary behaviorist or other qualified behavior professional can help you identify patterns and provide appropriate behavior modification. The key is to find the cause and create a situation in which your cat no longer feels threatened. It could be one particular circumstance triggering the aggression, or it could be that your cat feels he must remain on high alert at all times in any situation. Because there are quite a few types of aggression and the behavior can range from mild to severe, it's best to talk with your veterinarian about a referral to a behavior expert if you have trouble identifying the trigger or are unable to modify the immediate environment in a way that decreases the cat's perception of a threat.

Question:

Arnie and Abby are normally best friends, but when I brought Abby home from the veterinary hospital after getting her teeth cleaned, Arnie attacked her. What happened, and how can I be sure this won't happen again?

Pam's Answer:

This is a relatively common behavior issue in multicat homes. One cat comes home from the veterinary clinic and is either hissed at or actually attacked by a companion cat due to nonrecognition. For the unsuspecting cat parent (and for the victim cat), the aggression is terrifying because it comes out of nowhere. It's hard to imagine that the cat who stayed home would no longer recognize his best buddy, but although the returning cat may look the same, from a feline point of view, she isn't recognized because of how she smells. That may seem odd to a human, but when you understand how important scent communication is to cats, you'll see that this behavior, however frightening, is actually normal. Luckily, though, you can take steps to prevent it.

The Importance of Scent. To better understand the scenario that takes place when the returning cat is attacked, you have to appreciate how cats communicate. They are masters at it and use vocalization, visual signals, and yes, scent! In fact, scent is arguably at the top of the list.

The pheromones cats give off from their scent glands provide other cats with a huge amount of information. Every time your cat rubs her cheek along an object, she's depositing a scent; when cats flank-rub each other, they are exchanging scents; when one cat lovingly grooms another, he leaves a scent. In a cat colony, this mixing of scents through allogrooming, flank rubbing, etc., is important to the security and peace of the group because it creates a communal scent.

Have you noticed how your cat may sniff your shoes or your clothes when you return home? That's because you carry unfamiliar scents into the territory. If you were at a home with another cat, your cat may do some intense sniffing to gather as much information as possible. So imagine how threatening it must be for the cat who stayed home to see a strange-smelling cat emerge from the carrier. In fact, when it comes to not smelling like her normal self, the situation is made worse because the scents are those of a place that's very threatening from the cat's perspective. The returning cat doesn't smell the same and actually is carrying scents the other cat associates with fear. Not many cats look forward to a visit to the veterinarian.

The Offense and Defense. The cat who stayed home makes an initial attack. The returning cat doesn't know where this came from, and so she reacts defensively. The returning cat will be even more reactive if she's already stressed out from the veterinary visit, is sick, is recovering from an injury or illness, or is unhappy about having been in a car.

How to Prevent This Type of Aggression:

■ If the visit is for routine vaccinations or exams, schedule an appointment for both cats. That way they'll both have a similar scent.

■ Begin the use of Feliway Multicat cat-appeasing pheromone diffuser several days before the scheduled appointment.

■ If you take just one cat to the veterinary clinic, before leaving, take a pair of clean socks and gently rub her down, including around the cheeks, to collect the pheromones. Place the socks in a plastic bag.

■ When you return from the veterinary clinic, place the returning cat in a separate room and close the door. Take the socks out of the plastic bag and gently rub her down again to redistribute some of her own scent. Leave her alone in the room, or at least keep her separated from other pets in the household. This time alone will give her an opportunity to do some grooming so she can clean off more of the unfamiliar scents and redistribute her own, comforting scent. The time alone in the room will also give her a chance to acquire some of the normal household scents as well.

■ A note of caution: Do not use the socks to rub down the cat who stayed home after using them on the returning cat. This will not end nicely. You definitely don't want to distribute the veterinary clinic smell to any other cats. Just place those socks in your washing machine.

■ While the cats are separated, wash out the carrier to remove the veterinary clinic smell.

■ When you feel enough time has gone by and you want to reintroduce the cats, monitor their behavior until you're sure everyone is back to normal. Conduct an interactive play session, and offer a meal or treats for distraction. If, however, the situation still seems tense, separate the cats again for a longer period.

Question:
Why does my cat sometimes bite me when I pet him?

Pam's Answer:
I get more and more calls from cat parents who are confused about why they get bitten when petting their cats. Things start out just fine, and then suddenly, without warning, the cat lashes out with teeth or claws.

A quiet session of petting and affection suddenly turns violent as the cat sinks his teeth into the very hand stroking him.

Here are five steps to identify and correct petting-induced aggression:

1. Veterinary Visit. If this happens more than just occasionally, just to be on the safe side, have your cat examined by the veterinarian, because the sudden aggression may be the result of pain. He may be fine when you pet him in some locations on his body, but if you hit that tender spot, he may react aggressively.

2. Mood Matters. Sometimes the reason your cat may bite when you pet him is that you misinterpreted his intention when he approached in the first place. His approach may actually have been a play solicitation, not a request for physical affection. Perhaps he was being as tolerant as possible by allowing you to stroke him a few times, but if he was in play mode, then the stroking just increased his stimulation.

3. Read the Body Language. Even though it may seem that your cat attacked without any warning, there are usually several body language signals given first, which cat parents often miss. It may seem that his aggression came out of the blue, but from his point of view, he gave you numerous clear warnings. Watch his body language as you pet him. You can't become distracted, or you'll easily miss those physical warning signs.

Here are some body language signals indicating that your cat is reaching his petting limit:

- Cessation of purring
- Tail lashing
- Tail thumping
- Skin twitching
- Shifting body position
- Meowing
- Growling
- Ears in airplane mode
- Ears flattened back against head
- Cat looking back at your hand
- Dilated pupils

4. End on a Positive Note. The way to help a cat feel more comfortable with being petted is to pay attention to his tolerance level so you can stop petting well in advance of an attack. Pay attention to his body language and stop petting *before* the warning signals start appearing. For example, if you know you can typically pet your cat for about three minutes before he bites, then in order to keep this a positive experience, stop petting after about a minute and a half. Leave your cat wanting more. When you stop petting while the experience is still positive, your cat stops feeling that the only way to end the session is to be aggressive.

Pay attention to where on the body your cat likes to be petted and where he doesn't. He may enjoy being petted on the back of the head but not at the base of the tail. Petting in some areas may actually cause too much stimulation.

5. Never Punish. He isn't biting you because he's mean; he's biting because he feels he has no other option. From his point of view, all other forms of communicating with you have failed. He was left with no choice. If you watch his body language, pet where he likes it, and stop long before exhausting his tolerance, you stand a very good chance of changing his mind about physical contact. Punishment is inhumane and counterproductive.

Question:

I came home from work to find that my two cats must've had a huge fight. They normally get along very well. Why would they suddenly become enemies?

Pam's Answer:

Without witnessing what took place between your cats, I can offer only a general idea. There's a common type of aggression that results when a cat becomes agitated by something and then lashes out at the nearest human, cat, or dog. Redirected aggression is frequently misdiagnosed because the cat can stay reactive for quite a while. By the time the cat parent sees the aggressive display, there may be no trigger visible.

What Causes Redirected Aggression? The most frequent cause of redirected aggression is the sight of an unfamiliar cat in the yard. Your cat may be looking out the window when she spots a feline intruder hanging out by the bird feeder. Unable to gain access to the source of her agitation, the indoor cat becomes highly reactive. A family member walking by may casually pet the cat, or a companion cat may come near, thinking all is well, but both can become the surprised target of claws and teeth. The aggressive cat doesn't lash out because he mistakes his companion for his target, but rather because he's highly aroused and suddenly interrupted.

Check with Your Veterinarian. If your cat has suddenly become aggressive and you didn't see an initial trigger, it may not necessarily be redirected aggression, so have your cat examined by the veterinarian.

Unintended Consequences. When the unintended target of a cat's redirected aggression is a companion cat, a cycle of mutual aggression can develop. The victim cat is taken totally by surprise and doesn't understand why his companion has suddenly attacked. The understandably confused victim strikes back defensively, adding fuel to the fire. Now both cats don't really know why they're fighting; they know only that they're enemies. If the aggressive attack is severe enough, it can create tremendous fear in the victim cat, with long-term effects.

Ongoing Cycle. After the initial redirected-aggression episode, both cats may start posturing defensively, continuing the downward spiral. The cat who was the original victim may begin a routine of frequent hiding.

The cat parent may come home from work one day and suddenly find two cats who were always best buddies now growling and hissing at each other. Because the initial cause of the agitation (perhaps that outdoor cat, someone working outdoors, or any number of possible triggers) has long disappeared, the cat parent is at a loss as to why the relationship deteriorated.

Dealing with Redirected Aggression. First, make sure everyone stays safe. Separate the cats, so each has time to settle down. Next, do what you can to address the source of the redirected aggression if the cause is known.

Time to Chill. In my years of doing cat behavior consultations, I've found that the sooner the cats are separated, the easier it'll be to get them back together. If they're allowed to just keep agitating each other, you'll end up with escalating hostility that can become severe and continue indefinitely. Just gently (and safely) separate the cats. Don't attempt to pick up an aggressive cat, because you risk injury to yourself. Use a large piece of cardboard or a towel to block the cats from seeing each other. If the cats are fighting, bang a couple of pots together or make some other loud noise to frighten them into backing off. Then safely get them separated.

When everyone seems back to normal (performing normal daily functions, such as eating, playing, and using the litter box, not hiding or hissing), you can reintroduce them.

A Matter of Time

A cat can stay aroused for up to two days after an episode of redirected aggression.

Reintroduction. If the incident has just occurred, if it wasn't severe, and if you're able to separate the cats immediately, then the reintroduction won't take long. If, however, the incident happened days ago and the cats are still fighting with each other, then the process will have to be more gradual. A particularly severe episode will result in a longer reintroduction process. Keeping each cat safe is of the utmost importance. The key is to give them a reason to like each other again. That's done by offering meals and treats in each other's presence. This is all done slowly while you allow both cats to stay within their comfort zones. Go at the pace of the most fearful cat. Reward behaviors such as breaking a stare. Because a direct stare is a threat, give a treat if the aggressor looks away. Basically, reward behaviors indicating there is no threat.

Incorporate the use of cat-appeasing pheromones, which may help reduce conflict.

Aggression Redirected Toward a Human Family Member. Don't try to cuddle or comfort the agitated cat. Leave her alone to calm down. Turn the lights down, close the curtains, and give her time to hide and de-stress. If you try to comfort her, you risk more aggression. In addition to your risk of getting injured, comfort now will keep the cat's arousal level too high and actually reinforce the unwanted behavior.

When your cat has calmed down, you can offer food or begin a gentle, low-intensity play session with an interactive toy to change her mind-set from negative to positive.

> ## Safety Through Clicking
> Clicker training can be very effective when dealing with aggression-related problems because it keeps you at a safe distance during the training process.

Ongoing Redirected Aggression. If you know that your cat has a pattern of becoming reactive to certain things and as a result frequently displays redirected aggression, you'll need a long-term plan. If there's a cat outdoors, you may have to block viewing access for your indoor cat. If an outdoor cat routinely comes into your yard, you can set up a motion-activated sprinkler to deter him from getting close.

Gradually desensitize and countercondition your cat to noises or other triggers that cause stress. Begin at a very low level at which your cat is still relatively comfortable, and offer a treat or a play session. Very slowly you can begin to increase her exposure to the trigger.

If there's a particular spot in the house where redirected aggression tends to occur, the cat may now have formed a negative association with that area. If you can't change the association with that area, your best bet is to block off access to it.

Pam's CatWise Clue

Ten Tips for Calming an Out-of-Control Cat. Aggression in cats can have many causes, but here are some tips for dealing with any angry cat:

1. A veterinarian visit is crucial if your cat begins to show even a hint of behavior change involving more aggression. The sooner you detect the change and have it checked by the veterinarian, the greater the chance of avoiding an escalation of the aggression.

2. If you know your cat isn't feeling well or you can tell by his body language that he's getting agitated, prefers not to interact, or is getting stressed, provide a safe place for him. Be proactive and offer a place to safely chill rather than testing his tolerance.

3. If you have a multicat household where there are routine spats, have some helpful objects on hand to separate the feuding felines from each other. Keep some towels and pieces of cardboard around so you can block their view of each other. Sometimes keeping the cats from staring

each other down can be enough to quash the aggression. If it continues or worsens, a reintroduction may be necessary.

4. Young children and pets should never be left together unsupervised. Even if you know your pet is extremely tolerant and friendly, it takes only a moment for a tail to be pulled or a fistful of fur to be yanked. Animals in pain, especially when surprised, may react defensively.

5. If you have young children, there should always be elevated locations for your cat to get out of harm's way. As children get old enough, make sure they understand that there are certain cat-only areas in the house. Jumping or climbing to safety will almost always be a cat's first move to avoid confrontation. Children should also know when cats need their own space, such as while eating, sleeping, or using the litter box.

6. Teach children the appropriate way to pet the family cat. Teach open-handed petting that always goes in the direction the hair grows. As children get older, teach them about cat body language so they can avoid a cat who is giving clear signals to stay away.

7. If your cat is being reactive, give him time to himself. The best course of action is to leave him alone. Lower the lights and let him have some time to settle down. Don't try to comfort and soothe him, because your approach may just increase his agitation.

8. Never punish a cat for aggression. Punishment will only increase his fear of you and may increase the aggression level. Animals don't act aggressively just for the heck of it; they do so because they perceive a situation to be threatening. Figure out the underlying cause, remove the threat, and let the cat calm down—that's the safe, productive course.

9. Incorporate the use of cat-appeasing pheromones to increase positive social contact and reduce tension.

10. Seek qualified, professional help for ongoing aggression problems or if you're at all concerned about your cat's behavior. Start with your veterinarian so an evaluation can be made; then your veterinarian can refer you to a qualified behavior expert.

Question:

Why does my cat occasionally attack his own tail? I've noticed his skin twitching as well. Is this serious?

Pam's Answer:

Your cat needs a veterinary evaluation to rule out medical causes such as pain or injury. For one thing, the veterinarian will need to decide whether your cat is experiencing a condition known as hyperesthesia. This is also referred to as rolling-skin disease. It's a condition that typically affects younger cats. The cause of hyperesthesia syndrome is unknown, but some experts describe it as a neurotransmitter malfunction in the brain during periods of anxiety. It's not a common disorder, but if your cat is experiencing this, it's very frightening for everyone.

Hyperesthesia causes the cat to feel intensely sensitive to touch. The parts of the body most vulnerable are the spine and along the tail. Cats most at risk are those living in environments of ongoing stress.

Signs of Hyperesthesia Syndrome. With hyperesthesia, you'll usually notice that the cat engages in excessive grooming. Typically the cat will focus on the spine and tail, sometimes continuing to the point of self-mutilation. Other physical signs include tail lashing and skin twitching or rippling. Often, there will be sudden bursts of activity, which can escalate into aggression. The cat may attack other pets or even human family members. The cat may appear perfectly fine, then react aggressively as if a switch had been flipped, and may even display seizurelike behavior. Other signs may include dilated pupils, biting at the tail, and an increase in vocalization.

Treating Hyperesthesia Syndrome. When diagnosing hyperesthesia other underlying conditions must be ruled out first, such as epilepsy, arthritis, abscesses, cancer, spinal problems, injuries, and other skin conditions.

Hyperesthesia is usually controlled by antianxiety, antiseizure, or antidepressant medication. Environmental factors must also be addressed, reducing the cat's exposure to anxiety triggers. Environmental enrichment is also beneficial.

Question:

I think I need a professional to help me with my cat's behavior problem. How do I know which one to choose? Should I try to find a cat whisperer?

Pam's Answer:

Ever since Cesar Millan hit the TV screen with his popular show *The Dog Whisperer*, many people have claimed to have the special talent of knowing the dog or cat mind (or the rabbit, frog, gerbil, or ferret mind, for that matter). There has also been an increase in cat-related television programs. The problem is that, in this unregulated field, anyone can claim to be a cat expert, cat whisperer, cat therapist, cat psychologist, or cat counselor. Anyone can put up a Web site, make claims of expertise, and post testimonials, but how do you know their expertise is valid? The problem is, you don't. If you're having a behavior problem with your pet and your family life is in crisis because of it, you may be enticed by claims of "guaranteed" results or lots of testimonials (which may not even be real), but a wrong choice can result in making the problem worse.

Start at the Veterinary Clinic. If you feel you need professional help with a cat behavior problem, how do you go about choosing the right expert? The first place to start is at your veterinarian's office. I know it doesn't sound as glamorous as consulting with someone who claims to have had some sort of special rapport with cats since the age of two, but many behavior problems can be the result of an underlying medical problem. You'd be surprised how many times a litter box problem is due to lower urinary tract disease, renal failure, or diabetes. I've seen cases of aggression, as well, whose cause turned out to be periodontal disease, spinal pain, an abscess, hyperthyroidism, or arthritis.

Do Your Homework. Behavior modification is a powerful tool and, if done correctly, is an effective way to change unwanted behavior. It is science-based; there's no magic about it. A trained, professional expert can explain to you how and why it works and the science behind it. An ethical professional will not guarantee results, because much of the success of behavior modification depends on client compliance and the specifics of the individual case. A qualified professional won't promise a quick fix. Every case is unique. Your neighbor's cat with the same behavior problem might take twice as long as your cat.

Look for Qualified Experts with a Track Record. The best way to protect yourself from the multitude of so-called experts is to ask your veterinarian for a referral to a qualified behavior expert. Applied animal behaviorists are certified by the Animal Behavior Society. Certified veterinary behaviorists are certified by the American College of Veterinary Behaviorists. There are also other professional organizations that certify, such as the International Association of Animal Behavior Consultants.

Choose someone with documented experience in their field. Make sure that person is truly an expert in cat behavior and has a track record involving more than just shameless self-promotion or slick products. Is the person you've chosen recognized by colleagues in the field as a professional? Your cat can't speak for himself, so he's counting on you to find a qualified professional, not someone viewing the current popularity of animal behavior consulting as a ticket to fame. Those of us who have been in the business for many years know what's really involved in dedicating our lives to animal welfare.

What to Expect:

- Don't hesitate to ask the behavior professional you're considering about his or her background. Is this someone who has demonstrated true expertise in the field or someone who has put up an impressive Web site and claims to be good with cats due to having had many? Is the Web site advertising misleading, or does it provide factual information about the professional's level of expertise? Lately, I have come across some Web sites with very misleading claims. My heart breaks for the cats.

- Truly professional experts adhere to strict ethical guidelines. They don't make claims outside of their area of expertise, they respect your confidentiality, and they do not judge or blame. A behavior professional should not make a medical diagnosis (without having a veterinary degree as well) and should never guarantee results.

- You should feel comfortable talking with the behavior expert and also be comfortable with the proposed behavior modification plan. In order for behavior modification to be successful, it must be a plan that fits your abilities, schedule, and lifestyle. A qualified professional will work with you to establish a customized plan to fit you and your cat. There is no one-size-fits-all behavior modification plan.

- The behavior expert should explain why the proposed behavior modification is being chosen and the science behind it.

- Whether you do an in-home consultation, a clinic visit, or a remote video consultation, you should receive a behavioral and medical history questionnaire. This history form is important to help the behavior expert get as much background as possible. Even if a question on the form doesn't seem relevant, answer to the best of your abilities to help the behaviorist put all the pieces of the puzzle together.

- Pictures and video are extremely helpful. Don't provoke your cat in order to capture video of aggression, but have your phone handy to record episodes of the unwanted behavior if they occur. If the behavior professional isn't making an in-home visit, then pictures and/or videos of the environment are important. Take pictures of areas where problems have occurred, as well as litter box areas, feeding areas, favorite resting spots, and any other location that might help in the evaluation.

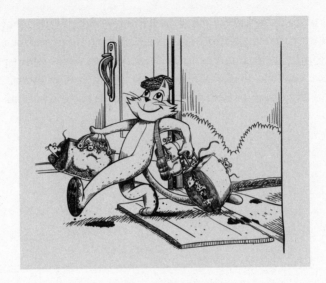

Chapter 14

Outside Influence

How to persuade your cat the grass isn't really greener on the other side

Question:
Isn't it cruel to keep cats indoors?

Pam's Answer:
I take a pretty strong position on indoor versus outdoor life for cats. In my opinion, indoor life is safer, healthier, and happier. Consider these twelve reasons to keep your cat indoors:

1. Indoor Cats Generally Live Longer. In general, a cat who spends his entire life indoors will live many years longer than a cat restricted exclusively to the outdoors. If your cat has indoor/outdoor access, he may live longer than the exclusively outdoor feline, but he still faces increased risks to his health and safety that can shorten lifespan.

2. Indoor Cats Won't Get Struck by Vehicles. The outdoor cat is always at risk of being struck by a vehicle. Even the most "street savvy" feline can become distracted while in pursuit of prey or while being chased by another cat or a dog. Cats get hit by cars at an alarmingly high rate, and even if the animal survives, the injuries are usually extremely severe.

3. Danger of Poisoning. Outdoor cats are at risk of poisoning by ethylene glycol (antifreeze), lawn pesticides, spoiled food in trash cans, mole and rodent poisons, and poisoned food placed out by people to kill cats.

Even though there's a risk of poisoning indoors, you're in much more control there and can remove toxic plants, toxic chemicals, and other dangers.

4. Outdoors Means Animal Fights. It's not unusual for an outdoor cat to become injured or develop a painful and serious abscess from fighting with another cat, a dog, or other animal. Even if you have your cat neutered or spayed, there are many intact cats outside, and they are extremely territorial.

5. Decreased Risk of Disease. If your cat isn't exposed to other outdoor cats, he has a greatly reduced risk of contracting a contagious disease.

6. Decreased Risk of Parasites. The chances of your cat becoming infested with fleas, ticks, or internal worms will be greatly reduced if he remains indoors, because he won't be coming in contact with infected feces, prey, grass, or soil.

7. No Danger from Predators. Cats are potential prey to some dogs, and if you live in certain areas of the country, they are also at risk of being attacked by coyotes or even owls.

8. Control over Diet. You can control what an indoor cat eats. If your cat goes outdoors, you have no idea whether he's munching on some cheap food left out on a neighbor's back porch for the local stray cats.

9. No Risk of Cruelty. Outdoors, your cat may easily become the victim of a cat-hating neighbor, people who think it's fun to abuse a helpless animal, or people who use cats for unspeakable things.

10. You'll Always Know Where Your Cat Is. If your cat is indoors, there's a greatly reduced risk of his getting lost, trapped somewhere, or stolen.

Why Cats Get Stuck in Trees

Because the front claws curve rearward, it's easy to climb up the tree but hard to get down unless the cat has learned how to climb down tail first. Ascending a tree is also aided by the cat's strong hind legs.

---

11. Better Health Monitoring. With an indoor cat, you can easily monitor what is or isn't happening in the litter box. That early detection of any change in your cat's litter box habits could mean less pain and suffering. You're also better able to monitor changes in food or water intake and activity level.

12. You'll Be a Better Neighbor. Not everyone wants a cat peeing in their garden, stalking the backyard bird feeder, or lounging on the car in their driveway. In most cases, your neighbors will be happier knowing your cat is quietly watching the outdoor activity from inside the house.

Question:

We've been feeding an outdoor cat for a few years and would like to bring her indoors now. Will she accept indoor life at this point?

Pam's Answer:

Making the transition from outdoor life to indoor life can be easy for a cat if you set up the indoor environment to be as interesting as the one she's about to leave behind and follow some important steps in acclimatizing her.

What If the Cat Has Never Been Indoors? First take the cat to the veterinarian to make sure she's healthy, to get her vaccinated if she hasn't already been, and to start her on flea control. The only newcomer you want to bring into the house is the cat, not fleas or ticks.

While you're at the veterinarian, talk about having the cat microchipped. That way, if she does escape, you stand a much better chance of having her returned to you. Spay/neuter surgery should also be scheduled if you're dealing with an intact cat.

If you're bringing in a stray cat or if you decide your exclusively outdoor cat should now live indoors, you can't just bring her in and let her have the run of the house right away. She'll need to get her bearings, and you may need to do a little training before she goes exploring in every room. Even though you may think that, after having access to the whole outdoors, she should handle your eighteen-hundred-square-foot house without a hitch, it won't necessarily be a seamless transition. First of all, in the great outdoors, she could pee and poop wherever she pleased. I don't think you'll want that to be the case in your house. Confine her to one area until you know she has adjusted to the litter box. The same applies to scratching. Outside she had every tree and fence post at her disposal. Inside, you'll want her using a designated scratching post, not your living room furniture.

Outdoors, the cat also had her own hiding places, favorite perches, and other locations. The indoor environment will be totally unfamiliar to her, and it can be overwhelming if you offer too much too soon.

If you're bringing in a stray or a cat who hasn't had much contact with you, confine her to a smaller area to allow you to start getting to know each other.

The Sanctuary Room. I've talked and written so much about how to set up a sanctuary room, especially as it applies to introducing a second cat to a resident cat. For a cat who has never set foot inside your home, setting up a sanctuary room will be needed to establish a comfort zone.

The sanctuary room is just a room you can close off, such as a bedroom. This is where all of the cat's necessities will be located.

Hideaways. The first thing the former outdoor cat may do when inside is to seek out a hiding place. This is important because, once she feels securely hidden, she can use that hiding place as her home base as she begins to get to know the environment. The hideaways can be as simple as open paper bags placed on their sides, boxes on their sides, boxes turned upside down with an entrance hole cut in one side, soft-sided pet tunnels, etc. The more hideaways you spread around the room, the less likely the cat will camp out under the bed.

Litter Box. If the cat has never used a litter box, then you have to make the setup easy for her to figure out. Use a large open litter box and fill it with unscented, soft litter. Although large, the box shouldn't be too high. The litter should resemble what the cat would use outdoors (garden soil, sand, dirt). This isn't the time to experiment with alternative litters or a high-tech self-cleaning litter box. Make the setup appealing and obvious. Don't use a covered box, and don't place the box in the closet. Keep everything convenient. In some cases with stray cats, you may even have to start out by filling the box with a sand and dirt mixture so it more closely resembles the substrate she used outdoors. Once the cat understands what the litter box is for, you can gradually start adding scoopable litter and reduce the amount of sand and dirt.

Scratching Post. A stray cat or one who was exclusively outdoors will have claws that have never been trimmed. This is a cat used to being able to scratch on whatever she pleases, so make sure there's a good, sturdy scratching post available. Sisal-covered ones are usually the most effective.

Cat Tree or Perch. Being able to climb up to a safe elevated perch was a crucial part of outdoor life for the cat. It provided safety and let the cat see what was going on around her. Provide a sturdy cat tree, or at the very least, install a window perch. If you don't invest in a cat tree now, you really will need to at some point. A cat tree may seem like a big expense, but it's a very important piece of feline real estate. It provides so much comfort and security.

Cat trees come in all shapes, sizes, and prices. When I brought in two feral cats many years ago, I attached some silk tree branches around the cat tree to give the cats more cover. They felt a little more concealed when up on the tree, and I believe that accelerated our trust-building process.

Shopping Tip

When shopping for a cat tree, look for one that provides comfort, stability, and security. Stay away from narrow, sleek ones.

Trust Building. Don't be in a rush to show the cat how much you love her. Let her set the pace. She needs to feel secure; then the bond of trust will start to grow. Use interactive playtime as a way to engage her in fun activities while still allowing her to stay within her comfort zone. The fishing pole–type design of the toy keeps you just far enough away from her so she can focus more on playing than on you. That's what you want. If she feels she can relax around you and not have to keep her eyes on you at all times, she'll see you're a friend and not a foe.

Cat-Proofing. Now that your cat is indoors, there are some dangers that you may not have paid attention to previously. Go around your home, check for potential risks, and make necessary changes. Make sure all window screens are secure, put plants out of the cat's reach, keep cleaners and chemicals stored away, and put the trash can under the sink or make sure it has a secure lid.

Because you aren't familiar with the cat's habits yet, when it comes time to bring her out of the sanctuary room, you'll have to pay attention to whether she tends to want to steal food off the counters or chew on things she shouldn't. You may have to do some training to keep the cat off the counter. In the meantime, make sure food isn't left out.

Watch for Escapes. When it comes time to open the sanctuary room door, you'll then have to deal with the risk that the cat may try to bolt out the front door when she sees an opportunity. Make sure the cat's whereabouts are known before anyone opens a door.

Creating a Safe "Outdoor" Experience. If you want to still allow your cat to have some exposure to the outdoors, consider doing it in a very safe way by creating or purchasing a sturdy outdoor enclosure. You can find all types of enclosures, from small to elaborate.

Maximize the Indoor Enrichment. To keep your cat persuaded that being indoors is a good thing, pay attention to environmental enrichment. Be creative in increasing the fun factor. Grow some kitty greens for your cat to munch on as she might have done outdoors.

Because the outdoor environment holds lots of opportunities for hunting, adventure, and exploration, provide some semblance of that stimulation (without live prey, of course) for the transitioning indoor cat. Don't allow the indoors to become boring.

Question:

Nicolette is an inside/outside cat. I don't really want to have a litter box in the house, but my wife says we should have one. Won't she do OK just being let out to eliminate like a dog?

Pam's Answer:

If you train your cat to eliminate exclusively outdoors, you may be setting yourself up for a behavior problem down the road.

Some cat parents who allow their cats outdoors have tried to do without an indoor litter box. They may have trained their cats to scratch at the door, use a pet door, or meow, or maybe the cats are just let out on a regular schedule. This can be shortsighted thinking, for the following reasons:

Foul Weather. Your cat may not enjoy going outdoors during extremes in temperature, rain, snow, or other severe weather. Forcing the cat to go out there for elimination can be stressful and even dangerous.

Threats from Other Animals. Your cat may not have a problem eliminating outdoors until one day when she comes face to face with another cat or dog. Going outdoors may then become a very stressful experience, if your cat has to worry about being ambushed by the neighborhood bully. A physical encounter can put her in danger of injury. If she anticipates trouble, she may become reluctant to go outdoors or may even start eliminating inside in inappropriate locations to avoid conflict with an outdoor animal.

Illness or Injury. Cats who aren't feeling well or have some type of injury will find it more difficult to go outdoors for elimination.

Senior Issues. Your cat may never have had a problem going outdoors to eliminate in years past, but as she gets older and less mobile, it may become more uncomfortable. Cold and damp weather will be especially aggravating to a senior cat's joints.

Garden Maintenance. When your cat eliminates outside, do you know where she goes? Does she eliminate in your garden? In the woods? In your neighbor's backyard? It can be unpleasant to have a garden filled with cat feces.

Lack of Monitoring. When you aren't scooping a litter box regularly, you have less information regarding your cat's health. You could easily miss potential issues. Scooping the litter box is an opportunity to notice any changes in your cat's elimination habits.

Question:
Can my cat be trained to walk on a leash?

Pam's Answer:
I'm not big on taking a cat outdoors, and even if you never plan to walk your cat around the block, there's a good reason to leash train her. Leash training can help with a new cat introduction, aggressive issues between companion cats, or even in introducing a dog to your cat. If you're dealing with a cat who displays offensive aggression toward companion pets in the home, you can leash train her to help her stay "checked in" with you. This training can keep her at a safe distance from the target of her aggression. The fact that she can't go after her intended target can also help the other cat relax. This may lead to an overall relaxation in body language communication between the cats.

Not Every Cat Is a Candidate for Leash Training. As with any type of training, there's a learning curve, but if your cat is easily stressed or you think she'll never be comfortable, then don't try leash training. You know your cat. Use that knowledge to make a sound decision that will benefit her and not stress or endanger her.

Leash Walking Indoors Is Vastly Different from Outdoors. Cats are territorial, and scent plays a huge role in their lives. When you take a cat outdoors, she'll be bombarded with endless unfamiliar scents. Some of those scents may be threatening. In addition, cats can easily be startled outdoors by dogs, loud noises, cars, and even people walking by. If you think trying to hold a terrified and defensive cat in your arms as you head back to safety indoors is easy, let me tell you, it isn't! This is how people and cats get injured. This is how cats escape from your control and get lost. Think carefully before you decide that walking outdoors is a good option. Know your cat, plan to walk only within your yard, and take precautions. At least place a heavy towel over your shoulder before you head out for the walk, so you can wrap the cat in it if she panics. Another thing to consider is that your indoor cat, if she's exposed to the outdoors, will be susceptible to parasites, such as fleas and ticks. Make sure you plan in advance and begin flea and tick and even heartworm preventives well in advance of going outside. Finally, the unthinkable can happen; your cat may escape, so make sure she's microchipped. Have visible ID on her as well. The ID should say "indoor cat" so anyone coming across her will know she isn't street savvy.

Unwanted Behaviors. Walking your cat outside on a leash may seem like the best of both worlds, but keep in mind that your cat may decide she should be in charge of the walking schedule. A few fun walks could start her meowing at the door at lunchtime. She could also become a door darter if she feels you aren't taking her outside often enough. Think carefully before rushing into this new adventure.

Have the Right Equipment. You'll need a harness made especially for cats or a walking jacket for cats. Don't use a collar, because your cat will easily slip out of it. The other danger with a collar is your cat could get strangled on a tree branch if she escapes from you. Your best bet is a cat harness or a walking jacket. I recommend the walking jacket because it provides more comfort, is more secure, and cradles the cat with an even amount of pressure. On a cat harness or walking jacket, the leash attachment is near the middle of the cat's body rather than at the neck as on a collar. This is more comfortable for the cat and much safer.

You'll have to get the right size harness or jacket. Measure your cat's girth just behind her front legs. Manufacturers of jackets and harnesses have specific instructions on exactly where and how to measure.

Start Slow. You can't just slap on a harness or jacket, hook up the leash, and expect a cat to be comfortable and know what to do. The training process involves gradual desensitization.

Initially, just leave the harness or walking jacket on the floor for your cat to sniff and investigate. When she's comfortable with that, you can put it on (but not too snug) while kitty eats dinner or gets yummy treats. Gradually increase the time she wears it. Work up to adjusting the harness or jacket so it fits appropriately. The next step is to attach the leash and hold it loosely while she walks around. It may be easier to let her drag the leash, but just be careful she doesn't get caught on anything, or else you'll have a panicky cat on your hands. Have treats with you so you can distract her and also reward her when she shows any sign of being calm. Remember this process is all to be done strictly indoors.

One way to entice your cat to walk alongside you is to hold the treat at her level just a few inches in front of her. She'll walk toward it hopefully. After she eats that treat, hold another a few inches away again. Keep in mind that as her hunger decreases, so will her level of compliance. You don't want to fill her up with treats, so break them into small pieces and keep your training sessions short.

It's not at all unusual for a cat to drop over on her side or freeze when a harness or jacket is placed on her. If this happens, see if you can entice her to stand up again by offering a treat. If she won't budge, remove the harness or jacket and just leave it on the floor. She may need more time with that initial stage of just having it lying around in the environment for a while. When you're ready to try again, be armed with treats. If your cat is always ready for a play session, have an interactive toy nearby or even just a peacock feather to see if you can distract her.

A Few Paw Facts

A cat's paw pads may feel rough, but they're extremely sensitive. Cats sweat through their paw pads. They also rely on the sensitive nerve endings in them to feel movement, texture, and temperature. The pads can suffer burns and frostbite.

Make It Fun and Monitor Your Cat's Stress. Training sessions should be short, positive, and fun. If you're training to control aggression between cats, don't rely strictly on the leash as a way to cut short behavior modification. You still need to do the behavior modification necessary to help cats in a multicat environment develop a good relationship. Leash training is just one tool in your toolbox.

A Cat Is Not a Dog. If you do decide to venture outdoors, don't expect your cat to walk next to you the way a dog would. She's going to stop and smell everything; she may bolt, freeze, try to climb up your leg, or hide under the nearest bush. Stay very close to the house, have treats, stay calm, and keep the session short and safe. Timing is also important here. Don't try to walk your cat at the same time your next-door neighbor lets his dog out for the afternoon or when the school bus stops on the corner to discharge the students. I also recommend that you pick up and carry your cat outside and back inside so she learns that *you* are the one in control of her entrances and exits.

Chapter 15

You Expect Me to Eat That?

*How to make the feeding
station a happy place*

Question:

Is there an easy way to switch my cat from dry food to moist without upsetting her?

Pam's Answer:

Cats are creatures of habit, and making any type of significant change can be tricky. Making a food change requires care to avoid the potential health complications that can occur if done incorrectly or abruptly.

A Gradual Transition. Even if you're going to change your cat over from a bargain basement dry food to the best quality wet food, it's important not to rush. Don't take the attitude that your cat will love the high-class stuff or will eat when she gets hungry enough, because she won't, and the consequences can be fatal. Hepatic lipidosis is a life-threatening liver condition that can develop when a cat goes without eating or eats only a small amount of food.

Going from dry food to wet food is a huge change. Going from one brand of dry food to another brand of dry is sometimes difficult enough because of smell, taste, and texture issues, so imagine how strange it might be for many cats to experience the very unfamiliar texture of wet food. So don't rush this transition, and don't take the tough-love stance.

Your Cat's Feeding Schedule. If you normally leave food down for meals ad lib, transition to scheduled mealtimes to let your cat get hungry enough to want to try the wet food. If she's able to nibble on the familiar food all day long, she may never feel the need to even taste the new stuff. Start on a schedule of three or four dry-food meals a day (unless you receive other directions from your veterinarian), and don't leave the food down for more than twenty minutes. Make sure that when you place the food down, you alert your cat to the fact that it's mealtime. Once your cat has accepted the new routine of scheduled mealtimes instead of free-choice feeding, you can then offer a wet-food meal.

Make the wet food as appealing as possible. Your cat may devour it the moment you place the bowl on the floor (and in that case, consider yourself very lucky!), but she may also turn her nose up at it. Warm the food slightly to release the aroma. Never serve canned food straight out of the refrigerator. Cats prefer food to be at room temperature or slightly warmer. Don't leave wet food down for more than twenty minutes, because it will dry and lose its taste appeal. Your cat certainly won't enjoy trying to pry out of the bowl food that's turned to concrete.

If your cat still doesn't touch the wet food, sprinkle a little dry food on top of the wet and offer the meal that way. You can also mix some dry food into the wet food so your cat has to work a little harder to get to the dry food and in the process tastes more of the wet food. Gradually reduce the amount of dry food you mix into the wet food each day.

Mealtime Monitoring in Multicat Homes. If you have more than one cat and you're doing the transition from dry to wet food, give each cat an individual bowl so you can be sure everyone gets an adequate amount. In some cases, that may mean feeding cats in separate locations.

Question:

My cat, Caroline, seems nervous when she eats around my other cats. Is there a way to help her feel more at ease?

Pam's Answer:

For your cat, mealtime should be healthy, tasty, peaceful, and secure. Some cat parents focus on the first two things but don't pay enough attention to the last two. When your cat walks over to the food bowl, she shouldn't have to worry about whether she can eat in peace or whether she's going to have to deal with a threat.

The Route to the Food Bowl. Here's something many people don't think about: evaluating the route your cat has to take to get to the bowl. When dinner is served, does she have to walk through a feline minefield where she's faced with potential threats from companion animals? In a multi-cat household where there are some tense relationships, a cat may not feel secure enough to walk through the room another cat tends to control. If that's the case, set up an additional feeding area where an intimidated cat feels comfortable.

To increase security during mealtime in a multicat home, don't feed out of one communal bowl. Cats feel more secure when eating alone. For us, eating is an opportunity for social engagement, but that's not the case for cats. Give each cat her own bowl to avoid intimidation and bullying. If there are still issues, set up additional feeding areas in multiple locations so one cat doesn't nose another out of the bowl and nobody feels the need to resource-guard. This is also helpful if specific cats are on special diets. If everyone has a personal feeding location, it's easier to make sure each cat gets the right food. Keep in mind that just because you may not see overt aggression doesn't mean your cat isn't experiencing it.

Nervousness + Mealtime = Unhappy Cat. Observe your cat's body language as she eats her meal. When does she look relaxed and when does she look nervous? Does she seem that she's in a hurry to get out of the line of fire? Is she looking over her shoulder repeatedly? Is she constantly lifting her head to watch out for potential attacks? Help her feel more comfortable by setting up the feeding station in a more secure area. Even in a secure location, if your cat seems nervous, slide the food bowl out from against the wall so she can look toward the entrance while she eats. This way, she doesn't have to have her back to the door or keep looking over her shoulder. Position the food bowl on the side of the room opposite the entrance so your cat has adequate warning if someone enters. For some cats, it helps to elevate the feeding station, and some feel more at ease when totally hidden while eating. Follow your cat's lead and pay attention to where she seems most secure. For a timid cat, close the door of the room during mealtime so there's absolutely no chance of another cat, a dog, or a person entering and startling her.

Mealtime must always be safe and secure. Never assume that your cat will eventually come out of hiding and eat when hungry enough. The result could be emotional and medical trouble for your kitty.

Question:
Why do some cats act as if trying to bury their food?

Pam's Answer:
It's a relatively common behavior and not one you need to worry about. It looks as if the cat were trying to bury waste. You may see him scrape one front paw on the floor around the bowl. In some cases, cats get so involved in attempting to cover that they actually start pushing the bowl around.

Is Your Cat Sending You a Message? Many people think their cats are saying they dislike the food, but this isn't true. You'll see cats perform this covering ritual even with food they have previously eaten and liked.

It All Comes Down to Survival. In the wild, a cat may attempt to bury or cover any uneaten food in order to avoid attracting any predators to the area. It's also an attempt to avoid alerting any other potential prey that a feline hunter is in the vicinity. Cats aren't scavengers, so they don't bury the food to consume later. They do it strictly to protect themselves and their supply of fresh prey. Even an indoor cat who has never set foot outside retains this survival instinct. It's just a matter of how much it concerns a certain cat; that determines to what degree the behavior is displayed.

Tips for Stopping the Behavior. It really is a harmless behavior, but if it bothers you or if your cat seems to become obsessed with burying the leftovers, here are some tips:

■ Offer smaller portions. Watch the amount he typically eats in a meal and don't overdo what you place in the bowl.

■ Don't leave food bowls out once the cat has given the signal that he's finished. Take the food bowl up, clean any spills on the floor, and leave fresh water available.

■ If you leave food out for free-choice eating, place some in puzzle feeders so your cat can "hunt" for his meal.

■ When you notice your cat begin to display the behavior, distract him with some playtime or another activity.

Question:
Why does my cat eat grass?

Pam's Answer:
I assume you have a cat who goes outdoors and at some point you've seen her nibble on a few blades of grass in your yard. Soon afterward you've probably seen her throw that grass right back up. It might seem odd that a cat would knowingly eat something that makes her sick, but there are a few theories that suggest that grass nibbling serves a valuable function.

It Must Be Something I Ate. Cats may eat grass to rid their digestive tract of something unpleasant or inedible. Grass nibbling may be of particular importance to outdoor cats who eat prey in order to get rid of any inedible parts that get swallowed, such as feathers or bones. It can also be a way for a cat to get rid of some hair that gets swallowed during grooming, thus cutting down on hairballs.

Speaking of Hairballs. Hairballs that don't get vomited out will go through the intestinal tract. Sometimes they don't pass easily out the back end. Cats might instinctively know that the added fiber from eating grass helps keep things moving in the south.

Providing Nutrients. Another theory is that cats eat grass for nutrients. Typically, when a cat eats prey, she also consumes the contents of the prey's stomach. The prey's belly usually contains grasses and grains.

Is Eating Grass Harmful? Eating grass is typically not harmful. If you have an outdoor cat, though, you wouldn't want her eating grass that has been chemically treated. The safest way to provide grass for your cat is to grow a pot of it for her. You can either purchase a kitty-greens kit at your local pet product store or grow your own using rye, wheat, or oat seeds. In fact, providing your cat with some safe kitty greens may help prevent her from nibbling on dangerous houseplants—which *are* toxic to cats.

Don't confuse grass eating with plant eating. All houseplants are toxic to cats, and most are poisonous. Keep plants out of your cat's reach.

Question:
Why should I get my cat a puzzle feeder?

Pam's Answer:
A puzzle feeder is simply a food-dispensing toy. The cat figures out what movement of the toy is required to get a food reward, and a game is born. You cat doesn't necessarily *need* a puzzle feeder, but for many cats, it can be a very effective tool for adding mental stimulation into daily life. Your cat is a hunter, and the natural way she would get her meals would be to hunt them down. In the wild, there are no stainless bowls filled with mice or serving trays holding beautifully prepared birds and chipmunks. For the hunter to get her meal, she must first stalk it, pounce, and capture her prize. For the hunter, a successful meal requires mental and physical stimulation. Many of us want our cats to stay indoors for safety reasons, but then we don't supply enough environmental enrichment to keep the cats mentally stimulated and physically fit. Using a puzzle feeder is just one aspect of an all-around enhancement of your cat's day-to-day life.

What Are the Benefits? Even the most basic food-dispensing toy can be valuable in a variety of behavior and health issues. A puzzle feeder can:

- Encourage a cat to eat slowly
- Incorporate some reward-based solo playtime into your cat's day
- Ease boredom
- Redirect a cat from engaging in destructive behavior
- Provide a little added exercise
- Encourage a cat to think and stay mentally stimulated
- Give a cat some choice about when to eat, without free-feeding
- Aid in weight control
- Help with cats who are prone to vomiting from eating too quickly

Which Puzzle Feeder Should My Cat Use? There are many puzzle feeders available at your local pet product store as well as online. They vary from simple to complex. The type to use will depend on how fast your cat gets the idea. Some cats take to puzzle solving immediately and can work the food-dispensing toys quite successfully in a short amount of time. My cat, Pearl, has been able to master whatever puzzle feeder I present to her. She seems to truly enjoy the challenge. Other cats, though, may need to start with the most basic container with a large hole from which the food falls out easily. The point isn't to frustrate your cat but rather to tap into her natural hunting skills.

Make a Dry-Food Puzzle Feeder. Homemade puzzle feeders are often the most entertaining and rewarding for both the cat and the cat parent. Before you go out and buy a puzzle feeder, try making a simple one at home. One method is to make a water bottle feeder. Take an empty water bottle and cut holes in it that are bigger than the pieces of dry food or the treats. To start, make lots of holes in the bottle so your cat will have immediate success just by touching it. Put in some dry food or treats and lay it on its side on the floor. Another option is to make a cardboard feeder using the tubular core of a paper towel roll. Cut holes along the cardboard tube, fold in one end, put some dry food in there and then fold the other end closed.

Even yogurt containers can become puzzle feeders as long as they have a lid that snaps back on. Cut a couple of holes in the container and you have an instant puzzle feeder. Note: Make plastic and cardboard puzzle feeders only if your cat doesn't tend to chew on plastic or cardboard. If she does, use a commercial puzzle feeder right from the beginning. When you do give your cat the homemade puzzle feeder for the first time, supervise so you can be sure she won't chew it.

Another homemade puzzle feeder can be made by cutting holes in a small cardboard box. Make the holes larger than the size of your cat's paws so she can easily reach in for the food prize.

More Complex Homemade Puzzle Feeders. Collect paper towel or bathroom tissue cardboard tubes, and tape them together in a pyramid shape. If using paper towel tubes, you'll have to cut them in half. Attach the pyramid to a flat piece of cardboard and you have a honeycomb-style puzzle feeder with many different compartments in which you can place treats. Use your imagination in creating puzzle feeders. Just keep in mind that you want the experience to be rewarding, not frustrating.

One commercial dry-food puzzle feeder that has tubes of various lengths is called the Stimulo. You can customize the tubes to make them shorter or longer, depending upon what challenge level you want for your cat. Instead of dry food, you can put treats in them. Putting a high-value treat in the tubes may motivate the cat to work harder to achieve the reward.

Another way to make the puzzles more challenging is to cut fewer holes in the water bottle, yogurt container, or tubular cardboard feeders. Just make sure each hole is larger than the size of the kibble or treat.

Safety Reminder

The first time you introduce a puzzle feeder to your cat, whether it's homemade or one you purchased, be sure she doesn't chew parts of it or get her claws stuck in it.

Wet Food with Puzzle Feeders. A simple wet-food feeder is easy to make using a muffin tin. Just place a little drop of food in each compartment so the cat has to walk around a little to discover each reward. Even just dividing up the wet food into various dishes and placing them around the cat's play area will create a game of reward-based hide-and-seek for her.

Some commercial puzzle feeders can be used with wet food, as well. I stuff a little wet food inside a Kong dog toy for my cat. I use the small size so she can hold it and get the food inside.

Where to Buy Puzzle Feeders. Get on your favorite search engine, type in "puzzle feeders for cats," and you'll find lots of companies that make them, as well as many videos with how-to information. Not all commercial puzzle feeders are good for all cats, though, so take into consideration your cat's age, personality, and health when choosing them. Many of the companies have videos on their sites so you can watch a tutorial on how the product works and decide whether it's a good match for your cat.

Question:

Do you have any tips for helping me put my fat cat on a diet? I'm worried she'll get depressed or stressed.

Pam's Answer:

You're absolutely right to get that weight off if you've got an overweight cat. It's stressful, and it puts her at increased risk for diabetes, arthritis, and heart disease. Here are some important tips and reminders:

Visit the Veterinarian. The veterinary clinic is the first stop you should make when determining whether your cat is at the right weight or whether she needs a dietary change. Your veterinarian will examine your cat and do diagnostic blood work. Ideal weight is determined by your cat's age, body type, activity level, and overall health. The blood work will help identify any underlying medical concern, such as diabetes. Your veterinarian may also do additional diagnostics to check the condition of the heart and other organs.

Follow Appropriate Feeding Guidelines. A big mountain of food in the bowl will accomplish two things: It'll increase your cat's chances of becoming overweight, and it will reduce her chances of staying active. It's all too easy to let obesity and inactivity jeopardize your cat's health.

The feeding guidelines on the bag, box, or can of cat food are general information. Your cat has specific, unique needs and may require more or less than the recommended amount. If you feed homemade or raw food, your veterinarian can help you determine portion size based on your cat's needs. Learn what your cat's ideal weight should be and then weigh her regularly to determine if the portions you're feeding are the right size. This is important whether you feed commercial cat food or follow a homemade or raw nutritional plan.

Hold the Veggies

Cats are obligate carnivores. They must get vitamin A from meat sources. They can't convert beta carotene into vitamin A the way humans and dogs can, so don't even think of going vegetarian or vegan with them.

Feed the Correct Food. Make sure it's the appropriate food for your cat's stage of life. Your veterinarian may instruct you to keep your cat on her current food but adjust the portions, or she may prescribe a special reduced-calorie food. Be sure to follow your veterinarian's advice, and don't sneak extra treats, because you won't be doing your cat any favors.

Feed Smaller Meals More Often. Instead of putting a large amount of food down once or twice a day, portion the food out by feeding smaller meals more often. Cats have small stomachs, and eating smaller meals will be more natural for her.

Work for Food. Putting food in the bowl should be only one way of feeding your cat. Cats are hardwired to work for food, to *hunt* for it, so instead of piling the food into the bowl, use puzzle feeders. In addition to giving the cat a chance to work for her supper, the puzzle feeder enforces slow eating. If you have a cat who gulps the food down the second you place the bowl on the floor, the puzzle feeder may be the solution.

Beware of Softhearted Family Members. In nearly every family there's someone (and maybe that person is *you*) who's a soft touch. It takes only a plaintive meow or a sad look to get that person to fill the food bowl or offer a treat. You won't be doing the cat any favors if you or anyone else sneaks extra food her way. Instead, offer her a bonus play session!

Increase Activity. When was the last time you played with your cat? If you didn't answer "today" or "yesterday," then you're missing a golden opportunity to help your cat stay healthy. Don't just dump a huge pile of toys in a corner of the room. They're dead prey. Purchase some interactive toys and get into the game with your cat. Move the toy like prey so your cat can respond like a predator. Interactive play therapy should be done at least twice a day.

Don't Forget the Importance of Enrichment. In addition to the puzzle feeders and interactive playtime, set up some solo games and opportunities for exploration to keep your cat active when you're not at home.

- A multiperch tree provides an opportunity for your cat to leap, climb, scratch, and thus get a little extra exercise.
- Paper bags or boxes left on their sides with toys inside will tempt her to explore. You can even cut out the bottoms and connect them to make tunnels.
- Place balls, fuzzy mice, and other little toys around the house for your cat to discover.

Training. Clicker training is a great way to work on behavior issues, but it's also a fun way to increase the bond you share with your cat and train her to do some physical activities. You can even use clicker training to create an indoor agility course for your cat. Start with something simple, such as going through a tunnel, and then gradually add new elements.

Take It Slow. Feline weight loss shouldn't be done quickly, because of the risk of hepatic lipidosis. No matter how much weight your cat needs to lose, follow your veterinarian's guidelines and help the cat do it gradually.

Question:
Sparklette was always a good eater, but lately she has become finicky. Why is she so picky these days?

Pam's Answer:
If your cat's appetite has changed, have her examined by the veterinarian, and think about anything else that might have changed besides her appetite.

Have You Switched Brands or Flavors? One of the most common reasons a cat becomes a finicky eater is a sudden change in the food. While variety is very helpful in avoiding fixed food preferences, abrupt changes can upset the digestive system. It's good to introduce different brands and flavors and rotate them, but make sure you do a gradual transition each time you introduce an unfamiliar food. Gradually add a little more of the new food into the current brand each day over the course of a few days. Once that food becomes familiar, you can include it in your meal rotation.

What's the Temperature? Food fed directly from the refrigerator is unappealing. Cats aren't scavengers; they use their nose to determine if their prey is warm enough to be safe to eat. If the food is cold, it's not very fresh. Cold food also releases fewer aromas, so there's decreased scent appeal. Wet food should be served at body temperature or slightly warmer. Dry food should be at room temperature. Wet food shouldn't be left out in the bowl to dry and harden.

Feeding Your Cat Table Scraps. Finicky eating can result if you've been giving your cat table scraps. Why in the world would a cat want to eat her bowl of boring cat food after sampling some delicious cooked chicken, cheese casserole, or a nibble of filet mignon? Supplementing your cat's diet with rich foods with high taste appeal is a sure way to get her to turn her cute little nose up at her regular meal offering. Then the cat parent often starts incorporating some table scraps into the cat's regular food in an attempt to get her to eat. This upsets the nutritional balance. Because your cat is very smart, she quickly learns to simply eat around the cat food to get at the tasty table scraps.

Finicky eating can also be the result of conditions at the feeding station. Merely adding more food to a dirty bowl can discourage your cat from eating. Be sure to wash the food and water bowls daily.

I Found That Pill You Were Hiding in My Dish! If your cat has to be on medication and you know from experience that trying to put a pill in her mouth results in one very angry cat and possible injury to you, then you may have resorted to disguising the medication in your cat's meal. Your cat has a keen sense of smell, and more often than not, she'll know that her meal has been tampered with. Moreover, many medications aren't meant to be chewed but are designed to go down to the stomach with their protective coating intact. Often the pill is bitter, making the food less palatable. Your cat is smart. If she's found medication in her food, she may reject that food in the future regardless of whether you have added anything or not. If you medicate your cat, do so separately from meals unless your veterinarian tells you otherwise.

Mixing Courses. Feeding your cat from a double feeder, with food in one side and water in the other, may make the food very unappealing to her. Some cats like their water in a location totally separate from the food.

Watering Down the Food. You may have thought it was a good idea to add water to your cat's dry food to increase her water consumption, but this ploy results only in uneaten, soggy food. Likewise, adding water to wet food changes the consistency too much and often makes it less appealing.

Too Close for Comfort. We don't eat in the bathroom, and neither does your cat. Eliminating away from the living quarters and covering the waste are very important aspects of survival. To eat near the elimination area can be very confusing for cats. In most cases, it leads to litter box avoidance, but it can also result in finicky eating, or at the very least, anxiety during meals.

Stressed Cat = Unhappy Cat. Stress can also play a factor in finicky eating. Make sure the feeding station is a safe and secure place for your cat. In a multicat environment, you may need to set up more than one feeding station if one cat overpowers another to claim all the food. The feeding station needs to be a place where a cat feels secure. Being nervous, afraid of being ambushed by a companion cat, a dog, or even the children, can affect her appetite.

Question:

Rather than drink normally from her water bowl, my cat likes to play with the water using her paw. She'll sit and lick water from her paw and then dunk it over and over again. How can I get her to drink the way other cats do?

Pam's Answer:

There are a couple of reasons why your cat may enjoy playing with the water. One reason is just that it's fun. Water moves, so the slightest touch of a paw or even a whisker can spark playful behavior. It may not have started as play, but when the cat saw that dipping her paw in the water made it swirl around, it might've turned into a fun activity. She may have originally dipped her paw in the bowl out of curiosity about light reflection or movement, or it might have been out of necessity if the bowl was too narrow to comfortably accommodate her whiskers. When water levels aren't kept consistent, some cats will dip their paws in if they can't see the water line. Check to make sure your cat isn't having any vision problems. Sometimes cats who have declining vision will use their paws to reach for water or food. The next step is to figure out whether your cat is doing this because of the size, shape, or location of the water bowl or whether it truly is play behavior.

Create an Appealing Water Station. Make sure the bowl is wide enough to comfortably fit your cat's whiskers. If she has had to share a water bowl with other pets in the home, increase the number of bowls and their locations to increase her chances of having one to herself. If you have a multipet household, she may not feel safe sticking her face into the water bowl and thus making it hard to see if another animal is approaching. If you think that may be the case, then in addition to increasing the number and locations of bowls, use clear glass bowls. If there's a dog in the household, create a safe water station for your cat by elevating a couple of the bowls.

Don't just refill water each day without first washing the bowl. Hair, dirt, saliva, and food can stick to the sides, contaminating the water and changing the taste. When you wash the bowl, be sure to remove all traces of dishwashing soap, because residue can burn the cat's tongue.

Maintain a consistent water level. Don't let it go down to the last few drops and then fill it to the brim. The inconsistent level can be confusing and may lead to paw dipping.

Don't use a double feeding bowl. It may seem convenient to have food and water close together, but cats don't like it that way. Besides the chance of contamination from food particles spilling into the water, your cat doesn't necessarily want the smell of food nearby when she goes for a drink in the middle of the day. A cat instinctively knows that the smell of food attracts predators. Even though you know there's no coyote lurking in your kitchen, your cat doesn't know that.

Paws and Effect

When you have a paw dipper in the household, you have to remember not to leave cups of water or other drinks around. Although you may not mind that your cat dips her paws in her own water, you probably don't want that happening to the glass of iced tea you left on the table.

Dealing with a Water Bowl Player. If you've created the ideal water station(s) and you find your cat still paw dipping, it may have become a habit. If you want to discourage this type of play, you'll need to increase the stimulation and opportunities for play in other areas of your cat's life. Provide stimulation through interactive play therapy twice daily, and set up food-dispensing puzzle toys for your cat to enjoy throughout the day.

To control drips and spills, or if your cat overturns the whole bowl, use a weighted bowl too heavy for her to tip over. To contain spills, put a pet place mat under the bowl. This type of place mat has raised edges to protect your floors or carpets from spills.

If you don't mind that your cat plays with the water but would like to stop him from pushing the bowl around the kitchen or knocking it over, consider providing a pet water fountain. There are several types on the market, and the flowing water creates appealing movement and sound. The flowing water also stays oxygenated, which can increase taste appeal. This can be a plus if you're trying to get your cat to drink more water.

Chapter 16

No Guilt Trips

Traveling with or without your cat,
without worrying yourself sick

Question:
How do I choose the right size carrier for my new cat?

Pam's Answer:
When shopping for a carrier for your cat, you may be tempted to think bigger is better. You might feel it would be far more comfortable for your cat to be able to stretch out during travel. That's not how she sees it, and in fact can be distressed in a carrier too large for her.

Bigger Isn't Necessarily Better. Cats prefer to feel their backs up against something for a feeling of security. When you look at a frightened cat in a shelter or veterinary clinic cage, she's in a corner with her back against the wall. There's security in knowing that at least no one can attack from behind. That same feeling helps her when in the carrier.

A carrier that's too big is uncomfortable for her because she ends up sliding around. It's awkward to balance a carrier that's too big. Have you ever tried to balance a large carrier with twelve pounds of cat sloshing from one side to the other? It's not good for her, and it's definitely not good for your back!

Two Cats in One Carrier? Not a Good Idea. If you have a couple of cats and you're planning to buy one big carrier so they can be together, don't. It would be better to buy two carriers that'll each fit one cat perfectly. There will be times when you're bringing only one cat with you (for example, if only one needs to visit the veterinarian), and being alone in that big carrier is awkward. Moreover, even cats who get along fine at home can show aggression if they're bottled up together and the journey becomes stressful. After the office visit, one cat may become aggressive toward the other on the ride back home.

The Trouble with Being Trendy

Soft-sided, zippered carriers may be easier to carry and look more fashionable, but they don't help reduce anxiety at the veterinary clinic. Plastic kennel-type carriers enable you to take the top off and leave the cat in the bottom half during exams.

Too Small. On the other hand, a carrier that was a good fit for your cat when she was a kitten may be too small if she has grown into a large adult. Being stuffed into a carrier that causes her to feel cramped will only add to whatever displeasure she feels about having to travel in the first place.

Just the Right Size. Generally, a carrier should be one and a half times the size of your cat. It should give her enough room to stand up and turn around. If you buy a carrier for a kitten, she'll grow pretty fast, so get a regular-size carrier that you think will be appropriate when she reaches her adult size. During those kitten months, you can line the carrier with a thick towel so she doesn't slide all over the place while in transit.

Question:

How do we help our cat adjust to being in a carrier? It's a huge battle every time we have to take her to the veterinarian.

Pam's Answer:

It starts out innocently. A carrier initially holds no negative association. In fact, it may begin as a positive object for a cat—something in which to hide. The problems begin with what happens once that carrier door is closed or the bag is zippered up. The cat is whisked away, placed in a moving vehicle (which may even cause the cat to vomit, pee, poop, or salivate excessively), and brought to the veterinary clinic. Besides the frightening smells and sounds, the cat endures unwanted handling and bright lights in the eyes. Her mouth is forcibly opened, and most likely she gets stuck with a few needles as well. Then it's time for another drool-inducing ride back home. At this point, the carrier might as well have a big sign on it that says CAT TORTURE DEVICE.

If You're Nervous, You Make Your Cat Nervous. To make matters worse, we, as pet parents, don't help the situation. Our own body language plays a big role in how the cat adjusts to a carrier. There are cats who seem almost psychic in their ability to know that a trip to the veterinary clinic is about to happen, before the carrier is even taken out of the closet.

Cats can pick up on very subtle signals from their human families. Their highly developed senses know when a cat parent isn't acting in the usual manner. The cat isn't reading the cat parent's mind; she's reading body language. If you tense up as you head for the closet to get the carrier because you're gearing up for the inevitable battle about to take place, your cat is well aware that you aren't your normal self. Your tense body language becomes a flashing neon warning sign that even a cat on the other side of the house will pick up on.

Change Your Cat's Association with the Carrier. Much of the problem stems from the fact that the carrier comes out only when it's time for that trip to the veterinary clinic. As we know, *nothing* fun ever happens there. Make the appearance of the carrier a little less awful. Don't let it be exclusively associated with veterinary visits. If you have room, leave the carrier out all the time, so it loses much of its fear factor. If you use a kennel-type carrier, take the door off, line the carrier with a towel, and make it a cozy hideaway for your cat. Get some totally irresistible treats and periodically place one near the carrier. Every once in a while toss another one, closer and closer until you eventually put it inside the carrier. Feed your cat her meals near and eventually inside the carrier during this training phase.

Once your cat is comfortable with being in the carrier, you can replace the door. In subsequent sessions, close the door when the cat is in the carrier, then immediately open it and offer a treat. Work up to being able to close the carrier door, walk around the room with the carrier, and put it back down.

It may help to also use synthetic pheromone therapy. Spray Feliway or use the towelette version in the inside corners of the carrier. Do this about twenty minutes before putting your cat in there, to allow the alcohol smell to dissipate.

Change Your Cat's Association with the Car. The next step is to get the cat comfortable with being in the car. Put the cat in the carrier. Next, bring the carrier out to the car and place it inside. Don't start the engine. Just let your cat adjust to being in the car for a few minutes. Offer a few treats. When your cat is comfortable with being in the car, start the engine during your next training session. When she's comfortable with the motor running, take a short drive around the block and back home. Always keep things positive, casual, and brief. Work your way up to longer drives.

Question:
Can I leave my cat alone for the weekend while I go out of town?

Pam's Answer:
Don't believe what you may have read—that cats do just fine staying home alone, as long as you've given them a mountain of food and a big bowl of water. Things can go wrong in a house with an animal left alone. Never mind a major medical emergency, fire, flood, or electrical failure; even if it's just a minor medical problem, you wouldn't want your cat suffering because no one checked on him over the weekend. In addition, it can be very stressful for a cat to be completely alone in a quiet home when he has been used to your return each day at a certain hour.

Too many people view cats as low maintenance and get them mainly because of the perceived convenience of not having to interrupt their lives too much. These cats are left alone for anywhere from just one night to an entire week. Imagine the risk these cat parents take with their cats' health and safety. Now also imagine the stress these cats endure. Cats aren't low-maintenance substitutes for dogs, and their health and welfare shouldn't be compromised. You should arrange for a reliable neighbor, friend, or pet sitter to come by twice a day to check on the cat and give her fresh food and water. Your veterinarian's office usually has a roster of sitters available, often including members of the staff.

Question:

We'll be going on vacation soon. Is it better to have a pet sitter or use a boarding facility for our cat?

Pam's Answer:

I generally recommend hiring a pet sitter, but the answer really depends on your cat's personality, her ability to handle change, and your specific circumstances. Here are some guidelines to help you make your decision:

Boarding Facilities. There are good ones, great ones, and terrible ones. If you choose to place your cat in a boarding facility, go there yourself and take a tour. For a cat, being placed in a cage, surrounded by unfamiliar animals, sounds, smells, and sights, can cause the stress-o-meter to go past the red line. Facilities that have condos with hiding places and elevated areas inside each cat's area can make a big difference in how secure your cat feels. Keep in mind how sensitive your cat's senses are and inspect the kennel with a keen CatWise eye . . . and nose!

- How does it smell?
- How loud is the environment?
- Are cages facing each other? This can be very stressful.
- Is the cage or condo big enough so the food bowl isn't right next to the litter box?
- What type of staff interaction is there?
- Do the cats get played with, petted, and held?
- What is done to help reduce stress and fear?
- Is there a veterinarian on call for emergencies?
- How is the facility monitored at night?

Some boarding facilities have great enrichment protocols. Others are stark and depressing.

The Comforts of Home. Hiring a pet sitter or having a friend come over to care for your cat is a great way for you to have the security of knowing your cat remains as comfortable as possible in her own surroundings. From the cat's viewpoint, her family has run off and disappeared without warning, but at least she still has her territory. Just having that security can make the difference, helping your cat take your absence in stride with minimal stress instead of freaking out. For some cats, a boarding kennel, no matter how well run, is terrifying. Don't get me wrong, there are some state-of-the-art boarding facilities that look better than many of the hotel rooms I've stayed in, but for a typical cat, nothing beats the familiarity of home. If it's in the budget, consider hiring an experienced pet sitter or work out an arrangement with a friend or neighbor.

You have to do your homework when planning to have someone come in to care for your cat. Don't just ask the kid next door to drop in every day to toss food into the bowl. You need someone who'll make sure your cat is safe, clean the litter box, feed, monitor how she's eating and using the litter box, interact with her (if she enjoys this), and try to minimize the stress of your absence. A pet sitter who takes the time to play with the cat or interact in whatever way that particular cat enjoys makes a difference in keeping the kitty stress level manageable. The pet caretaker who rushes in and back out in mere minutes isn't going to notice that your cat hasn't urinated all day, that she has pulled a patch of hair off her hind leg, that she's limping, or maybe that she's scratched her eye and is squinting in pain. The drive-by caretaker isn't much better than filling the bowls and taking your chances. Hire a pet sitter who cares deeply for the welfare of every client, or if you're choosing a friend or neighbor to help you, choose someone who can take the time to ensure your cat's safety and security.

Question:

I'm hiring a pet sitter for my cat while I'm away on business for a week. How often should I tell him to visit the house?

Pam's Answer:

Many people think a single visit to the home is adequate, but really you need two visits daily.

If your cat is used to scheduled meals, have the pet sitter come at those times to maintain the normal schedule. It's not healthy for his digestion to gulp down in one meal what he normally would eat in several.

It's also important to keep an eye on what's happening in the litter box. If there's any diarrhea, constipation, bloody urine, or a lack of evidence of elimination, it's better that it's noticed right away. The twice-daily pet sitter visit will also help ensure good litter box hygiene. If your cat is used to having a sparkly clean box, having to navigate mounds of soiled litter won't go over very well.

More than one visit per day also provides activity for your cat, which can make a difference in maintaining minimal stress levels. A visit in the morning to open curtains and do a little playtime, in addition to the normal feeding and litter box cleaning, and then an evening visit to turn lights on, close curtains, and spend some time petting or doing a play session can set your cat up for a nice night. Just hearing some normal household sounds—the faucet, a television or radio, a human voice—can provide a sense of security.

Last but not least, if there's any medical issue with your cat, wouldn't you rather it not take twenty-four hours before getting noticed?

When planning for your cat's care during your vacation or holiday travel, the extra precautions you take to minimize stress and help ensure safety and security can make all the difference in whether this is a positive or negative experience . . . for everyone.

Question:
I'm driving to visit my parents in another state and will be staying with them for a month. Do you have any tips for traveling by car with a cat?

Pam's Answer:
Here are some ideas to make car travel safer and less stressful:

Take the Time to Get Your Cat Used to Being in a Carrier. Leave the carrier out and start conditioning your cat to become comfortable going in and out, as well as having the carrier door closed. Work up to taking the cat (in the carrier) out to the car and then for short trips down the road. Every step of the process should be gradual.

Have Identification for Your Cat. No matter how careful you are, accidents can happen, and your cat can escape or get lost. The safest form of identification is a microchip. Inserting one is a quick procedure your veterinarian can do. In addition to microchipping, it's also a good idea to have a collar with identification. Cell phone numbers are the best ones to have on the identification rather than your home number, so you can always be reached when on the road.

Pack a Travel Bag for Your Cat. The bag should include a supply of any medication your cat is currently on, food, water, bowls, plastic bags for soiled litter, a litter scoop, litter, a travel-size litter box (which can be a disposable one), grooming supplies (very important for long-haired cats), treats, toys, pet wipes, and towels for cleanup.

Keep Your Cat in a Well-Ventilated Carrier. Even if your cat is calm and very well-behaved, it's not safe to let her loose in a moving car. A pet loose in the car is a distraction to the driver and can cause an accident. In addition, if an accident does happen, a loose pet has a greater chance of injury and of getting thrown from the vehicle. Line the carrier with a towel, and pack some extras in case that one gets soiled.

Secure the Carrier with a Seatbelt. A plastic kennel-type carrier is safest. Pull the seatbelt strap through the handle of the carrier and snap into the lock. If you go on a long trip and need to provide litter box access, you can use a dog crate or wire cage, but still secure the crate with straps if possible.

Never Leave Your Pet in a Parked Car. In hot weather, the temperature inside a car can skyrocket in seconds. Even a car parked in the shade with the windows cracked open can get hot enough to cause heatstroke in an animal. If the weather is cold, temperatures can plummet enough to potentially cause your cat to freeze.

Feed Your Cat About Four Hours Before Leaving. Make sure your cat has eaten a light meal early enough and has successfully used her litter box, so the car ride will be more comfortable. If you're going on a long trip, you'll have to provide access to a litter box during the ride.

Create a Comfortable Setup at Your Destination. When you get to your destination, set your cat up in a small area so she can begin to adjust without feeling overwhelmed. Arriving at an unfamiliar location will be stressful, so create a comfortable nook where she can relax and feel secure. If you can bring her box, bed, and favorite toys from home, that will make a new place less scary. Set up a sanctuary room for her so she'll have her own cozy little spot during your visit.

Question:

I'm moving to a new home soon. What's the best way to prepare my cat for this?

Pam's Answer:

Cats don't like change. They're also territorial, so when they suddenly find themselves in a totally unfamiliar location, they feel doubly lost. Heck, moving is stressful for humans, so you can understand how unhappy it makes a cat.

Even though a certain amount of stress will undoubtedly be involved in a move to a new home, there are things you can do to make the transition a little easier on the cat (and ultimately on you).

Prepare in Advance. If your cat doesn't like being in a carrier, spend time getting him comfortable with it. Because your move will likely involve either car travel or air travel, your cat will endure much less anxiety if he views the carrier as a safe place.

Start packing well enough in advance so the moving boxes can be out and about for your cat to investigate. You can actually make packing kind of fun if he can enjoy playing in empty boxes for a couple of weeks.

If your cat reacts negatively to unfamiliar scents, spray the corners of the moving boxes with Feliway.

If your cat is allowed outdoors, start keeping him indoors at least a week before the move. With all the packing and commotion associated with moving, it's not unusual for a cat to get nervous and disappear while outside.

Have the cat's new ID ready well in advance of the move, so you'll be able to attach it to his collar on moving day (if he wears a collar). For added safety, make sure the cat's identification contains your cell phone number, not a land-line number. If he's microchipped, update the online records for the service with your new address, etc.

During packing, make sure your cat's schedule stays as normal as possible. It will only add to his concern if meals are late or he doesn't receive the usual amount of attention from his family. In fact, incorporate some extra interactive play sessions to help with any increase in anxiety he may be experiencing.

If you're moving far enough away that you'll be switching veterinary clinics, get your cat's records to keep with you, or have them e-mailed to the new clinic. When you get to your new location, be sure you know the location of the nearest pet emergency clinic, just in case something unexpected happens in the middle of the night during your first few days in the new home.

Moving Day. To make sure your cat stays safe and doesn't bolt out the front door while you or the movers cart boxes and furniture out of the house, keep your cat in a separate room. You can empty the contents of that room ahead of time, leaving just his carrier, a couple of empty boxes (as extra hiding places), and his litter box, or you can make that the last room the movers will enter, putting your cat in his carrier before they do. Tell everyone involved where the cat is, and as an extra precaution, post a sign on the closed door. If you're concerned that someone might still open the door, keep the cat inside the carrier during the moving process.

If the moving process will totally freak out your cat, talk to your veterinarian about boarding him for the day if your new location will be in the same town.

The New Home. Cat-proof! Cat-proof! Cat-proof! Go through the house looking for potential dangers (window screens that aren't secure, places where the cat can get stuck, etc.) and make the necessary preparations so it will be a safe home for your cat.

Set up a sanctuary room so he'll have a safe and quiet place initially. Set up this room with some familiar furniture, his litter box, food and water bowls, a scratching post, toys, and some hideaways. Because the house will be totally unfamiliar, it will be less overwhelming for him to be confined in one room so he can get his bearings and start to feel some familiarity.

Exploring the New Environment. Your cat's level of stress or fear will determine when to gradually expose him to more of the new environment. When you do open the door to let him investigate, set up an additional litter box where you'll want to locate it permanently. Keep the one in the sanctuary room as well, so your cat will always have a safe place to return to if he isn't comfortable venturing so far out of his comfort zone.

Engage your cat in interactive play to help him form positive associations with the new house. If he's very frightened, you'll have to start these sessions in the sanctuary room and then work your way into the hallway. Go at your cat's pace. Don't ask him to venture too far out if he's not ready.

Use Familiar Scents. Help your cat find familiar scents in the home by either using Feliway or my sock method. Take a clean sock, put it on your hand, and gently pet your cat around the mouth to collect his facial pheromones. Then rub the sock on the corners of objects at cat-nose height.

They'll smell as though he facially rubbed there and may help him become more comfortable.

Should Your Cat Go Outdoors? If he was allowed outdoors in his previous home, this would be a good opportunity to make him an indoor cat. You don't know what kind of outdoor territorial issues might be going on with other cats, and he'll be the new kid in town. He'll also have no connection to his new territory, so letting him outside will greatly increase the chances of having him never returning home.

Chapter 17

Old Friends

Making the most of the golden years

Question:

What are some things I can do to make life easier for my senior cat?

Pam's Answer:

Cats tend to begin showing age-related physical and behavior changes at around seven to ten years of age. Cats older than this are considered seniors. When it comes to life expectancy, many factors must be considered, such as indoor versus outdoor life, veterinary care, genetics, health condition, and nutrition. The average life expectancy for cats is twelve to twenty years.

Physically, your older cat can start to have difficulty getting around and reaching places he normally loves. Jumping up to a favorite window perch may now be difficult. Arthritis can make it difficult for your cat to climb over the edge of the litter box. A geriatric cat may also lack bladder control, so he might not make it to the box in time. Arthritis or stiff joints can also make it difficult for the cat to rise to a standing position and walk to the box in time to empty his bladder. Older diabetic cats or ones in renal failure may not make it to the box in time because of increased water intake. Constipation is another common issue in older cats. This can lead to litter box avoidance if he associates the box with his discomfort.

Elderly felines suffering hearing loss typically sleep more soundly, and as a result, they don't get the message from the brain that the bladder is full. Cats with declining senses may also be more easily startled. You might notice a change in how your cat responds to his environment overall, due to sensory decline.

How Old Is Old?

The terms *geriatric* and *senior* aren't the same. A senior cat is beginning to display signs of aging. A geriatric cat is on the older side of the senior years.

Cognitive Problems. Cognitive dysfunction syndrome is something you may have heard of as it relates to dogs, but it can also affect cats. It can be as subtle as a periodic increase in vocalization or as obvious as complete disorientation.

Helping Your Geriatric Cat. If you don't already do this, get on a schedule of veterinary checkups twice a year. As cats age, medical conditions can appear quickly, so it's advisable not to wait for a yearly checkup but to see the veterinarian every six months. Many veterinarians have senior wellness packages to help with cost.

If your cat's behavior is worrisome and you think he may be experiencing cognitive dysfunction, consult with your veterinarian. There are treatments available, along with behavioral and environmental modifications, to help slow the progression.

Make life easier for your cat by providing steps to favorite perching locations. If your cat enjoys being on a window perch, but it's a drafty spot, install a heated window perch. These are available at your local pet product store and online.

If your cat becomes disoriented and starts vocalizing, call out to him to let him know where you are. It's not uncommon for cats with cognitive issues to start yowling at night when the house suddenly becomes quiet and dark. Leave nightlights on, especially near litter boxes, feeding stations, and favorite climbing areas. If your cat is very disoriented, take him into the bedroom with you and set up a cozy sleeping spot for him there—complete with a conveniently located litter box nearby.

Sensory Decline. For a visually impaired cat, use his own pheromones to help create familiar indoor road maps. Gently rub the sides of his mouth with a soft cloth or sock, and then rub objects in the environment.

Don't make changes to the environment or rearrange furniture. A visually impaired cat depends on his nose, ears, whiskers, paws, and other general tactile information to navigate now. He also largely depends on the familiarity of having things where he expects them to be.

For a visually or aurally impaired cat, the startle response will be much more sensitive. Make your presence gently known before touching him or picking him up. Use your voice to softly announce yourself to a visually impaired cat before touching him. If you have a hearing-impaired cat, come into his line of vision before picking him up. If a cat is sleeping when you approach, use a very gentle touch; never just scoop the kitty up.

Litter Box. Make the litter box setup for an older cat very convenient by increasing the number of boxes and locating them throughout the house, so he never has far to travel when nature calls. If he has arthritis or difficulty getting into a regular box, use a low-sided one. If you're worried about litter scatter, get a high-sided plastic storage container and cut a low entrance on one end. I've found Sterilite containers to be easy to cut, and they come in a wide variety of sizes. If your cat's aim is no longer accurate when in the box, place absorbent pads under and around it to catch spills.

If your cat has balance or mobility problems, you may have to decrease the litter depth in the box. He may find it easier to stand if there's only about an inch and a half to two inches in there.

Walk This Way

Even though healthy cats can see in what we would consider total darkness, your geriatric cat may have trouble navigating in the dark. Create lighted paths to resources using nightlights or rope lighting along the baseboard.

Changes in Grooming Habits. Elderly cats may not groom themselves as efficiently as in the past. Take time to brush your cat on a regular basis. This is also an excellent opportunity to do a physical once-over to check for any lumps or bumps that weren't there before. Keep in mind that older cats who have lost weight and muscle tone will be more sensitive to touch, so use a softer brush and go easy around bony areas. Besides getting rid of loose hair, regular brushing also distributes natural oils and helps increase circulation.

Maintain Good Oral Health. If you haven't been regularly brushing your cat's teeth, it's never too late to start. If you can't brush the teeth, talk to your veterinarian about using an oral hygiene spray. Loss of appetite could be related to periodontal disease, so it's important to maintain your cat's oral health. Periodontal disease can also affect the health of your cat's organs.

Regularly check your cat's mouth for signs of bleeding, broken teeth, sores, or gingivitis. If you notice that your cat tends to chew on only one side, has trouble keeping food in his mouth, drools, has bad breath, or is losing weight, the cause could be mouth pain or periodontal disease.

Food and Water. Your cat's food and water intake may change. Consult your veterinarian if you have questions about any dietary issues. If keeping weight on your cat is a problem, your veterinarian can advise you on whether to add flavor-enhancing products. Some older cats eat better when the food is warmed slightly to bring out the aroma. Your veterinarian may also suggest feeding smaller meals more frequently to make it easier on digestion. If your cat is overweight, your veterinarian will advise you on a safe weight-loss program. Added weight on an elderly cat is extra hard on the joints, but you don't want to restrict his calories too much, because doing so can cause serious liver complications.

Staying Active. Exercise is an important part of a cat's life at any age. Even if your cat isn't very mobile, you can still engage him in low-intensity play sessions. Any activity that gives him a little spark in his life is beneficial— even if he can no longer do those gravity-defying backflips of his youth. Your veterinarian may also advise you on the possible incorporation of massage or flexibility exercises.

Scratching Behavior. Your cat may have faithfully used his scratching post in younger years, but perhaps he has now lost interest in it. Help him out by keeping his nails trimmed. You can also add a horizontal scratch pad; he may no longer be able to reach up to scratch vertically.

The Safer Indoor Life. If your cat is an indoor-outdoor cat, he should now be kept indoors exclusively. With declining senses and limited ability to escape, he's at greater risk of becoming injured. His immune system is also not as strong as it used to be, so he's more vulnerable to disease. The last thing an older cat needs is to be infested with parasites. In addition, if you even suspect cognitive issues, being outdoors may increase his disorientation.

Temperature Intolerance. As cats age, they can become more sensitive to temperature changes. If your cat always loved to sit in the window to watch the outdoor activities, now it may be too drafty there in winter. Ensure that your cat's favorite windows are securely sealed to reduce drafts. You can also find heated window perches in several styles. Just curling up in a donut-shaped or pyramid-style bed can make some cats cozy enough and can help them retain warmth. If you've given him a heated bed, make sure you also offer unheated options so your cat can choose to move away from the warmth.

Monitor Your Cat. Older cats are prone to age-related diseases and conditions, such as chronic renal failure, diabetes, hyperthyroidism, and arthritis, to name just a few. Pay attention to behavioral changes, as well as changes in food and water intake and litter box habits, in order to catch medical problems in the earliest stages.

SIGNS OF CHRONIC RENAL FAILURE CAN INCLUDE:

- Change in behavior
- Increased water intake
- Change in litter box habits
- Increased urination

SIGNS OF DIABETES CAN INCLUDE:

- Increased water intake
- Increased urination
- Excessive hunger
- Weight loss

SIGNS OF HYPERTHYROIDISM CAN INCLUDE:

- Change in appetite
- Change in behavior
- Hyperactivity
- Increased thirst
- Hypertension

- Weight loss
- Change in litter box habits
- Vomiting
- Diarrhea

Routinely check your cat's rear, in case he needs help cleaning there. Some elderly cats groom less or dribble urine in their sleep. Longhaired cats may have feces stuck to their fur and will need help getting that removed. If your cat has started urinating in his sleep or on his bedding, cover the bedding with absorbent pads, such as puppy pee pads. Check his fur and skin frequently for signs of sores or rashes from urine staying in contact with the skin.

Minimize Stress. Stress can wreak havoc on health at any time, and as your cat ages, he's less able to deal with its effects. Be aware of potential stressful triggers in his environment so you can reduce his exposure. For example, if you have many guests coming over, put your cat in a separate room where it's quiet. In a multipet household, be aware of whether your older cat becomes the target of aggression or whether he gets nosed out of his food bowl or favorite napping areas. Changes in your cat's cognitive or physical abilities can result in a change in the relationships he may have with other companion pets in the home.

Be Patient. Most of all, be patient and understanding of missed litter box attempts, food spilled on the floor, a miscalculation while climbing that causes a picture on the table to get knocked over, or the increased desire to be close to you. These golden years can be absolutely precious, a time of tender closeness between the cat and his human family. You may find that the cat who in his youth was reluctant to be in your lap now seeks out your affection. Make the most of these years!

Question:
Can cats become senile?

Pam's Answer:
If you feel that your geriatric cat is showing signs of senility, there may be more to it than you realize. Cats can experience cognitive dysfunction

syndrome, similar to human dementia or Alzheimer's disease. More than just the typical behavioral changes associated with age, cats with CDS can display symptoms such as:

- Increased vocalization
- Litter box lapses
- Disorientation
- Pacing
- Restlessness
- Change in relationships with family members
- Uncharacteristic avoidance of physical interaction
- Constipation
- Incontinence
- Irritability
- Long periods of sleeping
- Altered sleep patterns
- Long periods of staring blankly
- Lack of interest in food
- New phobias

If you suspect your cat is experiencing CDS, an accurate diagnosis needs to be made by your veterinarian to rule out all other possible underlying medical issues, such as:

- Hyperthyroidism
- Renal disease
- Brain tumor
- Cardiac disease
- Decline in vision or hearing
- Degenerative joint disease

Other age-related conditions can look similar to CDS, so a thorough work-up is needed. There is no cure for CDS, but early diagnosis and intervention may slow the progression.

Helping a Cat with Cognitive Dysfunction Syndrome. To help a cat with CDS, keep the environment familiar and monitor the stress level to keep it minimal. Remember, it's not just the big stress triggers you should pay attention to, but the smaller ones as well.

You may need to increase the number of litter boxes to make things as convenient as possible. Create stairways and ramps for easy access to his favorite perches and windows. If he yowls at night or appears disoriented, you might need to confine him to a smaller area of the house. If there are dangerous areas in your home, such as second-story rooms that look out onto the first floor, block off access to prevent your cat from losing his balance on railings. Even some stairways may need to be blocked off if your cat has trouble with them.

Some cats become disoriented at night when the house becomes quiet and dark. It helps to have them sleep in the bedroom with you or at least leave nightlights on and a radio playing.

Help your cat with grooming if he has stopped maintaining the health of his coat. Regular brushing will help distribute the natural oils. It can also be an added way to keep the bond strong between the two of you.

Can You Hear Me Now?

A cat who yowls may be disoriented, but he may also have lost much of his hearing and simply doesn't realize how loud he's being.

Make sure your cat eats a high-quality species-appropriate and age-appropriate diet rich in antioxidants and omega-3 essential fatty acids. Talk to your veterinarian for advice on dietary changes that may be needed as your cat ages or if he shows little interest in food.

Routine veterinary care is essential throughout a cat's life, and it's absolutely a must during the older years to monitor your cat's organ functions and ensure that he never reaches the point of suffering and questionable quality of life. At the very least, plan on twice-yearly veterinary visits as long as things are going well. More frequent visits are needed if there are any signs of decline. Too many people don't think cats need to see the veterinarian as often as dogs do, but because cats tend to hide many signs of illness, routine veterinary care is crucial.

Cats with CDS are less able to cope with disruptions to their daily routines or changes to the environment. This isn't the time to move, renovate, or make lifestyle changes that will affect the cat.

Exercise That Brain. Mental stimulation is important, so regardless of whether you're trying to prevent CDS or are dealing with a cat with cognitive issues, keep up the interactive play sessions and make environmental adjustments that provide age-appropriate enrichment. Daily playtime will help your cat both physically and mentally. Environmental enrichment in the form of puzzle feeders and food treasure hunts can help keep your cat's mind healthy and active. Maintain a good schedule of daily physical interaction with your cat in the way he enjoys, such as petting or grooming. If he has never been a touchy-feely cat, then talk to him and keep him an active part of your daily life. It can be easy to let an older cat slip into disengagement with the family. It's never too late to keep your cat mentally active in family life.

Question:

Our twelve-year-old cat recently lost his brother to cancer. They had been together since they were littermates. Do cats grieve the way we do?

Pam's Answer:

Many people don't realize that animals grieve the loss of companions and family members. Even if companion cats had a hostile relationship, the surviving cat may still grieve the loss. There's confusion about where the other cat has gone. Whether they were close or not, the two had negotiated territories within the household, and now the surviving cat has to figure out whether to risk crossing onto that cat's turf.

The Household Dynamic. To add to the initial grief of the surviving cat, there's the fact that human family members are acting distraught. As the human grieves the loss of a pet, the household dynamic changes, and the grieving cat picks up on the elevated stress level. When the cat sees the cat parent crying and distressed, he knows that everything in his world has turned upside down. During our own grieving time, we may neglect normal routines, so mealtime may be late, playtime may be skipped, and interaction with surviving pets can become tense. You may clutch your surviving cat desperately as you grieve, but the message received by the cat is one of restraint and confusion, not necessarily love.

Here are some tips to guide you as you help your cat through the grieving process:

Monitor Your Cat's Routine. Observe your cat's eating and litter box habits. It's not unusual for a grieving cat to stop eating or to experience a change in litter box habits. If you notice either of these, contact your veterinarian. It's very dangerous for a cat to go two days without eating because of the risk of liver damage. Take care that your cat doesn't fall into depression as well. Stay in contact with your veterinarian if you're at all in doubt about how your cat is handling the loss of his companion.

When grieving a loss, it's not uncommon for a cat to experience altered sleeping patterns or show a strong desire to stay physically closer to human family members. He may even walk through the house looking for his companion. Keep an eye on behavioral changes, as well as changes in eating, grooming, and litter box habits to make sure the situation doesn't become serious or dangerous. Everybody, whether human, feline, or canine, grieves uniquely. Your best asset is your knowledge of your cat's typical patterns and behavior so you can be alert for potentially dangerous changes.

Maintain a Normal Schedule. Even if your cat doesn't seem as interested in interacting with you, it's important to keep schedules as normal as possible. Engage in your usual routine of interactive playtime, even if your cat doesn't seem enthusiastic. This is a time to maintain good nutrition, so resist the urge to entice your cat with unhealthy treats or a change in food. However, be sure to make the meal as appealing as possible. Don't leave canned food out in the dish to harden. Serve wet food at room temperature or slightly warmer to release enticing aromas. If you free-feed dry food, keep track of how much you put in the bowl so you'll know whether the cat is eating his normal amount. If several family members are responsible for filling the dry food bowl, it can be easy to lose track of how much is actually getting eaten. Designate one person to replenish the free-choice feeding bowl so amounts can be monitored.

Monitor Your Own Behavior. When we grieve, it's normal for us to want to embrace our family members and our companion animals as we cry. It's a typical way of giving and receiving comfort. When you hold your cat, beware of clutching so tightly as to alarm him. Your cat is very sensitive to your emotions, and too much clinging can create anxiety. Even though playing may be the last thing you want to do, it's important to keep him from falling into depression or becoming more stressed than he is already.

Create a Memorial. This is something that may help the humans grieve, indirectly benefiting the surviving cat. Honoring the cat who has passed may comfort you and can be especially helpful for children, who can easily feel left out and confused by what happens after the death of a pet. Anything you can do—creating a special garden, assembling a photo album, or making a special donation to an animal welfare organization—may provide a little more comfort and peace for you. The surviving cat, being the sensitive animal he is, will benefit from any body language signal of peace and comfort you display.

Don't Be Too Quick to Bring in Another Cat. To prevent the cat from being lonely or to ease family members' pain, it's not unexpected for the grieving human to want to bring home a "replacement" pet. This can be a recipe for disaster. The grieving cat may not be emotionally ready to handle the intrusion of an unfamiliar animal into his home. Territorial aggression could rear its head up in a big way. Under the best circumstances, cat introductions require good timing and positive associations. If the resident cat is grieving for a lost companion, the newcomer is in a no-win situation.

Don't rush to fill the void left by the cat who recently passed away. The best thing you can do for your surviving cat is to offer time with you in a normal way. He needs to know that not everything in his world has turned upside down and that much of his daily routine is still the same.

After allowing time for grief, you may then determine that your surviving cat would benefit from another companion. Then you can begin the gradual, positive introduction. Don't rush to get to this point, though. Take your cues from your cat, so you can be sure he's over his grief. It's also important that you and your family members have processed *your* grief, so that when and if you do decide to add another cat, that kitty has a good chance of being loved and accepted for who he is without comparisons with the cat who passed.

In a Multipet Home, Allow Time for Adjustments in Dynamics. In multipet homes, each relationship is unique, and the pets have worked out a way of time-sharing in the environment. Even if there was hostility over territorial rights, the death of a pet causes an upset in that normal routine. The pets need time to renegotiate territory and establish a new dynamic. Relationships may shift a bit during this time of uncertainty. Monitor to make sure no one gets picked on or ostracized, but let them have space as they find their new normal.

Carefully and Gently Introduce Neutral Items. While you certainly don't want to make major changes to the environment, it may be helpful to bring in a new interactive toy to spark some playtime interest or even a cozy bed or cat tree to place by a sunny window.

Don't Rush. We're all individual in not only the way we grieve, but also how long we grieve. You may notice that your cat seems back to normal in just a few days, or it could take weeks or months. If your cat seems unable to find the spark in his life again, talk to your veterinarian. You may need a referral to a veterinary behaviorist or other certified behavior expert at that point.

Appendix

BEHAVIOR RESOURCES

www.catbehaviorassociates.com
Web site of Pam Johnson-Bennett. Contains articles, podcasts, videos, and information on her books and lectures.

http://vet.tufts.edu/behavior-clinic
Web site of the Tufts Animal Behavior Clinic. Clinic appointments with a veterinary behaviorist are available. Veterinarian-to-veterinarian fax consultations are available as well.

www.clickertraining.com
Web site of Karen Pryor. Informative articles and videos on clicker training, as well as information on clicker-training expos.

www.dacvb.org
Web site of the American College of Veterinary Behaviorists. Information on finding a board-certified veterinary behaviorist.

www.animalbehaviorsociety.org
Web site of the Animal Behavior Society. Information on finding a certified applied animal behaviorist.

www.iaabc.org
Web site of the International Association of Animal Behavior Consultants. Information on finding a certified animal behavior consultant.

HEALTH AND SAFETY

www.catvets.com
Web site of the American Association of Feline Practitioners. There's a
section for pet parents with information on health and behavior, as well
as a list of cat-friendly veterinary practices.

www.catalystcouncil.org
Web site of a coalition of veterinarians, academicians, nonprofits, and
pet industry and animal welfare organizations.

www.aspca.org/pet-care/animal-poison-control
ASPCA Animal Poison Control Web site. Good information about many of
the poisons you may have around your home and how to safeguard pets
from them.
ASPCA Poison Control Hotline: (888) 426-4435, $65 fee.

PRODUCT MANUFACTURERS

www.nina-ottosson.com
Nina Ottosson makes puzzle feeders and toys for dogs and cats that pro-
mote mental activity and enrichment. Many of the products are available through various online retailers.

www.aikiou.com
Manufacturer of the Stimulo interactive cat feeder. The product is widely
available through various online retailers and many pet product stores.

www.go-cat.com
Manufacturer of Da Bird, a well-made interactive cat toy designed to
mimic a bird in flight. Available through various online retailers and
local pet product stores.

www.nekoflies.com

The company, Nekochan, is the manufacturer of the Nekoflies interactive cat toy, which is designed to mimic various insects. You can purchase different targets to attach to the wand. They also make a telescoping wand, which is great for travel. The wands are comfortable to hold, and the targets on the ends of the strings have high cat appeal. These toys are available through online retailers.

www.catdancer.com

Maker of one of the most basic but most effective interactive cat toys. Available through online retailers and at your local pet product store.

www.preciouscat.com

Manufacturer of Dr. Elsey's Cat Attract cat litter. This litter contains a natural herbal attractant that cats associate with a toileting area. This very low-dust litter is all natural and has excellent clumping ability. When my clients' cats are experiencing litter box issues, incorporating this litter is typically on my list of recommendations. Available through online retailers and at your local pet product store.

www.topcatproducts.com

Manufacturer of a top-of-the-line scratching post, a well-made, tall, sturdy product with a sisal covering that has strong cat appeal. In addition to vertical posts, they also make a horizontal scratching pad.

www.pioneerpet.com

This company manufactures SmartCat and Sticky Paws. The Smart-Cat Ultimate Scratching Post is a strong, durable post with a sisal covering. Sticky Paws is a double-sided tape product for use when retraining a cat away from scratching furniture. There is also a Sticky Paws product for planters to deter cats from digging in potted plants. Both products are widely available online and at your favorite pet product store.

www.petfountain.com

Maker of Drinkwell fountains, which come in ceramic, stainless steel, and plastic. Fountains keep water oxygenated and may encourage cats to drink more water. Available through online retailers and at pet product stores.

www.metpet.com
Maker of the WalkingJacket for cats. Well-made, comfortable jacket for taking your cat on outdoor walks on a leash.

www.greenies.com
Maker of Pill Pockets. These soft, tasty treats have a pocket in the center for hiding pills. Available for cats and dogs in different flavors.

www.catswall.com
Makers of the CatWheel exercise product and the Modular Cat Climbing Wall. The very creative modular wall is a good way to increase vertical space and provide some hiding places for your cat. The CatWheel provides exercise, although not all cats will naturally take to the device without some training.

www.throughadogsear.com
Creator of both the Through a Dog's Ear and Through a Cat's Ear series of psychoacoustic music albums. There are various CDs to choose from depending upon whether you want to calm, stimulate, or reduce noise fear. Available at the Web site and through online retailers.

www.thundershirt.com
Manufacturer of the Thundershirt for either cats or dogs. The product applies constant, gentle pressure similar to the infant swaddling effect. Used for calming fear of thunderstorms, travel, veterinary visits, and anything else the cat needs help remaining calm about. Available through the Web site, online retailers, and pet product stores.

www.ceva.com
Maker of Feliway and Feliway Multicat. Both products contain synthetic versions of feline pheromones to help in behavior modification and stress reduction. Ceva also makes the Adaptil diffuser and Adaptil collar for dogs to help in stress reduction and ease separation anxiety.

www.kongcompany.com
Maker of many treat-dispensing toys and other toys for your cat's enjoyment. I use their small puppy Kong toy for filling with wet food. It's sturdy and can handle the strong chewing tendencies of some cats.

www.mistermax.com

Manufacturer of Anti-Icky-Poo, a pet stain and odor eliminator. Available at many veterinary clinics and online retailers.

www.bio-proresearch.com

Maker of Urine-Off, a pet stain and odor remover. Available on the Web site and through online retailers.

www.legacycanine.com

Terry Ryan has wonderful sound effects CDs for working with fear of thunderstorms, vacuum cleaners, children, babies, fireworks, and more.

Index

AVAILABLE FROM PENGUIN BOOKS

Cat vs. Cat:
Keeping Peace When You Have
More Than One Cat

Hiss and Tell:
True Stories from the Files
of a Cat Shrink

Starting from Scratch:
How to Correct Behavior Problems
in Your Adult Cat

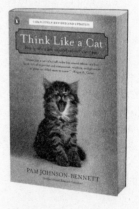

Think Like a Cat:
How to Raise a Well-Adjusted
Cat—Not a Sour Puss

PENGUIN
BOOKS